For Barbara H. Maxwell, whose commitment to future generations gave meaning to her own life.

Who Will Care for Us?

Aging and Long-Term Care in Multicultural America

Ronald J. Angel
AND
Jacqueline L. Angel

NEW YORK UNIVERSITY PRESS
New York and London

NEW YORK UNIVERSITY PRESS
New York and London

Library of Congress Cataloging-in-Publication Data
Angel, Ronald.
Who will care for us? : aging and long-term care in a multicultural America / Ronald J. Angel and Jacqueline L. Angel.
p. cm.
Includes bibliographical references (p.) and index.
ISBN 0-8147-0629-0 (acid-free paper)
1. Aged—Long-term care—United States. 2. Minority aged—Long-term care—United States. 3. Aged—United States—Social conditions. 4. Minority aged—United States—Social conditions. 5. Pluralism (Social sciences)—United States. I. Angel, Jacqueline Lowe. II. Title.
HV1461.F56513 1996
362.6—dc20 96-25333
CIP

New York University Press books are printed on acid-free paper, and their binding materials are chosen for strength and durability.

Manufactured in the United States of America

10 9 8 7 6 5 4 3 2 1

CONTENTS

List of Tables and Figures xi
Preface: Ethnicity and Aging in the Contemporary World xiii

ONE The Social Transformation Of Old Age 1

The Institutional Challenge 4
A Heterogeneous Older Population 7
The Changing Social Context of Aging 9
The Declining Significance of Marriage 12
The Loss of Women as Full-Time Care Givers 16
Cultural Change and Options in the Care of the Elderly 19

TWO A Longer and Better Life: Who has Benefited Most from Improvements in Health? 23

The Differential Prevalence of Chronic Conditions 26
The Meaning of Health and Functional Status 28
Disability and the Social Environment: Active Life Expectancy 35
The Health of Mexican American and Black Elderly: Some Recent Findings 38
A Longer and Better Life? 44

THREE Group Differences in Income and Wealth in Old Age: The Role of Public and Private Pensions 46

Employment Status and Retirement Income 52
Social Security 55
Supplemental Security Income (SSI) 59
Women, Minority Americans, and Social Security 60

FOUR Medicare, Medicaid, and Private Insurance: Group Differences in Health Insurance Coverage 63

Health Insurance in the United States 65
The Health Insurance—Employment Nexus 66
Medicare: Universal Health Coverage for the Old 69
Medicaid: Publicly Funded "Medigap" Insurance 72
Falling through the Cracks: Insurance Coverage among Blacks and Hispanics 73
Health Insurance Coverage in the Years before Retirement 77
The Future of Health Care Financing: Implications for Minority Americans 81

FIVE The Role of the Family in the Informal Support of the Elderly 88

The Cultural and Social Context of Social Support 92
Systems of Social Support 94
Cultural and Social Class Differences in Social Support 95
The Composition of Informal Networks 97
Living Arrangements and Social Support 100
Rural/Urban Differences in Social Support 103
Migration/Age at Immigration 105
Race, Ethnicity, and the Future of the Family in the Care of the Elderly 110

SIX A Refuge of Last Resort: Culture, Social Class, and the Use of Institutional Long-Term Care 113

Does Formal Support Replace the Family? 114
Options in Institutional Long-Term Care 117
Continuing Care Retirement Communities (CCRCs) 118
Variations on the CCRC 119
Paying for Long-Term Care: The Role of Private Insurance 121
Medicaid and Long-Term Care 124

Group Differences in the Use of Nursing Home Care 126
Institutional Alternatives or Alternatives to Institutionalization? 130

SEVEN Staying at Home: New Options in the Community Care of the Elderly 134

The Nursing Home or Community Care? 136
What Is Community Care? 138
The Potential of Induced Demand for Home-Based Care 139
National Policy and Program Options in Community-Based Long-Term Care 141
The Older Americans Act (OAA) and Other Federal Community-Based Programs for the Elderly 142
Transportation 143
Case Management 145
Nutrition 145
Respite Care 146
Adult Day Care 147
Other Residential Options 147
Housing Programs and Services 148
Reverse Equity Mortgages: Gaining Access to One's Home Equity 149
On Lok: The Ultimate Community-Based Model 150
Can We Afford Community-Based Long-Term Care? 153

EIGHT The New Pact between the Generations: Intergenerational Exchanges in a Multicultural Society 158

The Old-Age Welfare State and the Possibility of Intergenerational Conflict 162
The Consequences of Heterogeneity among the Elderly 163
Is the Modern Welfare State Equitable? 166
Inequalities in Health Care 167

Intergenerational Exchanges and the Rise of the "Third Age" 168
A New and Informed Public Discourse 172
The Consequences of Various Proposed Reforms of Social Security for the Poor, Minorities, and Women 173
The Moral Foundation of Our Interdependence: A Policy Agenda 177
An Opportunity for Imaginative Experimentation: Specific Recommendations 180

Bibliography 189
Index 223

TABLES AND FIGURES

Tables

1.1 Percentage of Elderly, by Country: 1990 to 2025 5
1.2 Income Sources for Persons 65 Years and Over: 1990 11
1.3 Single Women Living with Their Grandchildren in 1993 13
1.4 Percentage of Children Living in Single-Parent Families with a Divorced or Never Married Parent 15
2.1 Death Rates from Leading Causes, by Age, Race, Hispanic Ethnicity: 1980–1990 27
2.2 Percentage of Individuals with Problems with Activities of Daily Living, by Race and Mexican American Ethnicity 39
2.3 Percentage of Individuals with Major Mobility Impairments, by Age 41
2.4 Percentage of Men and Women Reporting Chronic Conditions 42
2.5 Self-Assessed Health, by Age, Race, and Mexican American Ethnicity 43
3.1 Income Sources, by Race and Ethnicity: 1989 48
3.2 Home Equity and Assets, by Race, Hispanic Ethnicity, and Household Type 51
3.3 Personal Income Sources, by Age and Nativity 62
3.4 Average Household Size by Age at Immigration and Nativity for Elderly Mexican Americans 62
4.1 Health Insurance Coverage of Male-/Couple-Headed and Female-Headed Households, by Race and Hispanic Ethnicity 68
4.2 Health Insurance Coverage of Individuals 65 Years and Over, by Race and Hispanic Ethnicity 75
4.3 Health Insurance Coverage, for Mexican Americans 65 Years and Over, by Nativity 76

4.4 Wealth and Income of Preretirement Age Male-/Couple-Headed and Female-Headed Households, by Race and Hispanic Ethnicity 78
4.5 Retirement Health Insurance Coverage of Male-/Couple-Headed and Female-Headed Households, by Race and Hispanic Ethnicity 80
5.1 Percentage of Unmarried Persons Aged 65 Years and Over Who Live with Their Children 102
5.2 Life-Course Stage at Migration, by Birth Cohort 107
5.3 Income Sources for Women, by Age at Immigration and Nativity 108
5.4 Depression, by Age at Immigration and Nativity 109
6.1 Where Older Mexican Americans Would Care to Live if They Became Incapacitated 127
7.1 Percentage of Persons 65 and Over Using Social Services in the Last Year 144

Figures

1.1 Projections of Persons Aged 65 by Race and Hispanic Ethnicity, 1995 to 2025 3
2.1 Projected Life Expectancy at Age 65 in 2030, by Race and Ethnicity 25
2.2 The Sociocultural Context of the Disablement Process 31
5.1 Elderly Hispanic Social Network, by Origin 100

Ethnicity and Aging in the Contemporary World

As the result of low fertility and increasing life expectancies among all racial and ethnic groups, the population of the United States, like that of other developed nations, is aging rapidly Suzman, Willis, and Manton 1992 (Manton and Vaupel 1995;). Even in nations like Mexico, where high fertility keeps the population relatively young, many more people than ever before are surviving to old age because of better living conditions and improved public health (Kinsella 1992). As a consequence, all over the world social welfare states are struggling with the increasing burden brought on by the economic and medical needs of this growing older population (Waldo et al. 1989; Ham-Chande 1994). In the United States the growth in the cost of long-term care for the elderly is one of the major forces behind recent increases in Medicaid expenditures, and any reformed health care financing system will have to find ways of providing high-quality long-term care to older Americans at a reasonable cost.

Each country's approach to the problem of old age dependency is structured by its culture, history, and economy. In Japan, for example, which has the longest life expectancy at birth of any nation on earth, and in which an estimated 25 percent of the population will be over sixty-five early in the next century, official policy looks to the family for the support of aging parents (Lock 1987). Because of the expectation that wives should care for their husband's parents, this policy results in an increased burden for middle-aged daughters-in-law, and as feminism makes inroads into even traditional Japanese society, predictable strains are emerging. Yet the situation of the elderly in Japan speaks directly to our topic. Whatever the eventual fate of Japan's official policy for the care of the elderly, it is clear that such a reliance on the family can only work in a culturally homogeneous nation with widely shared norms of reciprocity and duty between the generations.

In a racially and culturally diverse nation like the United States, official policy regarding the care of the elderly cannot be based on a common set of norms concerning the family's role in the care of its older members. In the United States, the federal government has assumed the major responsibility for insuring the economic welfare and physical health of the elderly through Social Security and Medicare. Yet despite this shift in financial responsibility, the family continues to provide the majority of day-to-day care for older family members.

In this book, we examine the great racial and ethnic diversity among the elderly in the contemporary United States in terms of living arrangements, economic well-being, and reliance on formal and family-based sources of support. Our goal is to assess levels of need for long-term care for the elderly among blacks, Hispanics, and non-Hispanic whites and to examine possible alternatives to institutionalization. One of our core objectives is to examine the possibility of assisting the family, when it is available and willing, to care for their older relatives in the community. One possible negative consequence of the increase in state-funded formal long-term care is a decrease in the family's committment to the care of the elderly and the shifting of responsibility onto already burdened tax bases.

Even among Mexican Americans and other groups who have traditionally cared for their aging parents at home, the economic and social forces that are changing the very structure of the family have significant implications for the role of the family in the care of aging parents. The possibility of involving the family in the care of the elderly differs from one ethnic group to another, because ethnic groups differ in average family size and expectations concerning responsibility for aging relatives. Larger families have potentially more younger individuals available to provide care to older individuals. Group norms and practices that encourage large families, therefore, directly affect the availability of informal care for the elderly. Any policy for the long-term care of the elderly must be informed by an understanding of the needs and preferences of older persons themselves as well as of their families.

As the proportion of the population over the age of 65 grows, the racial and cultural makeup of that population is also changing significantly. In years to come, a larger fraction of the older population than today will consist of blacks, Hispanics, and Asians (Angel and Hogan 1992). Their family situations, their health care needs, and their desires in living arrangements may differ significantly from those of non-Hispanic whites. Policies that are based on the assumption that the older population is homogeneous in terms of either needs or preferences will fail to take advantage of the opportunities that ethnic and cultural diversity offers and will minimize the individual's and the family's options in long-term care.

In this book we explore the possibility of a long-term care policy for the elderly in the United States that optimizes choice in living arrangements and makes the best use of community support systems, at the same time that it controls cost. What we would not want to see is a system in which poor black and Hispanic families shoulder the majority of the burden of caring for their aging relatives simply because family members are available, while more affluent non-Hispanic whites receive high-quality institutional care. Rather, we propose a system in which the quality of life of the older individual is maximized through increased options in community support that utilize family caregivers while at the same time easing the burden placed on them. Such a system should be available to all groups and not force any family or older person into situations they do not want. The data we review in the following chapters clearly show that older individuals prefer to live in their own households as long as possible, and that, while they do not wish to become burdens on their children, they welcome help from family members. In our opinion, a formal support system that offers assistance to the family in the care of older relatives is preferable to one which either provides inadequate services or forces an infirm older person into a nursing home.

The Meaning of "Ethnicity" in Contemporary America

Since the concepts of culture, race, and ethnicity are central to our discussion, it is imperative that we spend some time discussing what they mean in the United States today. Race and certain Hispanic ethnicities are clear risk factors for disadvantage in the United States today at every age (Angel 1995). It is simply impossible to pretend that our economic and political systems are race blind. The residue of years of discrimination seriously handicaps large numbers of individuals of color. Yet we do not wish to draw invidious distinctions between groups, nor do we wish to characterize any group in terms of social pathology. Rather, at the same time that we identifiy clear disadvantages, we also emphasize the opportunities for the care of the elderly that ethnic diversity provides.

Ethnicity, like race, has always been close to the surface in American life. It is an idea that has been hard to deal with, connoting a source of pride yet also something a bit parochial and even embarrassing (Waters 1990). In previous decades, and for blacks and certain Hispanics today, one's nation of origin determined where one lived, where and for how long one went to school, and even whom one could marry. Yet such ethnic parochiality violates the basic principles of America's political culture. This country was founded by individuals who wanted to create a nation of laws and not of men, a nation in which neither ethnic origin nor religious preference would restrict one's chances for advancement. The institution of slavery and the racism that has characterized America's incorporation of blacks makes it clear that this idealized self-image was in many ways naive. Yet, as an ideal, the principle of unity forged from diversity remains at the heart of our nation's moral character. To individuals who left a Europe characterized by a patchwork of national, linguistic, and social differences, in which ethnic and religious distinctions limited one's possibilities in life, these new principles represented a liberation from the unwanted chains of the past. Today, immigrants from other continents seek that same liberation and hunger for the political freedom and the economic security that America promises.

There are clear dangers in the divisiveness that a self-conscious and politicized racial or ethnic identification can lead to, however. In his book, *The Disuniting of America,* Arthur Schlesinger, Jr., points out the disastrous consequences of the recent erosion of our sense of unity and warns of what we will lose if our common civic purpose is sacrificed to more parochial loyalties based on race and ethnicity (Schlesinger 1992). Schlesinger and others correctly point out that the rejection of a sense of a common purpose or higher principles leads to distortions of the past, to increased hostilities between groups, and to political cynicism. The nation, to which we all belong, must be more than the sum of our racial and ethnic identities. The hope of the New Republic of 1776, and our continuing mission today, is to forge a sense of unity out of our cultural differences, at the same time that we respect and preserve the racial and cultural richness that makes our nation unique.

The task we face today, of defining a common purpose that can unite people of various racial and ethnic backgrounds, is hardly new. From our very beginning, we have had to incorporate new cultures and languages into our national character, and the process has never been easy. Each new group has had to overcome the prejudices of those who came before. Except for the Civil War, we have avoided the disastrous rivalries based on race and ethnicity that have always been part of human history, that beset the Balkans and postcolonial Africa today, and that threaten to tear entire nations and societies apart. Each new addition to our cultural mélange has redefined America, as much as America has redefined the immigrant. Despite slavery and their economic and political disenfranchisement, black Americans too have left their unique stamp on our culture. Today, a growing Hispanic population is introducing a new spice into the melting pot. In many parts of the country, Spanish is as common as English, despite the objections of those who would legislate English as our only official language. We will debate for years the wisdom of bilingual education and English-only initiatives. Yet, in the end, these debates merely reflect the inevitable conflicts that accompany the mingling of peoples. In the United States, English is essential for effective social functioning and advancement, and although new immigrants will always alter the national character in subtle ways, English (if not necessarily the Queen's) will always dominate. Other languages are not a threat when they are recognized and treated as additions to our rich diversity, rather than as potential barriers to communication between people.

Today we are presented with a new set of problems surrounding the incorporation into middle-class society of both new arrivals and economically disadvantaged longer-term residents. During our early years as a nation, immigration to the United States was primarily from northern and western Europe. Even then, immigrants were received by old-stock natives with suspicion. As immigrants from southern, central, and eastern Europe began to arrive on our shores, bringing with them their unfamiliar religions and customs, as well as their darker skins, the level of suspicion increased. Whatever differences existed among immigrants from Europe, however, and despite the difficulties they experienced in leaving their native countries and migrating to the New World, they were all European, and the incorporation of each new wave into the cultural and economic mainstream basically mirrored that of previous groups. New arrivals lived in the urban ghettos of an economically dynamic America and found ample opportunities for manual labor and a foothold on the ladder of opportunity. After one or two generations they had saved up a nest egg, educated their children as Americans, advanced socially, and left the ghetto to a new set of aspirants to the American Dream.

For immigrants from Europe, time has worked its inevitable leveling function, and ethnic distinctions that are based on European nationalities have ceased to have any meaningful economic, civil, or even social consequences. Today, a young woman whose great-grandparents immigrated from Ireland would encounter little opposition were she to choose to marry the grandson of immigrants from Italy (Alba 1990; Lieberson and Waters 1990). Although Americans of European ancestry may cling to a symbolic ethnicity out of a basic human need to preserve a tie to the past, such an identity is manifested in little more than rudiments of the culture of origin, including, perhaps, a few words of a nearly forgotten language or special ethnic dishes at holidays.

Richard Alba hypothesizes that what we are witnessing, in fact, is the rise of a new ethnic identity, "one based on ancestry from *anywhere* on the European continent" (Alba 1990, 3). The evolution of this new European identification among non-Hispanic white Americans has important implications for what ethnicity means in the United States today and for what we are dealing with in this book. This new European identity among non-Hispanic whites draws greater attention to the differences between white Americans of European ancestry and Americans of non-European origin. Today the central-city ghettos that were once home to Jews, Irish, Poles, and Italians are inhabited by blacks, Hispanics, and Asians who come from a vast array of nations and very different economic and political situations. The question that we must ask ourselves is whether the incorporation experiences of the new immigrants will be similar to that of their European predecessors or whether, instead, the racial and cultural distance between these new arrivals and longer-term residents of European-origin may be so great as to slow, or even permanently block, their assimilation into the social and economic mainstream. The answer to this question has clear implications for the welfare of the elderly in the years to come.

What the following chapters make clear is that, in addition to large differences between racial and ethnic groups, there are large differences among individuals within each group in terms of economic success and overall well-being. Although some members of each group are following the upward path of previous immigrants, others are not and are faring quite badly in comparison with their predecessors. It is also clear that the social experiences of the elderly are influenced by the historical period and their age when they arrived. Among ethnic Americans, the old tend to be much closer to their cultural origins than the young. Although we have begun our discussion focusing on the immigrant experience, most of those who make up the bottom layers of our economic hierarchy are not immigrants. Rather, they are long-term residents who, for numerous reasons that we will explore in later chapters, never achieved middle-class status. The barriers to economic success that these individuals and families face today, though, gives them much in common with immigrants. Many of those who are currently excluded from the economic and social mainstream not only are culturally foreign to Americans of European origin but also face the task of social and economic advancement at a time when the entry-level jobs that have traditionally formed the first rung on the ladder of opportunity are gone (Kasarda 1993).

In the last few decades the manual and manufacturing jobs that provided opportunities for economic and social mobility to immigrants in the nineteenth and early twentieth centuries have been lost to other countries where labor costs are lower. Ethnic differences in the United States today, therefore, take on a new aspect, one that is colored by social class. The concept of "minority group" and the special affirmative action programs designed to aid certain members of our disadvantaged classes are based on the recognition that certain groups face particularly difficult hurdles to economic and social incorporation. Throughout the book, therefore, the complex interaction of race, ethnicity, and social class informs all of our investigations of the welfare of the elderly.

Several interrelated themes inform the following chapters. Perhaps the most central is that the world as a whole is facing a set of social problems arising from a historically unprecedented growth in the number of individuals over sixty-five. Among this growing population of older persons, an ever increasing fraction is over eighty-five, a group that gerontologists refer to as the "old-old" (Bould, Sanborn, and Reif 1989). Although, as Socrates proved long ago, the inherent biological limit to life has always been somewhere beyond eighty years, until fairly recently in human history relatively few individuals survived to extreme old age. Not far into the twenty-first century, over one-fifth of the population of the United States will be over sixty-five (Day 1993). We are only now beginning to closely examine the economic, social, and political implications of such an unprecedented graying of the population.

Another general theme that informs the following chapters is that a special set of considerations arises from the increasing cultural diversity of the older population. For example, we now face the necessity of developing culturally appropriate forms of acute and long-term care for older persons from different ethnic groups and of optimizing their options in community living arrangements. The following chapters will also demonstrate that the situation of the elderly is directly tied to the situation of younger individuals. Those factors that impede the economic and social advancement of the young have clear implications for their ability to care for the elderly, as well as for their own situations in later life.

Throughout our discussion of the situation of the elderly and their relationship to younger age groups, we must keep in mind that our capacity to care for those in need has always been limited by economics. After the Second World War, the generous support systems for older individuals that have become an integral part of the social welfare systems of the developed nations were made possible by rapid economic growth. In periods of slow economic growth, national economies approximate zero-sum games, in which the gains of one group are financed at the expense of another. In the United States today, programs for the old and for the young compete for the same limited resources (Preston 1984; Hudson 1995). If real economic growth remains relatively low, increased outlays for the elderly can only come at the expense of other social goods, including programs for children. Although the United States remains at present the world's richest country, in the future slower growth and the inevitable tradeoffs will result in heated debates and potential conflicts between the generations over how our aggregate economic pie is divided.

An aging population incurs costs of many kinds. Although many individuals think of Social Security as an annuity, it has never in fact operated in that fashion. Retired individuals are supported by the current earnings of the working-age population. An increase in the ratio of older to younger individuals means that in the years to come there will be fewer employed individuals to support each retired person, and the result will be a disproportionate flow of resources from the young to the old. Traditional conceptions of the intergenerational resource flow as proceeding from parents to children in the form of inheritance may be seriously strained by the new demographic and economic reality. Yet direct income support represents only a part of the costs of caring for the elderly. For most individuals, the period immediately preceding death is characterized by physical decline and the extensive use of medical care (Lubitz and Riley 1993; Lubitz and Prihoda 1984). Unlike the routine problems of childhood, which are relatively inexpensive to treat, the management of the chronic diseases of old age is expensive. As the technical management of chronic illness continues to advance, the cost of caring for the infirm elderly will inevitably skyrocket (Rivlin and Wiener 1988a; Angel and Angel 1993).

In the United States, as elsewhere in the developed world, the old are consuming an ever larger fraction of our national wealth. Since Social Security payments were indexed to the rate of inflation in the 1960s, poverty among the elderly has decreased dramatically; poverty today is concentrated among families with young children. In recent years the cost of medical and long-term care of the elderly has grown at an ever accelerating rate. Since 1965, when Medicare was introduced, the rate in the growth in expenditures for medical care under this program has increased severalfold. In 1970 spending for Medicare totaled $6.8 billion, 3.5 percent of the total federal budget. By 1990, this figure had leaped to $107 billion, accounting for 8.6 percent of federal outlays (Moon 1993). During the 1990s, Medicaid expenditures for hospital and physician services, as well as long-term care, for the elderly poor have advanced in the same way. Today, although single women and their children make up the majority of recipients of Medicaid, the disabled and the elderly account for the majority of Medicaid expenditures.

Unfortunately, there is little reason to posit any implicit upper limit on the growth in medical care expenditure for the elderly.

Although officially defined poverty is low among the elderly, the retirement incomes of many older Americans are modest, and many, especially among the minorities, find their share of payments for medical care burdensome. Currently, Medicaid provides coverage to only a third of the older population in poverty (Feder et al. 1993). Those not covered by Medicaid must rely on Medicare alone, managing somehow to cover the premiums, deductibles, and copayments out of current income—or they must do without services. Providing supplemental coverage to all poor elderly Americans, either through Medicaid or some other program, will add greatly to aggregate health care costs and divert money from other uses. For the foreseeable future, therefore, the forces propelling the growth in health care costs, including an aging population and advances in technology, will make it difficult, and perhaps impossible, to contain the growth in health care expenditure (Mendelson and Schwartz 1993; Newhouse 1993).

However our health care system evolves, then, it is clear that the demands of caring for the growing population of older individuals will continue to be a major impetus to increasing costs. In the context of an aging population with an ever greater need for hospital and home health care services, the containment of costs will require innovations that maximize the use of less expensive community mechanisms of support. Innovative state and local programs, such as On Lok in San Francisco's Chinatown (see chapter 7), demonstrate that with aggressive community support even seriously disabled older persons can avoid institutionalization (Ansak 1990; Capitman 1986; Branch, Coulam, and Zimmerman 1995). Such programs persuade us that the family and the community harbor rich resources for the care of the elderly that have not yet been fully explored.

Numerous experiments in home and community-based care have been tried and will, no doubt, form a central part of any reformed health care system for the elderly. Unfortunately, the cost-effectiveness of such programs and their ability to keep infirm older persons out of nursing homes or to delay institutionalization has not been clearly demonstrated (Branch, Coulam, and Zimmerman 1995; Capitman 1986; Vertrees, Manton, and Adler 1989; Wiener and Harris

1990; Wiener and Hanley 1992a; Weiner and Hanley 1992b; Leutz 1986). Most programs that attempt to provide health services to the elderly in their homes have not, as yet, resulted in the delivery of high-quality care at lower cost than institutionalization. When home health care services are offered, they evidently tap a large reservoir of unmet need in the community. Under our current system, many infirm elderly individuals who might benefit from assistance simply do without it. Were assistance made available, many of these individuals would certainly take advantage of it, leading to even greater costs. Still, in light of the continuing growth in health care costs, especially those associated with long-term care, community-based support programs continue to hold great potential, provided that they are informed, as is the On Lok program, by a clear understanding of the cultural and social situations of the clientele they seek to serve.

One reason to be optimistic about the possibility of community care is the continuing involvement of the family. Although there is a widely held belief that American families are abandoning their elderly, the data clearly show that this is not the case (Doty 1986; Soldo, Wolf, and Agree 1990). The evidence is overwhelming that the family shoulders the majority of the burden of caring for infirm older individuals, rather than relegating them to nursing homes. Even when they suffer from fairly serious disabilities, older individuals prefer to live alone or in the community, rather than enter nursing homes. Although many receive some form of home health care, many others simply do without care or rely mainly on the assistance of family members. Many alternatives have been proposed for assisting the families who provide support to elderly parents in the community, and it is likely that in the future such proposals and programs will become common. In light of the aging of the baby boom generation, it will become necessary to determine how such informal mechanisms of support might be augmented, rather than replaced, by formal sources. Unfortunately, as we show in later chapters, the tremendous social and demographic changes that have reshaped the family may undermine its ability to provide the care that older parents need.

It is probably not much of an exaggeration to say that most current proposals for health care reform are predicated on the assumption that the elderly population is homogeneous in terms of needs. Yet clinical factors alone do not determine the need for services. One's family situation and living arrangements influence the number of individuals available to help with the simple physical activities of daily living, such as dressing and bathing, and with more complex instrumental tasks, such as shopping and dealing with finances. There is ample evidence that cultural factors influence the role of the family in the care of elderly individuals, thereby affecting the overall assistance package that elderly individuals need and will accept (Burr 1990; Becerra 1983; Burr and Mutchler 1992; Thomas and Wister 1984; Markides, Martin, and Gomez 1983; Mutchler and Frisbie 1987).

Attempts to develop a rational system of community care for the elderly must be informed by a better understanding of the total package of pathology that different groups of elderly individuals experience, as well as an understanding of the ways in which cultural, economic, and health care system factors influence the extent of need for long-term care and specific home health care services. A fragmented system with little understanding or appreciation of the great cultural and social heterogeneity within the older population will fail to address the needs of all elderly Americans and will incur ever mounting costs as the result of ineffective and inappropriate management.

The questions we address in this book are motivated by very practical considerations, yet we must keep in mind that they are also ultimately moral ones. They have to do with more than simple demographics or technical economics. Rather, they go to the very heart of our basic values and expectations. In previous decades the pact between the generations was dictated by culture and tradition; today it is in flux and a matter of public debate, largely as the result of the truly unprecedented dependency burden that an aging population represents. Yet the old are not strangers. They are our parents and our grandparents; they are the people whose sacrifices built this nation and provided us with the opportunities we now enjoy; and they are ourselves at a different point in our life course. We cannot turn our backs on them without turning our backs on ourselves. What is called for at this point in our history is a change in consciousness and a profound reconceptualization of what it means to be old, middle-aged, and young and of the ways in which different age groups relate to one another. We must also begin to understand diversity, to see that cultural difference can be a source of strength as well as weakness. Today we must begin preparing for the world of the future, a world in which we will need to provide children with security, education, material well-being, and the prospect of a productive place in the adult world, while at the same time insuring a rich and meaningful existence to those at the other end of the life course. Inevitable tradeoffs will have to be made but with due regard for the claims of all age groups, since any society that neglects the young is doomed to senescence, and any that neglects the old, to barbarism. Hopefully, this book will make a small contribution to understanding the problems we face.

In the following chapters we characterize the racial and cultural mosaic of America's elderly population and take a first step toward a deeper and more sophisticated understanding of the role played by social class and culture in the health and welfare of older Americans. In chapter 1, we document the growth in the proportion of the population over sixty-five in the United States and other developed nations and canvas the problems posed for all nations, developed or developing, by longer life expectancies.

In chapter 2 we document the great extension of the life span that has occurred during the twentieth century and summarize findings concerning how much of that extension consists of years in which a person can expect to suffer illness. We also document group differences in health status and explore those factors that result in different life expectancies. In this chapter, and in the book as a whole, we focus largely on blacks, Hispanics, and non-Hispanic whites. In chapter 3 we document racial and ethnic group differences in income and assets among the elderly and show that, although the income disadvantage among minority Americans is large, differentials in assets are truly astonishing and mean that older blacks and Hispanics have very little wealth to liquidate for their own care or to leave to their children.

In chapter 4 we document the fact that compared to non-Hispanic white older persons a far greater proportion of black and Hispanic older persons have no private health insurance and are dependent on Medicaid to cover the costs that Medicare will not pay. We examine the impact of the lack of private health insurance on the health care use of black and Hispanic older persons and discuss the potential consequences of health care financing reform on health care use by older blacks and Hispanics. Chapter 5 focuses on the role of the family and the informal social support network in the care of the infirm elderly and explores group differences in this regard.

In chapter 6 we survey options in institutional long-term care for the elderly and explore the reasons that older blacks and Hispanics do not use nursing homes at the same rate as non-Hispanic whites. Chapter 7 examines options in the community care of the infirm elderly and reviews the results of recent programs that provide help to even seriously impaired individuals in their own homes.

What are the limitations of health care financing reform in improving the lot of the minority elderly? Reforming our health care financing system is clearly important, as we argue in chapter 8, but reforming the payment system is only one component of the solution. What we need is a new philosophy of health care delivery and of the role of the community in the care of the elderly. In places like the Rio Grande Valley of Texas and in the inner cities, services are often difficult to obtain and worse yet, they are often culturally inappropriate, resulting in noncompliance or despair with the medical care system on the part of minority clients. Addressing the social and health care needs of elderly persons in these environments will take new and imaginative initiatives. Finally, in chapter 8 we summarize the threats to the family's ability to continue providing the majority of care to the elderly and propose a system of long-term care that both offers the older person options in living arrangements and supplements, rather than replaces, the family in its caregiving role.

ONE

The Social Transformation of Old Age

It would be difficult to overstate the potential impact of the rapid and extensive aging of the population that we will witness during the first few decades of the twenty-first century on nearly every institution that governs organized social life. Education, health care, housing, transportation, the marketplace generally, as well as local, state, and federal governments, will all be called upon to respond to a new set of needs represented by a large and economically and politically powerful senior population. Never before in history has humanity had to adapt to such a rapid growth in the number of individuals who survive to their eighth and ninth decades and even beyond. The extent of this demographic transition and the new social realities it will bring with it have only recently begun to attract public attention, and it is still unclear whether we will be able to adapt to the inevitable changes in resource allocation that an aging population requires without engendering conflict between age groups.

Although the potential human life span has always been somewhere beyond the biblical three score and ten, average life expectancies, even among those who survived beyond childhood, have historically been much shorter than they are today in the developed world, and the proportion of people who did not participate in economic life in one fashion or another because of advanced age has been relatively small (Fischer 1978; Laslett 1989; Laslett and Fishkin 1992). Since at least the eighteenth century, however, improved standards of living and the control of infectious disease have brought about a demographic transition that is well advanced in the United States and the rest of the developed world. Our successes in feeding ourselves and in eliminating early death have resulted in ever older populations (Martin and Preston 1994). Although this demographic transition has pushed the average age of the populations of the developed nations slowly upward for at least two centuries, the rate of population aging has accelerated since World War II. In all developed nations, and increasingly in the developing world, the number of individuals over the age of sixty-five is growing at a historically unprecedented rate (U.S. Bureau of the Census 1992a; Bourgeois-Pichat 1979; Ham-Chande 1994; Myers 1990). In the harsher world of the past, the burden that the old placed on the young was never excessive, simply because there was little the old could consume and, except for a few privileged individuals, the luxury of an idle retirement was never a possibility. The concern with how one should live one's life in the "third age," as the period of healthy and productive older adulthood has come to be called, is a very modern phenomenon (Laslett 1989). For most of human history, as is still the case for a large fraction of the world today, people worked until they could no longer participate in paid or domestic labor, and then they survived on the charity of family and community until they died.

Figure 1.1 displays the projected future growth in the proportion of the population over sixty-five and illustrates the dramatic increase in the elderly population expected early in the next century. We should remember that the impact of changing age structures on the welfare of both the young and the old is a function not only of the absolute number of older individuals but also of the fraction of the population that they represent. In countries like Mexico, for example, although the number of older individuals is increasing rapidly, the proportion of the population that they represent remains small,

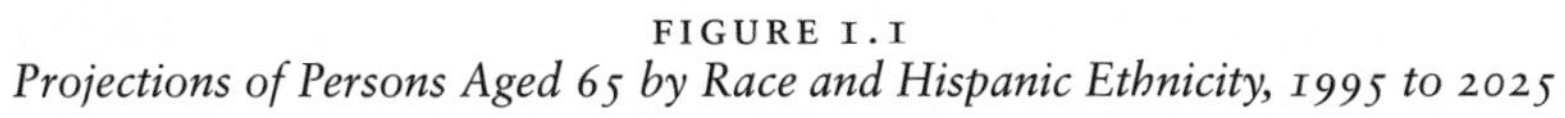

FIGURE 1.1

Projections of Persons Aged 65 by Race and Hispanic Ethnicity, 1995 to 2025

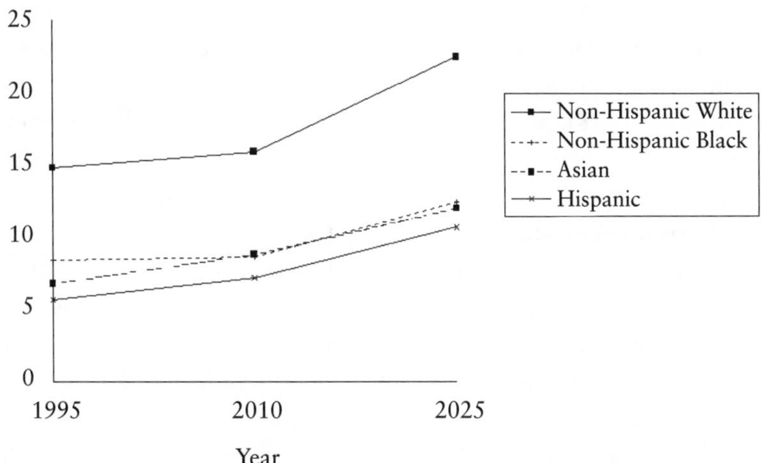

SOURCE: Jennifer Cheeseman Day, "Population Projections of the United States, by Age, Sex, Race, and Hispanic Origin: 1993–2050," U.S. Bureau of the Census, Current Population Reports, series P25-1104 (Washington, DC: Government Printing Office, 1993), table 2.

and the ratio of working-age to retirement-age individuals will, consequently, remain higher than in the United States, although the productivity of Mexican workers will remain lower because of that nation's lower level of development. The data in figure 1.1 show that, although the Hispanic, black, and Asian populations will age along with the population at large, they will remain younger than the non-Hispanic white population. In 1995, 86 percent of the older population was non-Hispanic white but by 2025 white Americans will make up nearly 75 percent of the population over sixty-five, meaning that the world of the elderly, like the working world, will be truly multicultural. The age disparities between racial and ethnic groups means that the needs and desires of the younger groups will be different from those of the older majority population. The older majority population may need institutional or intensive home health care, whereas the younger minority populations may need income support and housing assistance.

The huge preponderance of ethnic whites in the older population hints at what could become a major social problem in the years to come. In the future a larger fraction of the working-age population will consist of blacks and Hispanics, while the older population will remain predominantly non-Hispanic white (Hayes-Bautista, Schink, and Chapa 1988). It is possible, therefore, that racial and ethnic resentments could override age as a potential source of conflict between the generations, as a white gerontocracy draws upon the resources of a relatively poor black and Hispanic working class. Although this outcome is no more inevitable than is age-based conflict, we should be aware of the potential dangers implicit in the way we structure our systems of social rewards. If minority Americans are denied opportunities for good jobs, they will be less able to provide for a large older population than are today's workers.

Table 1.1, which provides information from the Bureau of the Census on the projected growth in the proportion of individuals over sixty-five and over eighty in a representative set of developed and developing countries, makes it clear that population aging is a worldwide phenomenon. In all countries, the percentage of the population aged sixty-five and older will grow into the twenty-first century. Even in developing nations, such as Mexico, Brazil, and India the proportion of older persons will double. Of course, the populations of the developed nations will age even faster. In Japan, the nation with the longest life expectancy at birth, over a quarter of the population will be sixty-five or older by the year 2025 and nearly 10 percent will be over eighty. Clearly, population aging of that magnitude presents nations with truly unprecedented challenges.

The Institutional Challenge

In the future no social institution will be spared the need to adapt to the unprecedented growth in the proportion of the population in the oldest age ranges. Every social norm, practice, and expectation will somehow be affected by the shift in social consciousness and resource allocation that an aging population brings about. Our traditional conception of the life cycle, with education, marriage, and fertility confined to the early years and retirement occurring in the mid-sixties, will change as individuals routinely pursue two or more careers, have multiple spouses, rear children later in adulthood, and continue working into what are now considered the retirement years. Improvements in health and in the quality of life mean that, for all practical purposes, sixty is still part of mid-life. In a society in which individuals in their sixties run marathons and engage in life to a fuller extent than did those in their forties in earlier eras, retirement at sixty-five will most certainly become less common. As the average life span increases, the life course itself becomes variable and, rather than following a prescribed set of transitions from youth to old age, individuals make or find their own pathways and may assume many different productive roles throughout their lifetime.

The entire concept of retirement must inevitably change as individuals who were once thought of as over the hill solely on the basis of

TABLE 1.1
Percentage of Elderly, by Country: 1990 to 2025

	1990		2010		2025	
	65 Years and Over	80 Years and Over	65 Years and Over	80 Years and Over	65 Years and Over	80 Years and Over
North America/ Western Europe						
Canada	11.5	2.4	14.3	4.1	20.7	5.2
Italy	14.6	3.2	19.8	5.8	24.1	7.5
Sweden	18.0	4.4	19.6	5.9	23.7	7.5
U.S.A.	12.5	2.8	13.3	3.8	18.7	4.3
Latin America						
Argentina	9.0	1.4	10.3	2.3	12.7	2.9
Brazil	4.2	0.6	6.2	1.1	9.4	1.7
Mexico	3.8	0.8	5.6	1.1	8.3	1.8
Asia						
China	5.8	0.8	8.3	1.6	13.3	2.5
India	3.7	0.4	5.3	0.7	7.8	1.1
Japan	11.8	2.4	21.3	5.7	26.7	9.3
Eastern Europe						
Azerbaijan	5.0	1.2	8.4	2.2	13.2	3.3
Hungary	13.4	2.6	16.7	4.4	22.4	6.1
Russia	10.0	2.0	13.5	3.5	18.9	4.3

SOURCES: U.S. Bureau of the Census, "*An Aging World II*," in *International Population Reports*, P95/92–3 (Washington, DC: U.S. Bureau of the Census, 1992), appendix A, 98–99; U.S. Bureau of the Census, *Aging in Eastern Europe and the Former Soviet Union*, P95/93–1 (Washington, DC, 1993), appendix A, A-1, A-2.

age are recognized as vital and productive workers. It is already clear that in a society in which the average life span is approaching eighty, routinely retiring large segments of the population in their mid-sixties is simply unrealistic. As economic necessity forces people to continue working longer, we may well find that the postwar pattern of retirement with which we are familiar was after all a historical fluke. In the future the very definitions of young adulthood, middle age, and old age will inevitably change, along with our notions of what is appropriate to each of these periods of the life course.

The aging of populations, regardless of where it occurs, brings about changes that affect the relative welfare of children and working-age adults, as well as that of the elderly. Work and career patterns are affected as opportunity chains are blocked; resources that might be devoted to education and youth are diverted to the care of the elderly; and working-age adults find themselves squeezed between the responsibility for their children and for their aging parents. In poor nations that are still struggling to provide the basics of a decent life to the young, the growing needs of the old represent a particularly difficult problem.

In the United States today many worry that too much of our aggregate economic pie is consumed by the elderly, and there is great concern that the situation will only get worse in the future, when our population will begin to age at an even faster rate. Perhaps because the United States does not have a universal social welfare system like those of other developed nations, conflicts between age groups emerge over the fact that older cohorts will reap far greater returns on their contributions to Social Security than will younger cohorts. Organized groups, such as the Americans for Generational Equity (AGE) and the Third Millennium, about which we will say more in chapter 8, were formed by working-age adults who believe that the old consume a disproportionate fraction of our aggregate income (Quadagno 1990). These individuals fear that today's workers will find that little is left for them when they retire (Kingson, Hirshorn, and Cornman 1986). Many young people feel that their contributions to Social Security will never be repaid and that the state-sponsored system of support for the old is age-biased and unfair.

Such a perspective clearly pits the young against the old and fails to appreciate the contributions that those who draw upon Social Security have made to our economy, culture, and society in the past. Yet the sentiment is not completely unfounded. Today's retirees will receive a very favorable return on their contributions to Social Security. The baby boom cohorts, who will retire after the turn of the century, will not. Such a system is inherently unfair since what is a right to a decent income for current retirees will not be a right for future retirees since their larger numbers will draw on more limited resources. In addition, younger cohorts will inevitably pay a far larger share of their lifetime earnings in taxes than older cohorts (Thomson 1993). However meritorious the contributions of the old to creating our modern world, such an age-based system of social rewards is bound to cause resentment. But perhaps that resentment can be defused by a more enlightened social policy and open conflict between age groups avoided.

A Heterogeneous Older Population

It is obvious that an economic and social system geared toward shorter life spans and smaller populations of elderly must change as our demographics change. Our expectations and outlook will evolve to conform to the reality of an older population, as will our political, economic, and social institutions. At one time, many individuals felt that the enfranchisement of women and their entry into the labor force spelled doom for our way of life. Today, both are an accepted fact, and anyone who would suggest a return to earlier gender roles would be considered hopelessly out of touch. As we adapt to changing demographic and social realities, the sense of crisis over the aging of the population that many now feel will pass. What is now new and unfamiliar will become the everyday reality, and we will develop new social institutions to deal with it.

For statistical purposes, the entire population of individuals over the age of sixty-five is often treated as dependent, but such a statistical definition of dependency is becoming less and less useful. Even today, many individuals continue to work and to pay taxes well past seventy. But stereotypes of the elderly as a homogeneous and nonproductive group still persist. Nothing could be further from the truth. The elderly are as diverse as any other age group. Not only do they differ in their employment status, but in race and ethnicity, in income and wealth, in health status, in migration history, in their living arrangements, and in their preferences in how they would like to spend their golden years. Treating age groups as if they were homogeneous is as erroneous as treating blacks or Hispanics as if they were all the same. People do not fit neatly into categories, and whether we are dealing with age, race, or ethnicity the differences between individuals within each category are far greater than the average differences between categories.

Our purpose in this and the following chapters is to elaborate the extensive variation among the elderly in terms of material and social resources and to show that the social disadvantages many individuals face in old age are continuations of the disadvantages they faced at earlier ages. In the United States today age, in and of itself, is not a dimension of disadvantage. The old, as a group, are fairly well off by any standard one might apply. As among younger age groups, though, certain individuals, especially older minority group women, face particular hardships. In what follows, one of our major concerns is to investigate the consequences of the increasing racial and ethnic diversity within the older population for resource allocation and health. One of our major objectives is to document how minority group status and gender interact to affect the health and welfare of older women in particular. To the extent that minority group status increases an individual's vulnerability to the negative consequences of rapid social and economic change, the welfare of a large segment of the elderly is at risk.

On the other hand, although race and ethnicity are often treated as risk factors for poverty and ill health, there are aspects of black and Hispanic culture that are particularly adaptive to the challenge of caring for the elderly and that potentially enhance their health and welfare and increase their ability to live in the community (Bagley et al. 1996). In chapter 5 we examine the supportive role of the family in the community care of the elderly and patterns of intergenerational exchanges of both material and emotional support. We begin in this chapter, however, by outlining the major post–World War II demographic and social transformations that have resulted in the rapid increase in the proportion of the population over sixty-five and by summarizing the potential impact of these changes on the elderly and especially on older women, blacks, and Hispanics. In later chapters we will elaborate the consequences of these changes in greater detail.

The Changing Social Context of Aging

The growth in the number of older persons has not occurred in a vacuum. Rather, it has been accompanied by a large number of other demographic, social, economic, and political changes that have potentially profound implications for the welfare of both the old and the young. Among these changes are alterations in family size, structure, and function. Since the end of the Second World War, the number of individuals who live alone has increased dramatically, as has the number of single parent households (Angel and Angel 1993; Kobrin 1976; Garfinkel and McLanahan 1986). Today the two-parent household with children is no longer the norm. Increases in housing stock, rising divorce rates, and the rise in extramarital fertility mean that the traditional family, consisting of husband, wife, and children, makes up a smaller and smaller fraction of all households (Saluter 1994). These rapid changes in family structure have affected the welfare of children and adults across the life course (Angel and Angel 1993). More and more individuals are spending a greater portion of their lives unmarried and entering the later years of life without a spouse (Worobey and Angel 1990a).

These new patterns of marriage, divorce, and extramarital fertility have important implications for the economic and social situations of individuals during the later stages of the life course. The economic and social situations of never married or temporarily married individuals in later life depend upon their own accumulated resources and not upon the joint accumulation of two spouses. Although some of these individuals will be well off in retirement, for others old age will bring a continuation, and perhaps even a worsening, of the poverty that they suffered during their younger years. Until women achieve equality with men in the labor force, those with limited work experience and disrupted marital histories will face particular hardship in later life (Angel and Angel 1993; Myers 1982). Because of the compounded disadvantages they face, many minority group women will fare even worse (Worobey and Angel 1990b).

Most governmental and private retirement plans are based on the traditional family form in which two people marry early in life and jointly accumulate assets during their working years. In retirement, the couple lives off the accumulated assets of their joint efforts, which may or may not have included active labor force participation by the wife. Her domestic contribution, however, will have freed her spouse to devote more time to work and, thereby, will have enhanced their aggregate economic well-being. After the death of a spouse, the surviving partner (usually the wife) continues to draw upon their joint assets and receives at least a portion of the deceased partner's retirement income.

Today the reality is very different for a large number of older persons. As a result of rapidly changing patterns of marriage and fertility, for many individuals this traditional pattern of asset accumulation does not apply, and many individuals have little or no private retirement income. In 1990, for example, 51 percent of the population aged sixty-five or older received only Social Security, unsupplemented by any private retirement income (Grad 1992). As always, the situation is particularly serious for the minority elderly. Table 1.2 shows that one in five minority elders make do with Supplemental Security Income, the portion of Social Security intended for the poor who have not contributed the amount required to qualify for regular benefits during their working lives. Less than one in twenty non-Hispanic whites rely on this source for their retirement income.

As the result of lifetime economic disadvantage, minority elderly also have fewer assets than do non-Hispanic white elders. Nearly three-quarters of non-Hispanic whites report income from assets, as compared to only one-third of minority elderly Americans (Angel 1995). This huge difference in lifetime asset accumulation among

TABLE 1.2
Income Sources for Persons 65 Years and Over: 1990

Percent who receive:	Non-Hispanic whites	Non-Hispanic blacks	Hispanics
Earnings[1]	22	20	20
Social Security	93	87	80
Income from assets	74	29	38
Supplemental Security Income (SSI)	5	20	23

SOURCE: Social Security Administration, Office of Research and Statistics, "Income of the Population 55 or Older, 1990," SSA Publication no. 13–11871 (Washington, DC: Social Security Administration, 1992) table 1.3, pp. 8–10.
1. Earnings include wages, salaries, and self-employment.

minority Americans has profound implications for the social mobility of groups as a whole. Young adults whose parents cannot help them buy into the American dream may be locked out forever, and such disadvantage can be passed on from one generation to the next. The failure to accumulate an estate is clearly one of the major consequences of the occupational disadvantages suffered by American blacks and Hispanics.

In the United States today gender, in addition to race and Hispanic ethnicity, forms one of the major dimensions of economic disadvantage. An individual who never marries, who has children early in life, and who receives only a minimal education clearly has no chance at a career that provides generous retirement benefits, nor is she likely to accumulate the assets that will provide an economically secure old age. Even middle-class individuals, who begin life with all of the advantages for educational and occupational achievement, can find their situations in later life seriously undermined by divorce and its negative consequences for income and asset accumulation. Divorce is very expensive for everyone involved, but women suffer especially sharp declines in income after divorce (Martin and Bumpass 1989; Holden and Smock 1991). In recent years the number of second and subsequent divorces has increased, resulting in even greater threats to income security in old age (Martin and Bumpass 1989; Saluter 1994).

We must, therefore, abandon old stereotypes of the life course, involving one marriage and a well-planned retirement. Today, the marital and fertility histories, as well as the economic situations, of the elderly are far more complex. The changes in family life that we have witnessed since the Second World War, including smaller families and an increase in the number of individuals living alone, have important implications for the economic and social welfare of the elderly that we must begin to understand. Ongoing debates over options in long-term care for the elderly have increased our appreciation of the diversity in needs among the older population. As the average life span continues to increase, the diversity in health, economic situations, and preferences in living arrangements among various segments of the older population will increase as well.

The Declining Significance of Marriage

In addition to the aging of the population, profound changes in family and marital patterns are the most significant social forces that will affect both the young and the old as we enter the twenty-first century. Since the Second World War we have witnessed a decline in the traditional two-parent household and an increase in the number of older individuals who live alone (Angel and Angel 1993; Worobey and Angel 1990a). An increasing housing stock and an apparent preference among older persons not to live with their children, even when they suffer significant declines in health, mean that today the family and living situations of the elderly are very different than they were only a few decades ago. The extended household of the past, containing a married couple, their children, and one or more grandparents, is increasingly rare (Ruggles 1987; Laslett 1972).

Yet for certain groups, the multigenerational household is still here and, if anything, growing in importance. But it is not the multigenerational household of the past. Rather, it is a product of the rise in unwed young motherhood and reflects a new and disturbing trend. Table 1.3 reveals large group differences in the number of families headed by women. It also shows that a substantial fraction of these households include grandchildren. As the data reveal, the trend is particularly pronounced among blacks and Hispanics (Angel and Angel 1993). In a considerable number of these households the second generation, the child's mother, is either literally or functionally

TABLE 1.3
Single Women Living with Their Grandchildren in 1993

	White	Black	Hispanic
Percent of families headed by women	13.6	46.7	23.3
Percent of female-headed households with grand-children	6.3	13.1	10.0

SOURCE: U. S. Bureau of the Census, Unpublished tabulations, Washington, DC, 1993.

absent, and the grandmother herself is quite young (Burton 1992; Saluter 1994). The general social disintegration of our inner cities and the rise in extramarital fertility, especially among very young women, means that the number of such households will increase.

Such a situation has serious implications for both the children and for the older adult. A grandparent can obviously fill the role of the parent, and throughout history grandparents have successfully raised their orphaned grandchildren. Today, though, some grandmothers must assume the responsibility for their grandchildren not because the parents died but because they have ceased to function as parents. In many of these situations drug addiction, incarceration, extreme youth, little education, and few job skills take the mother out of the picture as an even minimally adequate parent (Baydar and Brooks-Gunn 1991; Minkler, Roe, and Price 1992).

Many grandmothers who find themselves in this situation are quite young (Burton and Bentgson 1985). This family form has serious implications for the lifelong economic and social welfare of everyone involved, and again, insofar as a larger fraction of black and Hispanic families than non-Hispanic white families are female-headed and poor, the negative consequences will fall upon them disproportionately. To the extent that having to raise one's grandchildren, often by oneself, reflects blocked opportunities and a generally disorganized social environment, it is unlikely that either the grandmother or the grandchild will ever be in a position to greatly help the other or that the grandmother will be able to save for her own retirement. The grandchildren in such households will probably be exposed to the same disruptive forces that claimed their parents, and it is unlikely that the senior female will be able to greatly increase their opportunities. One wonders, of course, if the growth in the number of grandmothers raising their grandchildren is not a self-limiting phenomenon. Once the currently absent mothers become biological grandmothers themselves, it is unlikely that they will be in any position to care for their own grandchildren or to help their aging parents and grandparents. In such a situation responsibility for the care of the elderly will fall entirely on the state.

In a relatively few decades, then, we have come from a regime in which one married at a young age, had children quickly, and stayed married for life to one characterized by much more marital disruption and extramarital fertility (Cherlin 1991). Perhaps the most disturbing trend, and one that has serious implications for both the young and the old, is the increase in the number of births to never-married mothers. Table 1.4 shows that since 1960, the number of children living with a never-married mother has grown to the point where there are as many children living with a never-married mother as with a divorced mother. It is clear that for a large fraction of our population marriage and childbearing have become uncoupled. Many young women simply do not expect to wait until they are married to have children (Angel and Angel 1993).

Single mothers, whether divorced or never-married, face serious economic problems. After a divorce a woman's income usually drops precipitously (Holden and Smock 1991). Yet divorced mothers are usually older and have better job skills than never-married mothers, and although many fathers abandon their children after a divorce, many others provide at least some child support. The situation of most never-married mothers is truly grim. Of course, professional women with high incomes have the resources to cope with single motherhood quite well. Unfortunately, the majority of never-married mothers are not professionals, nor do they have high incomes. They are, for the most part, very young women with little hope of providing the material, emotional, or social support that their children need to become productive adults. Many of these young mothers are part of the growing underclass in which welfare dependency is chronic.

TABLE 1.4
Percentage of Children Living in Single-Parent Families with a Divorced or Never Married Parent

Year	Children Living with a	
	Divorced Parent	Never Married Parent
1960	23.0	4.2
1970	30.2	6.8
1980	42.4	14.6
1990	38.6	30.6
1993	37.1	35.0

SOURCE: Arlene Saluter, "Marital Status and Living Arrangements: March 1993." U.S. Bureau of the Census, *Current Population Reports,* P20–478 (Washington, DC: Government Printing Office, 1994), table G.

These women are unlikely to ever be able to support themselves, nor are they likely ever to be in a position to care for their own parents. Because of a lifetime of blocked opportunities, in old age they will have no savings upon which to draw, and they will be entirely dependent on public support.

Yet it is not only never-married mothers who face difficulties in old age. The increased incidence of divorce and remarriage has important implications for inheritance patterns and the intergenerational accumulation and transfer of assets. In the traditional family, a couple's assets were normally controlled by the surviving spouse after one or the other had died and then ultimately bequeathed to the children. Marriages that unite individuals with children from previous marriages lead to more complicated patterns of inheritance. The very meaning of family is changing, and the transfer of assets from one generation to the next may increasingly be governed by prenuptial agreements and other legal instruments, rather than by tradition. Of course, the transfer of a substantial estate has never been an option for the poor, who, at most, may pass on some real property; for them inheritance is not a means of generational upward mobility. One of the major problems faced by minorities and the poor is the difficulty in accumulating an estate that would serve as the basis for a family's mobility out of poverty (Crystal and Shea 1990a, 1990b). One of the most disturbing aspects of inequality between the races in the United

States is the fact that black Americans have very few tangible assets. Even middle-class blacks have far less equity in their homes than do whites (Myers 1995; Angel 1995).

The lack of an estate is part of a package that often includes the inability of the younger generations to contribute on a day-to-day basis to the care of their elderly parents. The necessity for women to work to make ends meet and the increase in extramarital fertility and marital disruption mean that often there is no one available to care for older parents. For poor older persons, purchasing such services is not an option, and for many of these individuals life in the community simply means learning to cope as best one can with whatever limitations they suffer. As for the poor generally, for minority single mothers the accumulation of an estate is never a realistic option. Getting ahead in life in any sense is often difficult, since low educational levels and a lack of job skills place well-paying work out of reach of these women and, as even its defenders concede, the welfare system itself becomes a trap from which one has difficulty escaping. For these individuals, and for the growing number of female-maintained households in which men never play a significant role, the intergenerational transfer of assets is a meaningless concept. For the poor all of their income is consumed in the purchase of day-to-day necessities. Exchanges between the generations for the most part consist of immediate instrumental support. The long-term consequences of the inability of such families to accumulate wealth means that neither the young nor the old are in any position to greatly assist one another. If one generation is unable to assist the next to move up economically, we may see a continuation or even exacerbation of the racially and ethnically stratified social class system that we have today.

The Loss of Women as Full-Time Care Givers

The problems of poverty, the failure to accumulate an estate, and a large number of poor female-maintained households are clearly serious problems for minority Americans. Other trends, however, affect the middle class as well as the poor. One of the major postwar changes that has affected the family and the lives of women in particular is the growth in the number of women who are full-time workers. Today even the mothers of small children work, and many middle class women are in jobs that provide retirement benefits. Clearly, such women will be in a much better economic situation during their retirement years than women without private pension plans. Unfortunately, since minority group women are more likely than nonminority women both to become single mothers and to hold jobs without adequate pension benefits, the benefits of work will accrue disproportionately to middle-class white women.

Although the increased labor force participation by women today will insure the economic security of many middle-class individuals during retirement, it also means that they are no longer available to care for aging parents on a full-time basis. As in the other areas we have dealt with, there are large social class differences in the consequences of female labor-force participation. Middle class individuals with adequate retirement incomes and numerous assets are in a better position to purchase the care they need and do not have to draw upon their children's resources. Women with high family incomes, whether they work or not, are in a better position to purchase care for their parents than women with lower family incomes. Again, as in other areas of life, the big losers are the poor, among whom neither the old nor the young are able to purchase home care services and among whom adult children are less able to care for their parents themselves because of competing responsibilities and the need to work.

Social class and labor force participation by women, therefore, clearly affect the welfare of the elderly. The impact of these factors, though, is compounded by an overall decrease in fertility, a feature of the "demographic transition" that has led to the lowest total fertility rates in the history of the developed world. Before this transition occurred, the care of aging parents could be farmed out to several adult children. Today, smaller families and greater mobility mean that children are often not available to provide day-to-day care.

All of these changes mean that in the future the elderly will have little alternative but to turn to the state when they become dependent. Although there will always be transfers of resources from one generation to another in the form of inheritance and gifts, in all likelihood those will continue to be from parents to children. Relatively few working-age adults are likely to be in a position to contribute significantly to their parents' acute or long-term care. The necessity of providing for their children's education and welfare and of preparing for their own retirements means that, at the individual level, the young are limited in their ability to contribute financially to the care of the elderly. Proposals that would require children to contribute substantially to their parent's long-term care represent a short-term solution that merely moves the crisis up one generation. If a working-age adult's asset accumulation is impaired because he or she is required to make large contributions to the care of aging parents, those individuals will in their turn have no choice but to draw upon their own children's resources or rely on the state. A system that impoverishes future generations assaults one of our core values—that we should provide for our children and grandchildren and insure that their lives are at least as good, if not better, than our own (Yankelovich 1994).

For this reason we, as a society, have chosen to socialize financial support for the elderly. Since the 1930s when the Social Security Act was passed, public expectations concerning children's financial responsibility for aging parents have changed dramatically (Crystal 1982; Treas and Spence 1989). In surveys conducted during the 1930s, a majority of individuals indicated that they believed that children should assume financial responsibility for their aging parents (Cowart 1994). Today, similar surveys reveal that a majority of individuals do not believe that children should be personally responsible for their parents in old age (e.g., Marshall, Rosenthal, and Daciuk 1987). Although it is still true that the family provides a large amount of instrumental and practical support to older individuals, when it comes to financial support we expect the state to step in (Crystal 1982; Wisensale and Allison 1988). The costs of acute and long-term care for the elderly are enormous, and the trend toward smaller families has reduced the number of individuals who can share the burden of this care. Even middle-class families are quickly impoverished when required to pay for a protracted nursing home stay. Today, when an aging parent finally requires such care, the only realistic alternative is Medicaid (Rivlin and Wiener 1988a).

Cultural Change and Options in the Care of the Elderly

We end this chapter by summarizing certain social forces that are changing the way in which we view the elderly and the way in which their long-term care is financed. These forces are changing not only our material and social worlds but our culture and the norms and expectations that govern relations between the generations (Popenoe 1994). Here we merely set the stage; in later chapters we will examine these social forces in greater detail. Discussions of ethnicity are often couched in terms of culture to emphasize the fact that individuals of different national origin bring with them their own beliefs, practices, and ways of life. After some time in this country, those differences tend to diminish and one's cultural identity becomes more that of mainstream American society. This process of acculturation results in very different orientations within groups with a recent immigration history. Among recent immigrants a traditional cultural orientation is associated with larger families and a familistic orientation that includes clear norms governing children's responsibility for aging parents (Trevino and Fielder 1986–87; Mindel 1979). For those who move up the ladder of social and economic success, patterns of marriage and divorce, fertility, and labor force participation begin to resemble those of long-term residents.

Although Hispanics have larger families than non-Hispanics on average, those with more education and higher incomes are, like the rest of the middle class, curtailing their fertility (Bean and Tienda 1987). Along with these demographic changes we would expect to witness the rejection of norms requiring children to care for their parents. Even for traditionally familistic groups, therefore, demographic changes and the potentially overwhelming burden of the financial responsibility that frail, aging parents represent will likely result in an increasing reliance on the state for the care of the elderly.

The process of cultural change is rapid and obvious among immigrants, but it affects the native as well. For them cultural change is not a matter of physical migration but of adopting the new world view that accompanies social change. We end this chapter by reiterating our observation that, along with the growth in the older population we will inevitably witness a cultural change in the social definition of old age and in the pact between the generations. Such changes inevitably occur in all areas of life as a function of material, demographic, or economic changes. Examples abound, from conceptions of the role of women in the workplace, to acceptable social intercourse between the races, to the role of religion in public life. Cultures and societies have no choice but to adapt to changing demographic and material realities. The impetus for cultural and social change that an aging population represents is irresistible, and the person who was considered old during a previous historical period will in the new age be considered middle-aged (Foner 1986). In years to come, retirement in the sixties will come to be viewed as is retirement in the forties or fifties today, justifiable only in the case of disability. Of course, many individuals will no doubt be ready to retire in their sixties, and, if they can afford to, they can always exercise that option. Already, though, we do not force professors to retire at sixty-five, and in the years to come many professionals and even nonprofessionals will undoubtedly continue working into their seventies, if only for the satisfaction that they receive from their work.

Cultural change will also manifest itself in the way we live and how we interact with different age groups. In the coming years we will witness large-scale experimentation with various options in living arrangements and work patterns among the able-bodied elderly. We will also witness experiments in new ways of caring for the infirm elderly. Already there is much discussion concerning the role of long-term care insurance for the elderly (Cohen et al. 1992; Rivlin and Wiener 1988a). The expectation that one should insure oneself against the need for long-term care clearly indicates that we are beginning to appreciate the limitations in the family's ability to provide it. Today very few people are even aware of the existence of long-term care insurance, although the data clearly show that most of us will need it. As of yet, long-term care policies are expensive and include so many exclusions, restrictions, and limitations that they are unlikely to address the needs of more than a small fraction of the elderly (Cohen et al. 1987). In the future, though, if coverage under such policies improves and if the cultural and social changes we anticipate create incentives for people to purchase such policies, they will become more common. Long-term care insurance will further change norms and expectations concerning the family's role in the care of the elderly. Of course, such policies will always remain out of reach for the poor and for the vulnerable groups with which we are most concerned. As in other areas, when it comes to the financing of long-term care, the old will comprise two unequal groups, and the least advantaged will be disproportionately black and Hispanic.

Other suggestions for financing long-term care for the elderly also imply profound cultural changes in the way we think of old age and the responsibility of the family for the elderly. In the future, reverse mortgages will become more common (Rivlin and Wiener 1988b). In such arrangements an older person basically sells his or her home to a bank or mortgage company in exchange for a lump sum or a monthly payment based on the equity he or she owns in a home. He or she then remains in the home until death or for some contracted period. Such plans are based on the liquidation of the equity and mean that the older person's estate will be largely depleted during his or her lifetime. Little or nothing may be left to pass on to heirs, potentially weakening the tie between generations. Individuals who are unable to amass a substantial estate will, of necessity, be thrown back upon the state. The equity one might have in an inexpensive house is not likely to provide for a long period of specialized nursing home care.

Although long-term care insurance, reverse mortgages, and other approaches that draw upon individual resources hold out some promise for the middle- and upper-class elderly, they will never address more than a small fraction of the need among the poor. The family will, of necessity, have to pick up the slack. One of the most promising avenues for providing support for the elderly on a long-term basis is enhanced community care that supplements, rather than replaces, the family. There is ample evidence that the elderly prefer to live in the community rather than enter an institution (Angel et al. 1996; Kendig and Yan 1993; Wolf and Soldo 1988). This attitude is very ingrained in our culture and reflects the almost universal desire for independence and autonomy. The challenge we face is to develop ways of providing high-quality community services that assist the family to care for its older members at a reasonable cost.

Community care is very recent, and effective and efficient ways of providing it have not yet been developed. Various demonstration projects indicate that providing care to the elderly in the community can be as expensive as institutionalization (Greene, Lovely, and Ondrich 1993a; Liu, Manton, and Liu 1985; Weissert, Cready, and Pawelak 1988; Vertrees, Manton, and Adler 1989). Other experiments, however, such as the On Lok program in community care in San Francisco's Chinatown, which we describe in greater detail in chapter 7, hold out much promise for the community care of even fairly impaired elderly people (Ansak 1990; Koff 1988; Capitman 1986). This program uses cultural and community resources to assist even the seriously impaired elderly to remain in the community.

We are particularly intrigued by such experiments in community care, because they hold out the promise of accomplishing at least two goals. First, they allow the older person to remain in the community and to participate in the life that he or she has come to know. Second, the availability of community care optimizes the choices that an older person's children have. With some formal assistance, the smaller families of the future may be able to keep their frail elderly parents at home in the community. As we will show in later chapters, groups differ in the extent to which they would be receptive to such arrangements. If programs for the elderly were designed to offer culturally appropriate community support services to families as an alternative to institutionalization, the range of possibilities for both the young and the old would be greatly enhanced and the quality of their lives improved.

TWO

A Longer and Better Life: Who Has Benefited Most from Improvements in Health?

The dramatic increase in life expectancy and the rapid growth in the older populations of the developed world that we documented in the last chapter are largely the result of better health. As standards of living have improved over the last century, death rates from both acute and chronic causes have declined and people are living not only longer but healthier lives. Yet even if we were able to achieve a health care utopia, people would still grow old, and age brings with it an increased susceptibility to degenerative and chronic illness. Health is central to an active and productive life, and it represents a real form of wealth at any age. Since health and illness are so central to discussions of the well-being of the elderly, in this chapter we take a closer look at the health consequences of the aging process and ask whether the gains in the quantity of life that we have enjoyed in the aggregate during the last few decades have been shared by all groups equally.

Although life expectancy at every age is at a historical high, the number of years one can expect to live varies for different racial and ethnic subgroups (Taeuber 1990). Between 1900 and 1989, the average life expectancy at birth for black men doubled from thirty-three to sixty-five, and for black women it increased from thirty-four to seventy-four. For whites, whose life expectancies were higher to begin with, improvements in life expectancy have also been dramatic. White men can now expect to live to seventy-three, as compared to forty-seven in 1900, and white women can expect to live to seventy-nine, as compared to forty-nine in 1900. These increases in life expectancy at birth are largely the result of declines in infant mortality, but they also reflect increases in overall life expectancy at later ages (Lubitz, Beebe, and Baker 1995; Manton and Vaupel 1995).

As with gains in life expectancy at birth, though, gains in life expectancy at age sixty-five have benefited racial and ethnic groups differentially. For white males aged sixty-five or older the remaining years of life increased by nearly three years from 1950 to 1989, while for black men the increase in life expectancy was only half a year. For women the increase has been even greater. For white women life expectancy increased by almost four years between 1950 and 1989; for black women, over two years. The two major dimensions of health disadvantage that these and other data reveal, then, are gender and race. Due largely to discrimination, class-based health risk factors, and the accumulated disadvantages of a lifetime, black men have benefited the least from improvements in longevity.

Projections into the twenty-first century indicate that, again due to improved living conditions, life expectancy will extend even further for all groups. Figure 2.1, though, reveals great variation in the gains projected for each group. The gender differential will persist, and women will continue to live longer than men. Gains will be substantial for Hispanic men and women (86.1 and 89.2 years) and for Asian-American men and women (88 and 92.2 years). American-Indian men and women will also benefit greatly (87.1 and 92 years). Unfortunately the gains for blacks will be more modest (80.4 and 84.5 years) (Day 1993).

These projections are consistent with the rather dramatic health differences that we already can observe between racial and ethnic groups at all ages. Hispanics, whose aggregate socioeconomic profile is poor, have mortality rate similar to those of non-Hispanics. Blacks,

FIGURE 2.1
Projected Life Expectancy at Age 65 in 2030, by Race and Ethnicity

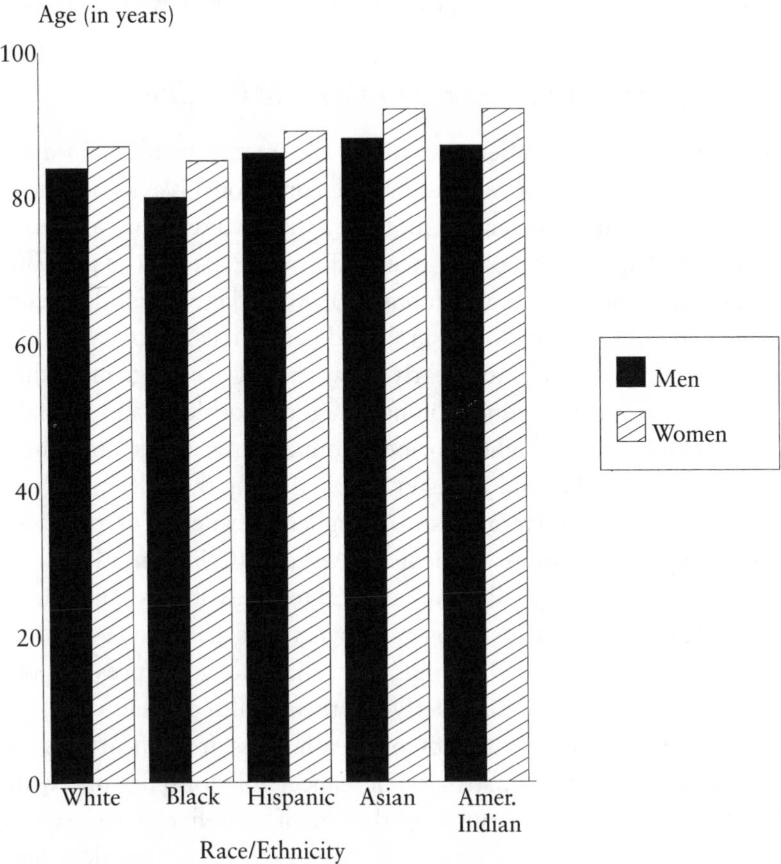

SOURCE: Jennifer Cheeseman Day, "Population Projections of the United States, by Age, Sex, Race, and Hispanic Origin: 1993–2050," U.S. Bureau of the Census, *Current Population Reports,* series P25-1104 (Washington, DC: Government Printing Office, 1993), table B-2.

on the other hand, fare far worse than either Hispanics or non-Hispanic whites and suffer serious health consequences as the result of their lower socioeconomic profile. Health and functional capacity, then, are not simple functions of either biology or socioeconomic status. Something about culture and group membership mediates the impact of biological and social risk factors on health. It is important that we begin to understand not only the health risks but also the health-*protective* aspects of group membership (Bagley et al. 1996).

The Differential Prevalence of Chronic Conditions

Among older adults differences in life expectancy result from differential death rates from various chronic conditions. Blacks, for example, continue to suffer higher mortality than whites from all causes, except perhaps at the oldest ages (Elo and Preston 1994; Gibson 1994; Manton, Patrick, and Johnson 1989). These racial differences in mortality are due to well-established health risk factors associated with social class. The data clearly show that at every age individuals with low income and education have higher morbidity and mortality rates than those of higher socioeconomic status (Link and Phelan 1995; Rogot, Sorlie, and Johnson 1992). Among the elderly, the poor have higher mortality rates and a higher prevalence of functional impairments than more affluent individuals (Crimmins, Hayward, and Saito 1994; Guralnik et al. 1993; House, Robbins, and Metzer 1982; Pappas et al. 1993; Rogers, Rogers, and Belanger 1990). The evidence is rather overwhelming, then, that race influences not only the material welfare of the elderly but their health as well.

Table 2.1 presents statistics on death rates from heart disease, cerebrovascular disease, stroke, and cancer for non-Hispanic white, black, and Hispanic persons over the age of sixty-five in 1980 and in 1990. We all must die of something, if not one cause, another. Since we must eventually die of something, if death rates from heart disease and stroke decline, as they did between 1980 and 1990, rates for some other cause must go up. The drop in death rates from heart disease and stroke among the elderly between 1980 and 1990 were accompanied by an increase in death rates from cancer. The data also reveal important differences between racial and ethnic groups both in base rates of mortality from the various causes and in rates of change in mortality, which tell us something about the health risks these groups face. At all ages after sixty-five, Hispanics have had and continue to have lower mortality rates than non-Hispanic whites or

TABLE 2.1
Death Rates from Leading Causes, by Age, Race, Hispanic Ethnicity: 1980–1990
(Deaths per 100,000 resident population)

	Non-Hispanic White			Non-Hispanic Black			Hispanic		
ause of death	1980–82	1988–90	Percent Change	1980–82	1988–90	Percent Change	1985–87	1988–90	Percent Change
eart Disease									
65–74 years	1166.7	913.8	−21.7	1434.4	1316.2	−8.24	681.0	649.7	−4.64
75–84 years	2896.8	2381.9	−17.8	2895.4	2689.2	−7.12	1662.0	1603.0	−3.58
85 years and over	7633.1	7036.7	−7.8	5814.5	6042.2	3.91	4514.0	4660.0	3.23
erebrovascular isease									
65–74 years	190.3	136.9	−28.1	380	288.8	−24	127.5	116.9	−8.31
75–84 years	714.1	507.5	−28.9	900.7	681.3	−24.4	376.8	349.3	−7.3
85 years and over	2164.9	1697.2	−21.6	1758.8	1503.8	−14.5	1021.0	971.6	−4.82
Ialignant Ieoplasms									
65–74 years	807.7	850.6	5.3	987.5	1105.5	11.95	472.2	505.5	7.05
75–84 years	1226	1312.2	7.0	1336.1	1534.8	14.88	831.5	887.0	6.67
85 years and over	1592.4	1696.3	6.5	1544.7	1890.5	22.39	1192.0	1326.0	11.3

OURCE: National Center for Health Statistics, *Health, United States, 1992*, (Washington, DC: Government Printing ffice, 1993), table 31.

blacks, a pattern that is inconsistent with their aggregate socioeconomic profile. Consequently, their rate of improvement between 1980 and 1990 was slower. As we noted above, this mortality advantage among Hispanics appears in other data and suggests a health-protective aspect associated with traditional Hispanic culture (Markides et al. in press). In contrast to Hispanics, blacks have higher base mortality rates than non-Hispanic whites, and their rates of improvement between 1980 and 1990 were consistently lower. These data, therefore, clearly demonstrate a serious mortality disadvantage among older blacks that is largely a function of low socioeconomic status. But why is low socioeconomic status translated into elevated mortality for blacks, but not for Hispanics?Although mortality statistics are useful in characterizing a group's overall quality of life, they do not tell us everything. With appropriate medical care an individual can live for some time with serious functional impairments, especially if they have a large informal social support network. In the United

States today those with little education and income are at greater risk of illness and death than those higher in the social hierarchy (Crimmins, Hayward, and Saito 1994; Angel, Angel, and Himes 1992; Manton 1993). Although most people remain healthy until relatively late in life, aging necessarily increases the risk of chronic illness, functional disability, and institutionalization. Social class differences in health risks have cumulative effects over the life course, resulting not only in higher mortality during the adult years but in diminished functional capacity in old age (Crimmins, Hayward, and Saito 1994; Manton 1993). One study of Puerto Rican nursing home residents in New York, for example, found that they were younger than non-Hispanic residents, suggesting that their functional capacity had deteriorated to a greater degree at an earlier age than was the case for non-Hispanics (Espino et al. 1988). Other evidence indicates that, once they are admitted to a nursing home, blacks are less likely than whites to be discharged, again suggesting that their functional status is worse than that of whites (Greene and Monahan 1984). These findings also indicate caution against assuming that all groups are the same. Puerto Ricans may age in a very different way than Cuban Americans or Mexican Americans, and their long-term care needs may be very different.

The Meaning of Health and Functional Status

The consequences of aging, therefore, are not solely the result of biology. Although all organisms age biologically in accordance with an innate clock, the rate at which they lose their functional capacities is extremely variable and depends upon numerous cultural and social class factors. It is important, therefore, to understand exactly what health and illness are and how they are affected by these nonbiological determinants. Each of us has an intuitive and immediate sense of what health is, but for our purpose we need greater conceptual precision. Like most other authors, although we speak of health, we are really concerned with its absence and focus on those risk factors that increase one's susceptibility to illness. Although it is certainly possible to offer a positive definition of health, for our purposes health is really no more than the absence of illness; it is that state of affairs that we take for granted until ill health intervenes. In order to understand the consequences of ill health it is necessary to differentiate between its clinical, psychological, and social components. At a strictly clinical level ill health consists of, or is at least revealed by, signs and symptoms that a physician uses in conjunction with laboratory tests to arrive at a diagnosis. Ill health at this level is often referred to as "disease" and is understood in terms of basic and fairly reductionistic physiological or psychological models.

Subjectively, the consequences of disease are experienced in a more diffuse somatic and emotional way. When we are ill, we do not experience a diagnosis, but rather become aware of uncomfortable sensations, whether vague or distinct. We refer to this subjective experience of poor health as "illness." It is important to distinguish illness from disease because it is this subjective sense that something is wrong that leads one to seek help or that at least results in the awareness that one's health has changed. It is also useful to distinguish between illness and disease because a large body of research shows that the subjective experience of illness, or at least its external manifestations, are affected by cultural and social factors (Angel and Angel 1995; Angel and Idler 1992; Dutton 1986; Idler and Angel 1990; Kleinman 1986). One's subjective sense of one's physical and mental well-being is affected by culturally conditioned beliefs about what is normal and abnormal, as well as by the general health of one's reference group, which includes those individuals to whom one compares one's own health to determine whether it is, by comparison, good or bad. For example, a backache is much less remarkable among agricultural workers than among professors and is less likely to be construed as pathological.

At the social level disease and illness manifest themselves as the inability to carry out one's prescribed social roles and duties. At this level illness has consequences for others as well as for the individual who must be cared for and who requires help with basic activities of daily living. Because our focus is primarily social, we focus less on the clinical aspects of aging and more on its social and functional consequences. Although none of us welcomes illness, it is probably fair to say that any specific physical pathology becomes a substantial problem for the individual only once it begins to seriously interfere with his or her functioning.

Conceiving of ill health as consisting of at least these three components—biological, social, and functional—is very useful for understanding the causes and consequences of its various manifestations. As one moves from the strictly biological level to the more social and functional levels, the number of factors that structure the consequences of disease and illness increases. Researchers working in the area of disability have developed conceptual schemes of the process by which a specific disease or set of diseases results in an inability to perform one's age-appropriate social roles (Nagi 1991; Nagi 1979). Lois Verbrugge and Alan Jette summarize these and offer a more comprehensive model of what they term the "disablement process" (Verbrugge and Jette 1994), a model that illustrates how the consequences of disease and illness are mediated by various social factors and how disability is as much a function of environmental demands as of individual impairments. This way of looking at the consequences of disease is based on the realization that the extent to which a specific disease or illness interferes with one's life depends not only on the disease itself but on the context in which it occurs. For a manual laborer a serious back problem quickly becomes disabling, due largely to the demands of the job. For someone with slight difficulty in walking or dressing, having someone available to help with these tasks can make the difference between a high-quality independent life in the community or a lower-quality life of struggle and, perhaps, institutionalization.

Figure 2.2 builds upon Verbrugge and Jette's model by specifically emphasizing the cultural and social class context within which disability occurs. It also distinguishes between the more objective and subjective components of the disablement process, since culture and social class potentially influence each of these components differently. Although disability is usually defined in purely medical terms for official purposes, it has clear subjective aspects that can affect the extent to which functional limitations become disabling. Two individuals with similar levels of pathology or functional limitation can

FIGURE 2.2
The Sociocultural Context of the Disablement Process

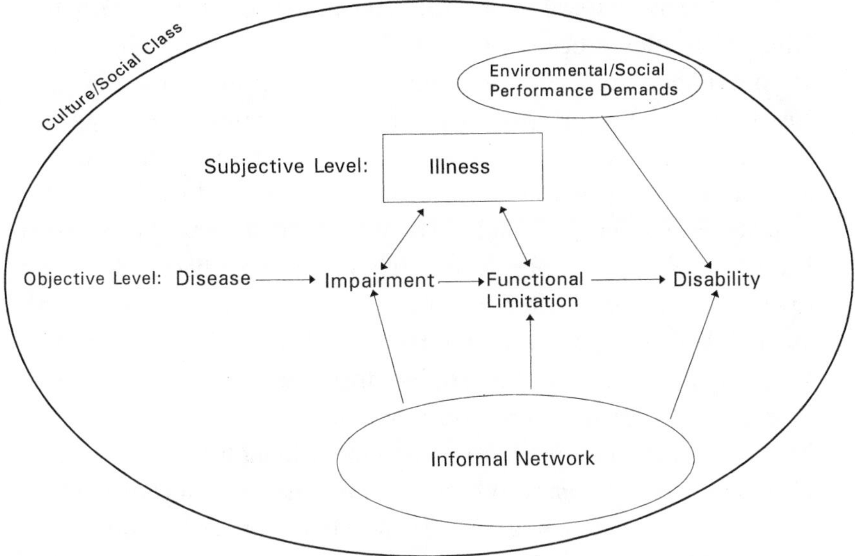

differ greatly in whether they view themselves as disabled (Idler and Angel 1990; Mechanic and Angel 1987). Cultural and social class factors, as well as one's social network and even one's own psychological makeup, influence whether a potentially disabling condition actually interferes with one's life.

In our model culture and social class influence each stage in the disablement process, both by affecting the probability of the occurrence of each stage and by influencing the timing of the transition to the next stage. Culture and social class, then, are contextual factors and not simply two more variables that affect only parts of the process. The model begins with disease, which is the actual pathological process that manifests itself as impairments. Impairments are physiological abnormalities such as brain damage, heart disease, or the loss of motor control. These can manifest themselves as functional limitations, which are problems in carrying out basic physical and mental functions like walking, bathing, and eating. If they are serious enough, these functional limitations can result in disability, which is the inability to carry out one's social roles.

Let us be more specific concerning the impact of race and Hispanic ethnicity on this process. Blacks and Hispanics have lower average socioeconomic statuses than non-Hispanic whites, and the data clearly show that the poor have higher mortality rates than the middle class. Blacks have higher rates of hypertension than whites and, consequently, a greater incidence of stroke and cardiovascular disease (Franco et al. 1985; Frerichs, Chapman, and Maes 1984; Kittner et al. 1990; Siegel 1993). They also have higher mortality rates from cancer (Center for Disease Control 1990; Jepson et al. 1991). Hispanics have higher rates of diabetes, which can lead to kidney failure, the loss of limbs, blindness, heart disease, and death (Samet et al. 1988). On the other hand, certain data indicate that Mexican Americans appear to enjoy a mortality advantage over non-Hispanics when it comes to both heart disease and cancer (Frerichs, Chapman, and Maes 1984; Forbes and Frisbie 1991; Markides et al. in press; Mitchell et al. 1990). This advantage is usually attributed to the protective aspects of traditional Mexican American culture, which are, unfortunately, lost as individuals absorb the values and habits of the U.S. mainstream. These differences between blacks and Hispanics illustrate the fact that group-specific behaviors influence the risk of disease. For example, Mexican Americans report low rates of smoking, a high-risk behavior that has been associated with numerous diseases.

Once a disease has manifested itself, cultural and social class factors influence the probability that symptoms will be recognized as serious and that help will be sought (Angel and Thoits 1987; Mechanic 1980). They also influence the quality of health care that one receives and one's compliance with recommended medical regimens. All of these factors operate to determine one's functional status. If one gets treatment for a chronic condition early in its course, effective management is often possible. Survival rates for many cancers are quite high if they are treated in time. Someone with coronary heart disease can live a full and active life with proper management and with proper treatment someone with diabetes need not suffer its more debilitating consequences.

Perhaps most important for our purposes, cultural and group factors influence the availability of social support and an individual's ability to purchase care, thereby influencing the probability that a disease will progress to a disability. Where families are large and children tend to stay close to their parents, an older person is more likely to receive help in dealing with functional limitations. Cultural norms that emphasize the obligation to care for an ailing or needy parent are likewise an advantage to the impaired elderly, tending to insure that they will get the kind of assistance that keeps diminished functional capacity from becoming crippling disability.

It is important to distinguish between the subjective and objective aspects of the disablement process, since a large body of evidence clearly shows that social support decreases morbidity and mortality, as well as depression. Although there are clear practical reasons for this, the simple fact of being part of a family and a social network improves an individual's mood. Depression is a common problem among all age groups, and the isolated elderly are at particular risk (Berkman et al. 1986; Feinson 1985). Depression has also been shown to be associated with higher mortality (Murphy et al. 1988). Isolated and depressed individuals are unable to engage in life fully, and they can easily come to view themselves as invalids, further compounding the depression. Adequate social support can prevent this outcome by keeping the older persons engaged with others and providing the help they need to keep from viewing themselves as invalids.

This model of the disablement process is very useful in emphasizing the crucial distinction between what Verbrugge and Jette call "intrinsic" versus "actual" disability. Intrinsic disability refers to difficulty with basic activities of daily living. At bottom, such difficulties constitute a potential for disability, which may or may not manifest itself. A person for example, may have trouble walking and may report that fact in a survey. Such a limitation, however, does not inevitably imply disability. If one has trouble walking one can use a cane and still go for walks. If one has trouble opening jars because of arthritis in the hands, can purchase a jar opener. The point is that one can compensate for physical impairments and continue living as one is used to. If the task can be changed to make it easier or if a device or a person can help, difficulties in functioning need not become disabling. If, on the other hand, the environmental demands are too great and if help is unavailable, one may be forced to change one's life radically.

Disability, therefore, is partially a social construction, and this model clearly emphasizes that environmental demands can be altered greatly by one's social network. If one has trouble buttoning one's clothes, help getting dressed can make the difference between doing well and becoming discouraged. If one cannot drive oneself to the grocery store, having a son or daughter who will provide transportation makes all the difference in the world. Cultural and social groups differ, both in the number of children older parents have and in the likelihood that those children will live close enough, and be willing, to provide assistance. The likelihood of disability, and the quality of one's life generally, depend upon both the social factors that affect the onset of disease and those that mediate its impact.

Most survey research that attempts to identify the risk factors for disability among the elderly asks about an individual's ability to carry out simple physical activities of daily living (ADLs), such as walking, bathing, and feeding oneself, or more complex instrumental activities of daily living (IADLs), such as preparing meals and taking care of finances. Although such questions address intrinsic rather than actual disability, the assessments based upon them are reliable, easy to gather, and extremely useful in studies of community health. They are ideal for our purpose since we are less interested in clinical pathology than in the consequences of disease for one's ability to live one's life to the fullest. We will therefore employ this sort of data to explore those mediating cultural and social factors that determine when, where, and how a disease begins to limit one's ability to function normally; when, in short, a potential disability becomes an actual one.

Disability and the Social Environment: Active Life Expectancy

One of the more useful ways of addressing the question of whether longer life has meant better life is offered by researchers who try to determine how much of the increase in average life expectancy that we have experienced in this century is disease free (Crimmins, Hayward, and Saito 1994; Katz et al. 1983; Manton, Stallard, and Liu 1993). We would probably all welcome twenty more years of healthy and active life as an addition to our expected life span. Twenty years characterized by mental and physical decline and poor health would be far less desirable. This approach focuses on what is termed "active life expectancy" and is based upon life table techniques, a statistical approach to studying aggregate mortality patterns in which demographers estimate how long a hypothetical cohort of individuals born at any one time would live if they experienced the age-specific death rates current at that time. One's active life expectancy consists of that period of life during which one can expect to live free of any significant illness or functional incapacity. Such an approach is particularly useful for those interested in improving the quality of life, not just increasing its length. Given innovations in modern medical technology, debates over the quality of life and the determination of when extraordinary measures should be abandoned will inevitably affect us all (Verbrugge 1994).

Most empirical studies of active life expectancy are based on survey data designed to determine the presence of cognitive impairment or functional incapacity. Most of these studies define disability as the point in the disablement process at which cognitive impairment or physical health problems seriously interfere with one's ability to engage in age-appropriate social activities without help (Land, Guralnik, and Blazer 1994; Rogers, Rogers, and Belanger 1990; Verbrugge and Jette 1994; Robine, Bucquet, and Ritchie 1991; Manton, Corder, and Stallard 1993).

Estimates of active life expectancy vary greatly, depending upon the definition of disability used in a particular study and the population studied. Robine and Ritchie (1993), for example, report that on average one spends 80 percent of one's total life span in an active state and 20 percent hampered by some significant limitation. In Sweden over 90 percent of the average life is active. Each nation and each group within each nation has its own active life expectancy, reflecting in each case its overall standard of living. Again, such radically different estimates may reflect the way in which disability is defined and measured rather than any real difference in the number of years one can expect to live in good health. Despite these international differences in estimates of active life expectancy, however, the data are unambiguous in showing that women, though they live longer than men, also spend more years in poor health (Verbrugge 1989).

These studies of active life expectancy also lead us to temper our expectations concerning extended longevity. Estimates of historical changes in active life expectancy for Great Britain, Australia, and the United States indicate that the years recently added to our overall life span are not characterized by activity and health but by mild or moderate disability (Robine, Bucquet, and Ritchie, 1991; Crimmins, Hayward, and Saito 1994). Longer life, therefore, may not mean better life. Again the data reveal significant gender differences. Although men are at greater risk of death at every age, they are also more likely than women to improve in functional capacity. Women pay for their longer life spans by enduring more years in poor health.

Unfortunately, there are few studies of active life expectancy that provide comparative information for different racial and ethnic groups. One recent study examined racial differences and found that blacks have shorter active life expectancies than whites because of the earlier onset of functional limitations (Crimmins, Hayward, and Saito 1994). This study, though, found that higher-status older persons have both longer lives and fewer inactive years. These findings are consistent with much of the previous research that we have reviewed, which indicates that the risk factors associated with minority group membership are largely due to lower socioeconomic status and poverty.

The sobering findings of research into active life expectancy might easily lead one to ask why, with all the scientific and medical advances that we have witnessed in recent years, the prevalence of disability is so high among the old. The answer is that, ironically, our successes in managing chronic illness have themselves increased its prevalence. Acute diseases typically kill their victim quickly, or the afflicted person recuperates and is cured. In either case the episode of illness is short. With chronic disease, for which cure is not an option, our object is to increase the length and quality of life. If a larger fraction of individuals with a chronic condition live longer lives, its prevalence in the population will of course invariably increase. Such an increased prevalence, then, is not a sign of failure but, rather, of success. Today, individuals with heart conditions, diabetes, and even cancer live longer than they used to. The increased prevalence of these conditions, however, represents an increased medical care burden and is one of the driving forces behind the rapid growth in medical care spending that we will discuss further in the next chapter.

Our success in increasing life expectancy, then, almost inevitably increases the number of years characterized by mild and moderate disability. The only way to decrease the number of years characterized by some disability while maintaining longer life spans is to delay the onset of chronic illness. If our current awareness of the consequences of health risks earlier in life results in such a delay in the onset of chronic illness, active life expectancy could increase in the future. If, on the other hand, chronic illness is, at a population level, an inevitable concomitant of aging, then we will continue to see an increase in the number of older individuals who are mildly to moderately disabled and an increase in the number of years they spend in that condition. Clearly, each of these potential outcomes has different implications for social policy and for the cost of caring for an aging population.

Although most observers are well aware that functional capacity and disability are influenced by the tasks one must perform and the social support one receives, few studies of active life expectancy have dealt with these issues in any detail. Someone who is employed in heavy manual labor will be more seriously affected by a back injury than is a professor of sociology. Someone who lives in a rural area will be much more seriously affected by an inability to drive than someone in an urban neighborhood. Environmental challenges and community structure, therefore, clearly affect the onset of functional incapacity and disability.

Since we are dealing with group differences in this book we could hardly ignore potential group differences in social support. Obviously, an older individual with family members close by to help deal with the functional consequences of declining health is in a much better position than someone without such assistance. Group differences in family size, migration patterns, and expectations concerning responsibility for parents clearly affect the availability of social support. An older Mexican American widow with several children nearby will be much more likely to move in with one of them in the event that she becomes incapacitated than a woman with no children or children who have moved far away. The woman with family nearby will, in all likelihood, receive help from them as she ages and as her health declines. Clearly, understanding how best to address the needs of the growing population of older individuals requires that we begin to understand how group membership affects the environmental challenges a person faces and the social support he or she has at their disposal.

The Health of Mexican American and Black Elderly: Some Recent Findings

As we have seen, then, health is a complex construct that is influenced by one's cultural and social context. Because of the almost complete lack of data on the comparative health of Mexican American elderly individuals, we and some colleagues recently conducted a study of three thousand Mexican Americans over the age of sixty-five in the five southwestern states of Arizona, California, Colorado, New Mexico, and Texas (Markides et al. in press). This study was one of a series carried out as part of the Established Populations for Epidemiologic Studies of the Elderly (EPESE) program and designed to assess the prevalence of chronic diseases, levels of functional capacity, and medical care use among elderly Americans. They provide some of the first findings concerning the comparative health levels of older Mexican Americans in the United States. Here we compare levels of functional incapacity among Mexican Americans to that of non-Hispanic blacks and whites in North Carolina (Cornoni-Huntley et al. 1990).

Table 2.2 presents data on problems with activities of daily living (ADLs) for black, Mexican American, and non-Hispanic white men and women in three age groups. With certain exceptions, the data indicate higher levels of disability among Mexican Americans than non-Hispanic whites and blacks. Many researchers have noted a mortality crossover between blacks and whites at the oldest ages. Our findings too indicate that the oldest blacks are a hearty lot who are functioning quite well. A much larger fraction of Mexican Americans, on the other hand, experience some incapacity at the older ages. These data are consistent with observations that we re-

TABLE 2.2
Percentage of Individuals with Problems with Activities of Daily Living, by Race and Mexican American Ethnicity
(Unweighted Ns in parentheses)

	65–74			75–84			85 or over		
ADL	White	Black	Mexican American	White	Black	Mexican American	White	Black	Mexican American
WOMEN									
Bathing	5.0	7.6	7.7	11.9	12.8	16.5	20.8	16.0	49.2
Dressing	5.4	5.5	7.0	8.0	6.7	11.6	16.1	11.6	36.0
Walking	6.6	8.8	6.9	12.6	11.8	11.7	29.3	25.7	39.0
Grooming	2.1	4.5	5.6	4.8	6.0	9.4	10.2	9.5	33.4
Transferring	4.8	6.7	6.2	8.0	8.2	10.6	15.1	10.3	33.6
Toileting	3.1	5.4	5.2	8.0	8.3	10.5	15.2	11.0	28.9
Eating	1.3	1.5	4.2	1.8	1.0	4.4	1.8	2.6	18.3
N	(6,661)	(3,558)	(1,140)	(3,459)	(1,826)	(493)	(737)	(455)	(118)
MEN									
Bathing	10.5	6.0	7.1	9.9	7.6	13.6	23.6	12.0	27.4
Dressing	4.8	5.4	6.1	5.3	3.9	13.4	13.7	12.7	18.4
Walking	6.7	8.4	6.7	8.3	7.5	14.6	12.3	15.1	19.6
Grooming	1.2	1.8	4.7	1.0	1.0	9.0	4.9	6.0	13.2
Transferring	3.7	5.5	6.1	4.0	3.4	11.3	4.9	6.6	18.8
Toileting	2.1	3.4	5.3	1.7	3.8	9.3	4.9	6.6	12.1
Eating	1.2	1.4	4.7	0.0	1.0	8.4	2.1	3.0	7.8
N	(4,491)	(2,398)	(861)	(1,741)	(965)	(334)	(284)	(166)	(94)

SOURCE: Kyriakos S. Markides, *A Longitudinal Study of Mexican American Elderly Health* (Washington, DC: National Institute on Aging, 1992).

ported earlier that, even in light of their favorable mortality experience, Mexican Americans may on average suffer earlier and more serious functional declines than the rest of the population.

In table 2.3 we compare the groups in terms of their ability to engage in tasks that require a fair amount of mobility. The table shows the percentage of individuals who report difficulty doing heavy housework, walking half a mile, or climbing stairs, i.e., Rosow. These items are designed to identify more serious functional incapacity than the questions concerning problems with activities of daily living. Again we leave the detail to the interested reader and provide only a global interpretation. A much larger percentage of Mexican American women than non-Hispanic black or white women report difficulty with these tasks. These data corroborate anecdotal evidence that Mexican American women are sedentary and, consequently, suffer more serious mobility limitations than non-Hispanics in old age. For the men the differences are less pronounced, but again the data provide evidence for greater functional incapacity among Mexican Americans. Blacks report more functional incapacity than non-Hispanic whites, but their rates are lower than those of Mexican Americans.

Table 2.4 presents information on chronic conditions and basically corroborate the patterns we reported earlier. Blacks report more high blood pressure than non-Hispanic whites and Mexican Americans far less, except at the oldest ages. This is consistent with the lower incidence of heart attacks and strokes among Mexican Americans. Mexican Americans report far less cancer but much more diabetes, a condition for which they are at very high risk.

Finally we asked these individuals how they would rate their own health. This very popular measure is useful because it tells you about the individual's subjective experience. As we noted in presenting our model, individuals with similar levels of functional incapacity can assess their health very differently, depending on numerous psychological and social factors. Table 2.5 presents information on self-assessments of physical health for the three groups and reveals dramatic differences between them. Black elderly report generally poorer health than non-Hispanic whites, but Mexican Americans rate their

TABLE 2.3

Percentage of Individuals with Major Mobility Impairments, by Age

(Unweighted Ns in parentheses)

	65–74			75–84			85 or over		
	White	Black	Mexican American	White	Black	Mexican American	White	Black	Mexican American
WOMEN									
Heavy housework	34.5	41.2	42.2	59.5	53.5	65.4	81.9	81.7	89.5
Climbing stairs	13.6	19.2	21.1	27.3	29.7	41.5	52.7	48.0	77.3
Walking half a mile	18.6	23.0	23.3	41.5	40.9	48.4	66.3	66.1	82.4
N	(6,703)	(3,659)	(1,129)	(3,452)	(1,912)	(490)	(728)	(575)	(117)
MEN									
Heavy housework	27.7	28.3	22.8	38.4	48.5	49.6	50.6	78.0	73.1
Climbing stairs	10.8	14.3	12.0	14.6	20.1	27.5	25.0	23.4	46.0
Walking half a mile	14.3	17.6	14.8	21.9	30.9	32.3	32.8	40.2	55.1
N	(4,526)	(2,479)	(854)	(1,909)	(1,049)	(331)	(308)	(214)	(96)

SOURCE: Kyriakos S. Markides, *A Longitudinal Study of Mexican American Elderly Health* (Washington, DC: National Institute on Aging, 1992).

TABLE 2.4
Percentage of Men and Women Reporting Chronic Conditions

	White		Black		Mexican American	
	Males	Females	Males	Females	Males	Females
65–74 years						
High blood pressure	44.8	53.4	53.8	71.5	37.4	49.5
Cancer	17.2	13.7	8.0	9.3	5.8	7.2
Diabetes	19.2	15.1	20.0	29.8	32.1	28.1
Hip fractures	2.8	3.9	2.3	1.9	1.9	2.7
Fractures other than hip	19.8	29.4	14.9	16.3	12.0	16.3
Heart attack	24.9	10.1	13.3	11.5	10.9	8.3
Stroke	10.6	4.0	9.3	9.5	6.9	4.1
N	(4,526)	(6,703)	(2,479)	(3,659)	(862)	(1,139)
75–84 years						
High blood pressure	42.3	51.2	46.1	66.7	32.1	53.0
Cancer	26.0	18.0	5.4	6.2	7.8	6.2
Diabetes	11.0	9.8	22.8	23.6	21.8	24.1
Hip fractures	3.8	6.8	3.9	2.9	5.5	9.4
Fractures other than hip	21.7	35.5	13.2	16.2	10.1	16.8
Heart attack	12.8	15.8	14.6	15.1	13.3	15.1
Stroke	14.2	6.1	10.1	8.2	11.9	13.3
N	(1,909)	(3,586)	(1,049)	(1,912)	(336)	(497)
85 or over						
High blood pressure	25.0	50.7	42.1	59.1	32.5	55.3
Cancer	22.7	16.1	9.3	8.2	7.7	12.2
Diabetes	10.4	14.3	13.6	13.7	17.4	17.2
Hip fractures	8.1	17.1	6.5	4.0	4.6	15.8
Fractures other than hip	15.3	34.2	18.7	20.0	11.9	15.7
Heart attack	10.1	14.4	13.6	19.8	17.1	10.7
Stroke	19.8	16.9	10.7	9.0	10.1	13.5
N	(308)	(918)	(214)	(575)	(96)	(118)

SOURCE: Joan Cornoni-Huntley, Dan G. Blazer, Mary E. Lafferty, Donald F. Everett, Dwight B. Brock, and Mary E. Farmer, *Established Populations for Epidemiologic Studies of the Elderly: Resource Data Book,* vol. 2, National Institutes of Health Publication No. 90–495 (Washington, DC: National Institute on Aging, 1990); Kyriakos S. Markides, *A Longitudinal Study of Mexican American Elderly Health* (Washington, DC: National Institute on Aging, 1992).

health as far worse than either of the other two groups. We suspect that this is, to at least some degree, the result of semantic differences between the English and Spanish versions of the question. Over 80 percent of the Mexican Americans answered the questions in Spanish. Even with careful translation it is impossible to convey the same meaning in Spanish and English, and it is likely that many Mexican Americans who feel just fine rate their health as fair, a reasonable descriptor in Spanish (Angel and Guarnaccia 1989). Clearly we will have to do much more qualitative research to determine the extent to

TABLE 2.5

Self-Assessed Health, by Age, Race, and Mexican American Ethnicity

	65–74			75–84			85 or over		
	White	Black	Mexican American	White	Black	Mexican American	White	Black	Mexican American
WOMEN									
Excellent/very good/good%	77.1	58.2	38.8	69.1	52.3	26.8	66.4	—	18.8
Fair%	16.8	26.3	39.0	21.9	25.1	41.3	23.0	—	31.6
Poor%	6.1	15.5	22.2	9.0	22.6	31.9	10.6	—	49.6
N	(9,011)	(932)	(1,140)	(5,321)	(451)	(496)	(1,648)	—	(118)
MEN									
Excellent/very good/good%	74.5	57.6	46.2	68.1	53.5	29.8	64.4	—	31.6
Fair%	17.5	29.0	36.2	20.5	25.3	34.5	21.8	—	27.7
Poor%	8.1	13.4	17.6	11.4	21.3	35.8	13.8	—	40.7
N	(7,375)	(711)	(862)	(3,498)	(286)	(336)	(687)	—	(96)

SOURCE: Kyriakos S. Markides, *A Longitudinal Study of Mexican American Elderly Health* (Washington, DC: National Institute on Aging, 1992).

which poorer self-assessed health among Mexican Americans reflects the true state of affairs.

A Longer and Better Life?

Health is a multifaceted phenomenon with both biological and social components. It is also very difficult to measure in populations. Although the data are sparse, certain consistent patterns emerge and it is beginning to become possible to piece together a comparative health and functional capacity profile of the minority elderly. The data clearly show that blacks are at higher risk of illness and death at all ages, except perhaps the very oldest. It is also clear that their health disadvantage is a legacy of the historically blocked opportunities for social and economic advancement. Black society has borne the burden of racism and its consequences, and the epidemiological record proves that, although we have removed the legal barriers to advancement for black Americans, disadvantages that are the result of centuries of oppression will take longer than a few decades or one or two generations to overcome for the population as a whole.

During the twentieth century, all groups have benefited from increases in life expectancy, and unless some serious economic or environmental disaster seriously exacerbates health risks, life expectancy should continue to climb for all groups at all ages. Although blacks have benefited along with the population as a whole, improvements in their life expectancy at birth and at later ages have lagged behind those of whites. Blacks have shorter active life expectancies, primarily because they suffer functional declines earlier in life. Overall, then, the picture is one of great improvements in health for black Americans, but persisting elevated risk of illness and death from causes such as stroke, heart disease, and cancer.

Hispanics, on the other hand, have an aggregate socioeconomic profile that would lead us to expect that they would also suffer elevated rates of morbidity and mortality. Mexican Americans do suffer high rates of diabetes and its consequences, yet their rates of heart disease and cancer are the same, if not lower, than those of non-Hispanic whites. This favorable morbidity and mortality experience suggests that there are protective aspects to traditional Mexican American culture that we must begin to understand and preserve if possible. The Mexican American elderly tend to be cared for at home, and they are typically well integrated into extensive family and community networks. These networks may account for the fact that their health is better than we would expect from their aggregate socioeconomic profile. As Mexican Americans assimilate into mainstream culture and adopt the life-style of middle-class Americans, these protective aspects of their traditional culture may be lost.

But, not all of the data point to better health among Hispanics. Certain evidence suggests that, like blacks, Hispanics may suffer functional declines earlier in life and be more functionally impaired in old age. The evidence, therefore, is mixed and leads us to the inevitable conclusion that we need further research, perhaps of a qualitative kind, to identify the predictors of better and worse functioning among the elderly. The most consistent finding in all of the research we have reviewed is that socioeconomic status is a major predictor of morbidity and mortality at all ages. Individuals with higher educations and incomes live longer and better than those with little education and income. The affluent are more likely to make it to old age and, once there, are more likely to function at a high level. Older individuals with sufficient assets simply have more control over their environments and their health. In the next chapter we continue our investigation of the situation of the elderly by examining group differences in income and assets and reveal large differences in the economic well-being of older blacks, Hispanics, and non-Hispanic whites.

THREE

Group Differences in Income and Wealth in Old Age: The Role of Public and Private Pensions

Since 1935, when the Social Security Act was passed, the economic situation of the elderly has improved dramatically, and today the official poverty rate among the elderly is lower than among families with small children (Angel and Angel 1993; Clark 1990; Crystal and Shea 1990a; Moon 1977; Schulz 1995; Smeeding 1990). Prior to the introduction of Social Security, old age frequently meant destitution and dependency, and retirement was not something ordinary folk looked forward to with anticipation. Without a guaranteed retirement income, a person had little choice but to work for as long as possible, and when he or she could no longer work or when a woman became a widow, there were few options other than to move in with relatives or face a life dependent on the charity of others. Numerous studies reveal that until fairly recently, individuals feared retirement, largely because of the economic uncertainty it involved (Friedman and Orbach 1974; Riley and Foner 1968; Atchley and Robinson 1982).

As their economic security improved, though, people came to look forward to retirement, and today most individuals no longer fear poverty in old age or the possibility that they will have to depend on their children when they can no longer work (Atchley and Robinson 1982). Of course, many individuals continue working into their seventies and even later, some because their work is a central part of their identity and others to supplement otherwise inadequate retirement incomes. These individuals, though, are the exception rather than the rule, and today the fear of destitution is no longer the primary motivation for staying in the labor force. The increasing acceptance of retirement has led to a remarkable decline in labor force participation among older men since the 1930s (Achenbaum 1986; Graebner 1980; Pampel 1981; Quadagno 1982; Quinn and Burkhauser 1990; Quinn, Burkhauser, and Myers 1990; Tuma and Sandefur 1988). Even as late as 1950 nearly half of all men over the age of sixty-four were in the labor force, but by the late 1980s fewer than 20 percent were still working (Schulz 1995). Today over half of working men retire before the age of sixty-five (Schulz 1995). This trend toward early retirement among men stands in contrast to an increase in the proportion of women between the ages of fifty-five and sixty-four who are working (Schulz 1995).

A series of amendments to the original Social Security legislation, including the indexing of benefits to the rate of inflation and programs such as Medicare and Medicaid, have made the program much more than the minimal income supplement it was originally (Danziger 1984; Smeeding 1990). Greater income security has fundamentally changed the meaning of retirement, and older persons today are able to travel, to give their children and grandchildren gifts, and to indulge their desire for privacy by remaining in their own homes (Worobey and Angel 1990a; Myles 1984). Yet as table 3.1 shows, this general improvement in the economic situation of the elderly has not benefited everyone to the same degree. Although Social Security has improved the lot of the elderly generally, there is a great deal of inequality among the older population, largely following racial and gender lines (Catchen 1989; Crystal and Shea 1990a; Dressel 1988; Meyer 1990; Taylor and Chatters 1988). Minority group elderly have lower household and personal incomes, lower earnings, fewer dividends, and less income from private and Social Security pensions

TABLE 3.1

Income Sources, by Race and Ethnicity: 1989

	Non-Hispanic White	Non-Hispanic Black	Mexican American	Cuban American	Puerto Rican	Other Hispanic	Asian
Household income	29,166	19,386	23,184	28,199	23,543	24,168	28,625
Personal income	15,261	8,300	8,228	9,043	8,904	8,315	13,470
Earnings	2,460	1,677	1,707	2,852	2,041	1,962	2,340
Interest and dividends	3,964	366	735	895	841	820	3,462
Social Security income (OASDI)[1]	5,308	3,819	3,633	3,137	3,775	3,296	4,707
Supplemental Security Income (SSI) and AFDC[2]	205	563	637	947	707	794	459
Private retirement income	2,532	1,564	1,108	734	1,206	1,044	1,924
All other income[3]	237	185	155	90	174	264	210
Mortgage payment[4]	69	64	91	169	105	79	117
N	(825,061)	(67,275)	(16,372)	(4,438)	(1,698)	(1,777)	(60,931)

SOURCE: U.S. Bureau of the Census, 1993. *1990 Census of Population and Housing: Public Use Microdata Samples, United States* (Washington, DC 1993).

1. Old Age Pension, Survivors Benefits, and Disability Insurance.
2. Supplemental Security Income and Aid to Families with Dependent Children.
3. Unemployment compensation, VA payments, alimony, and child support.
4. Monthly dollar amount.

than do non-Hispanic whites. By contrast, they receive a higher amount of Supplemental Security Income (SSI). As is the case among younger age groups, certain of the elderly remain in poverty or precariously close to it, and their retirement years are plagued by economic uncertainty. This highly vulnerable group consists disproportionately of blacks, Hispanics, and single women.

Women are at particular risk of poverty after widowhood, since fewer women than men are covered by pensions (Even 1994; Reno 1993; Holden and Smock 1991; Zick and Smith 1991). Yet even when they have long work histories, women—and especially minority women—are at greater risk than men of poverty in retirement (Logue 1991). Although only a small fraction of the elderly depend on public assistance, a disproportionate number of those who do are black (Abbott 1977). Other characteristics, often associated with minority group status, greatly increase the economic insecurity of certain older individuals. These include (1) a lack of supplemental health insurance to cover medical costs that Medicare does not pay, (2) the need for long-term care, (3) a reliance on Social Security as one's only source of income, (4) a large mortgage late in life, and (5) physical or mental disability (Angel and Angel 1993; Catchen 1989; Holden and Smeeding 1990). Individuals in these situations have very little slack and are at high risk of poverty if anything goes wrong.

In this chapter we examine the sources of income for elderly individuals in the years prior to and after retirement. We compare the basic economic situations of blacks, Hispanics, and non-Hispanic whites and document large differences in economic well-being among these groups that result from their reliance on different sources of income, as well as differences in lifetime asset accumulation. We also show that individuals without a private pension, a disproportionate number of whom are minority Americans and women, face far more serious economic difficulties in retirement than those who have one. Individuals with private pensions not only have a source of income in addition to Social Security, but since jobs that offer retirement plans are also those in which one pays higher Social Security taxes, these individuals tend to receive higher Social Security benefits than retirees without pensions, even though Social Security is designed to return a higher proportion of lifetime contributions to those with low incomes than to those with higher incomes.

Blacks and Hispanics earn far less on average than non-Hispanic whites throughout life and they are much more likely than non-Hispanic whites to be employed in jobs that do not offer a retirement plan. After they stop working, they are more often dependent on Social Security alone than are non-Hispanic whites, and the amounts they receive often leave them very close to poverty. The earnings disadvantages experienced by blacks and Hispanics are dramatic and have clear implications for all aspects of health and welfare, but the situation is even more serious when it comes to assets and property. Blacks and Hispanics have far fewer accumulated assets than do non-Hispanic whites by the time they reach retirement age. For most Americans a home represents their largest asset, and the typical middle-class white family has substantial equity in their home by the time the family's main breadwinner retires. In addition, by the time most middle-class individuals retire, they have at least some income from a private pension, and many have income from stocks, bonds, and rental property.

Among blacks and Hispanics, and especially among households headed by women, average home equity is shockingly low and income from stocks, bonds, or rent is nearly nonexistent. Table 3.2 presents comparisons of the total income and assets of preretirement age non-Hispanic black, non-Hispanic white, Mexican Americans, and other Hispanic households in 1992. These data are from the first wave of the Health and Retirement Survey (HRS), which provides detailed asset information for a large representative sample of individuals between the ages of fifty-one and sixty-one and their spouses (Juster 1993). Unfortunately, even with a large oversample of Hispanics, the number of Hispanics is modest, so we combine them into two groups, Mexican Americans and all other Hispanics. These data clearly show that race, Mexican American ethnicity, and gender form three dimensions of disadvantage in terms of household income and assets. As low as income and asset levels are for minority couples, the situation for minority female-headed households is far worse. Single

TABLE 3.2
Home Equity and Assets, by Race, Hispanic Ethnicity, and Household Type

	Non-Hispanic White	Non-Hispanic Black	Mexican American	Other Hispanic
SINGLE MALE OR COUPLE				
Housing equity				
Proportion	0.873	0.673	0.693	0.552
Mean	90,151	54,454	56,846	91,818
Nonhousing assets				
Proportion	0.995	0.890	0.901	0.904
Mean	235,609	75,539	58,396	142,333
Unweighted *N*	(4,390)	(893)	(340)	(203)
SINGLE FEMALE				
Housing equity				
Proportion	0.659	0.453	0.510	0.253
Mean	77,545	39,778	53,758	54,963
Nonhousing Assets				
Proportion	0.942	0.746	0.702	0.630
Mean	79,202	42,363	23,298	35,610
Unweighted *N*	(877)	(535)	(91)	(85)

SOURCE: Thomas F. Juster, "The Health and Retirement Survey" *ICPSR Bulletin* 14 (1993): 1–2.

black and Mexican American women have very few resources to carry them through the later years of life, and they are consequently at extremely high risk of dependency. These data make it clear, therefore, that gender and marital status, in conjunction with race and Hispanic ethnicity, represent major dimensions of economic disadvantage in the United States today. Throughout the life course single women have far lower incomes than either married couples or single men, and this pattern persists into old age. Women tend to outlive their husbands, and many widows are economically secure because they retain their husband's estate. Yet, as is the case in divorce, most women suffer a substantial drop in economic status following widowhood (Holden and Smock 1991; Logue 1991; Zick and Smith 1991). For single poor and minority women the economic hardships that often plague their earlier years continue into retirement (Burkhauser, Butler, and Holden 1991; Holden and Smock 1991; Logue 1991). Because of their more limited work histories and employment in jobs without pensions, many women often receive minimal Social Security or survivors benefits and are at high risk of poverty (Choi 1992; Schwenk 1992). Since low income is associated with diminished asset accumulation, few of these single older women have substantial assets.

If one cannot draw upon accumulated wealth, one must rely on current income and as table 3.2 shows, Hispanics fall far below non-Hispanic whites in income from private pensions. Private pensions are clearly the core of a package that includes higher Social Security benefits and frequently income from other sources. Among those who are better off, income from pensions and assets makes up a large fraction of total income (Clark 1990; Ycas and Grad 1987). The economic profile of older minority Americans, therefore, appears bleak.

Employment Status and Retirement Income

Our system of support for the elderly is quite complex, and it is necessary to know how it works in order to understand why blacks, Hispanics, and unmarried women are handicapped. In this section, therefore, we outline the system of private pensions and Social Security and point out why certain individuals benefit more than others. For most older individuals the primary source of income and wealth during retirement is from work-related retirement plans. Almost by definition, a good job is one that offers not only a decent salary and health insurance but a retirement plan as well. Private employer-based pensions represent one of the major sources of income for the middle-class elderly, and as the data in table 3.2 revealed, they can make the difference between a minimally adequate income and one that allows a person the freedom to enjoy his or her retirement.

Since the Second World War private pension coverage has increased greatly, and today most middle-class Americans take their retirement plans for granted. Yet large-scale pension coverage is a fairly recent phenomenon, and even today large segments of the labor force are not covered by employer-based plans. Indeed, a retirement plan represents as real an asset as any other. Although private pensions were introduced at the end of the last century, few workers were covered until after the 1920s when changes in the federal tax code induced large employers to adopt employer-funded pension plans. Early in the century the public sector led the way in offering pensions (Achenbaum 1986; Graebner 1980; Quadagno 1982). Federal government workers, professors, and teachers were among the first public occupational groups to receive pensions (Achenbaum 1986; Graebner 1980). By 1900 pensions for firemen and police officers were common, and by 1916 pensions for teachers were offered by thirty-three states (Achenbaum 1986). The Federal Civil Service Retirement System was established in 1920, and by 1930 15 percent of the labor force was eligible for a pension.

These early plans did not require contributions by the employee, nor did they typically provide for spouses or dependents after the pensioner's death. The primary motivation for the introduction of pensions by both private and public employers was to make it possible to retire older workers while providing them with a decent standard of living (Graebner 1980). Retirement has always served the dual purpose of removing from the labor force older workers who can no longer keep up with the pace of work and opening up opportunities for younger workers. Since those early days the extent of private pension coverage has greatly expanded, and employer-based pensions have become an important supplement to Social Security and personal savings for retired Americans. By 1990 57 percent of couples in which one spouse is over the age of sixty-five and 34 percent of unmarried older persons reported pension income. Among single older individuals 41 percent of men and 32 percent of women receive pension income (Reno 1993). Private pensions are rarely the major source of income among the elderly, but they can make the difference between just surviving and having enough money to buy needed medical and other services.

There are many variations in the way private pensions are funded and in the way they make payments. Although there are other options, we will focus on the two major types of pensions: defined benefit plans and defined contribution plans (Clark and McDermed 1989; Clark 1990; Schulz 1995). Defined benefit plans are the most common and are so named because once they are vested they guarantee a retiree a set benefit, either as a lump sum at retirement or in the form of a regular payment, usually based on a proportion of the individual's highest salary (Schulz 1995). Since such plans have traditionally not been transferable, from an employer's perspective they have the desirable characteristic of binding the employee to the firm. On the other hand, such plans limit the freedom of employees to change jobs, and if the payment amount is small or does not increase to compensate for inflation, one's economic situation in retirement might deteriorate over time. There are other dangers as well. If an employer goes bankrupt or is unable to pay the full amount of the pension, a retiree is simply out in the cold. In recent years pension legislation has guaranteed the vesting of such pension plans, but workers still cannot easily take their plans with them from one employer to another (Clark 1990; Schulz 1995).

Because they guarantee a basic income, defined-benefit plans are favored by many workers. Today, however, economic considerations, as well as changes in the tax laws governing an employer's contribution to pension plans, have led to a shift from defined benefit to what are termed "defined contribution" plans (Clark 1990; Schulz 1995). These plans are basically savings or investment plans administered by an insurance company or some other body. The employer contributes a set (or defined) amount, based on the employee's salary, and the employee also contributes. The administrator invests in mutual funds or other instruments in the employee's name, and upon retirement the employee begins to draw upon the accumulated value of the investments. In such plans the employee is often an active participant in choosing the investments to which the contributions are made.

Unlike a defined-benefit plan, though, in which one's income level is guaranteed, the only guarantee offered by defined-contribution plans is that the employer will contribute to the plan while the employee is working. If the financial advisers the employer hires invest wisely, the employee will reap strong earnings. If, on the other hand, the money is invested in ways that do not earn a high yield, the employee could conceivably lose much of the value of his or her savings and be seriously underfunded at retirement. Despite this insecurity, though, such plans have the advantage of limiting the employer's financial obligation to a certain contribution during the time that the employee is working. In addition, such plans are highly portable and provide the employee with the greatest possible mobility among employers.

But whatever the type of pension, one is clearly better off with some source of supplemental income in retirement than without it. Because private pensions are so closely tied to one's employment history, blacks, Hispanics, and women, who are less likely than non-Hispanic white men to have spent their working years in jobs that provide either defined-benefit or defined-contribution plans, are at greater risk of low income in retirement. Consequently, minority Americans are highly dependent on Social Security and on Supplemental Security Income. It is important, therefore, that we review how these programs work and understand those aspects of the public pension system that both penalize and benefit low-income individuals.

Social Security

When the Social Security Act was passed in 1935, the Old Age Insurance (OAI) component, Title II, covered only retired workers over the age of sixty-five who had been employed in commerce and industry (excluding railroad workers, who had their own retirement program). Four years later, in 1939, the first of many amendments to the Social Security law extended coverage to widows and dependent children. This Survivors Insurance (SI), along with OAI is funded by a payroll tax on employers and employees that has risen steadily over the years. Amendments enacted in 1956 created a permanent Disability Insurance program (DI) that authorized payments to disabled workers at age fifty (Achenbaum 1986). Subsequent amendments have extended the original Social Security program even further. The original program did not include domestic and farm workers, the self-employed, or federal employees. Today coverage has been extended to nearly the entire labor force. In addition, the original retirement age of sixty-five has been lowered to sixty-two, at which time one is eligible for benefits, though at a reduced rate. Perhaps one of the most significant changes is that since 1972 benefit levels have been indexed to the rate of inflation, so that the real value of Social Security benefits does not deteriorate (Achenbaum 1986; Clark 1990; Schulz 1995).

In order to qualify for OAI a worker must have contributed to the system for at least ten years, or forty quarters. The amount he or she receives is based on a complex formula that begins by mathematically equating a worker's earnings between the ages of twenty-one and sixty-five to current wage levels. This "indexing" procedure is used to adjust for the fact that average earnings have increased over time. The five lowest years of indexed earnings are dropped, and the remaining total earnings are averaged to calculate what is called the "average indexed monthly earnings," or AIME. The AIME is used to calculate the actual amount one receives, and the formula applied to it is designed to replace a larger fraction of the average earnings of individuals with low lifetime earnings than of individuals with higher lifetime earnings. For example, the formula for computing the retirement benefit for someone who reached age 62 in 1995 was the sum of (1) 90 percent of the first $426 of AIME, plus (2) 32 percent of AIME over $426 and below $2,141, plus (3) 15 percent of AIME over $2,567. The AIME dollar amounts are adjusted each year to stabilize the proportion of preretirement income that is replaced by the benefit. Thus, the replacement rate, or the proportion of preretirement income represented by one's Social Security benefit, is higher for individuals with low earnings than for those with higher earnings.

Several things can alter the amount of one's benefit. Since 1956 women have been allowed to retire at the age of sixty-two with actuarially reduced benefits. In 1962 this privilege was extended to men, and today over half of all men applying for Social Security benefits are below 65 (Schulz 1995). Those retiring early receive reduced payments to compensate for the longer period they are expected to receive benefits. Conversely, those who delay retirement beyond sixty-five receive larger benefits to compensate for the shorter period they are expected to receive benefits. A minimum benefit is provided to workers who reach sixty-two and who have ten or more years of covered earnings above a minimal level. Since Social Security is a retirement program, an earnings test reduces the benefits of individuals under the age of seventy who earn over a certain amount.

Today Social Security insures the income of far more individuals than just the covered worker. A spouse or child under eighteen (nineteen if the child is an elementary or secondary school student) is eligible to receive 50 percent of a worker's basic benefit, up to a maximum allowable amount for the family. Aged parents, disabled adult children, and divorced persons are eligible for dependent coverage under specified conditions. A widow or widower is eligible for survivor's benefits at age sixty under normal circumstances and at fifty if she or he is disabled. Disabled adult children or nondisabled children under sixteen are also eligible for survivors benefits. This benefit is 100 percent of the basic benefit for widows over sixty-five or for widows with dependent children. Benefits for individuals in the other categories vary.

Even from this brief description it is clear that Social Security is a complex program that provides income security for a large number of old and dependent Americans. It is a progressive income redistribution program in that it replaces a larger fraction of preretirement income for individuals with low lifetime earnings than for those with high lifetime earnings. It is regressive, however, in its financing, since the Social Security payroll tax is a flat rate for everyone. Additionally, one pays Social Security only on income up to a maximum. Income above the Social Security maximum is exempted, with the effect that individuals with low income pay Social Security taxes on all of their earnings while those with higher earnings pay on only a portion.

The designers of Social Security were keenly aware of the political vulnerability of programs geared only to the poor and wished to portray the program as an insurance or annuity scheme into which a worker would contribute during his or her working years and from which he or she would draw in retirement as an earned right. Such a system would avoid the stigma of welfare. The question at the time Social Security was designed, and one which continues to be debated today, is whether the current contributions of working individuals should go directly to retired workers or into a trust fund invested either in Treasury bonds or some other instruments. There was much concern in many circles over the size of such a fund, and many feared that control over such a large pool of money would give the government too much power. Ultimately, the designers opted for a pay-as-you-go system with a limited trust fund designed to cover short-run imbalances.

The current concern over Social Security has to do with the funding of the program, especially early in the next century when the baby boom cohorts will begin drawing benefits and the ratio of workers to retired persons will be low. Numerous radical proposals that would change the program fundamentally have been offered (Kingson and Quadagno 1995). The debate reflects both differences in basic values and differences in estimates of how serious the funding crisis is or how best to address it. Changes introduced in Social Security during the 1980s, including raising the retirement age to sixty-seven early in the next century, taxing the benefits of high-income recipients, and delaying the automatic cost of living adjustment (COLA), have alleviated some of the more serious mid-range funding problems. Actuarial projections show that with these changes the Social Security trust fund will grow rapidly into the early part of the next century and then deplete rapidly as the baby boom cohorts retire (Hambour 1987; Schulz 1995).

It is clear that Social Security is a massive program that has served the elderly well (Bernstein and Bernstein 1988). It is also clear that the cost of supporting the elderly will draw heavily on our aggregate resources in the future. For the most part, though, the more dramatic portrayals of a system in imminent danger of bankruptcy are based on the assumption that the program will not be modified to deal with emerging demographic realities. As is clear from the measures taken in the last two decades, we have already begun to modify the program in such a way as to insure its solvency, and alarmist projections are in all likelihood unfounded. The system is basically sound, although we will all have to expect to pay more for coverage, especially those with income from other sources. Because middle-class Americans generally have income from various sources, potential restrictions in Social Security will have less of an impact on them than they will on poor single women and minorities.

Supplemental Security Income (SSI)

The original Social Security Act had two major components to deal with income insecurity among the elderly. Although the designers of the program did not want to portray Social Security as a welfare program, in reality a large fraction of the elderly population would never contribute to the system and yet needed immediate help from it. In response, Title I of the Social Security Act established Old Age Assistance (OAA), a means-tested program that provided funds to states for the purpose of supporting older individuals in need (Achenbaum 1986; Orloff 1988; Quadagno 1982). As with other welfare programs, the determination of eligibility and benefit amounts were left to the states, and again as with other welfare programs, eligibility and benefits varied in consequence.

In 1974 OAA was replaced by the federally funded and administered Supplemental Security Income (SSI), which provides a standardized guaranteed income to poor elderly individuals who choose to participate (Clark 1990). Unlike OASI, the insurance component of Social Security, SSI is financed from general revenues. Many states supplement the federal SSI payment, and one need not have been employed or paid Social Security taxes in order to qualify. Rather, as with other welfare programs, eligibility is determined by income and asset tests. Blind and disabled individuals are also eligible for SSI. SSI proves that the designers of Social Security were correct in assuming that if it were viewed as a welfare program, rather than an insurance program, fewer individuals would participate. Because of the welfare stigma associated with SSI, a large fraction of individuals who qualify do not participate. Although estimates vary, it appears that at least 40 percent and probably more of poor elderly do not participate in the program (Leavitt and Schulz 1988; Menefee, Edwards, and Schieber 1981). In light of the economic disadvantages we have documented among single women and minorities, these groups are particularly dependent on SSI and, as of yet, we have very little information on rates of participation among those who are potentially eligible.

Other programs provide in-kind support to low-income elderly. Individuals who qualify for SSI also qualify for food stamps and various social services provided by the federal government. Many also qualify for public housing. But by far the most important programs in addition to OASI and SSI are Medicare and Medicaid, which we will discuss in the next chapter.

Women, Minority Americans, and Social Security

There is a general consensus that the Social Security program is poorly designed to address the needs of women, largely because of changing social realities. The program was devised at a time when few women worked outside of the home and when marriage and family patterns were much more traditional than they are today (Flowers 1977; Schulz 1995). The assumption that a woman will spend her life in one marriage and not work is obsolete and causes real problems when it continues to shape social policy. Today women work for at least part of their lives, and many are divorced or never marry. Women who are married for less than ten years have no claim to their ex-husband's benefits. Consequently, a woman can spend many years out of the labor force raising children and taking care of a home only to find that she gets no Social Security credit for her efforts. In computing one's level of benefits, years with no earnings are averaged in with years in which one has earnings, meaning that individuals with sporadic work histories qualify only for the minimal benefit, if any at all. As a consequence, many women find themselves dependent on Supplemental Security Income alone. Although SSI provides a minimal safety net, the levels for eligibility are set below the poverty threshold and few individuals are elevated above that threshold by receiving SSI (Schulz 1995).

Perhaps the most serious reason that many potentially eligible individuals do not receive SSI is the income and asset test. This test includes all income from Social Security, wages, and pensions. It also includes noncash items such as food, clothing, or shelter. One's spouse's income and assets are also taken into account. Even a small savings account is enough to disqualify an individual from receiving benefits (Leavitt and Schulz 1988). In order to receive SSI, therefore, one must be destitute, and the program itself does not provide sufficient income to elevate one above poverty.

This dilemma plagues our social welfare system and is the basis of much misunderstanding and resentment between the haves and have-nots in our country. The aggregate cost of programs like SSI is immense, and taxpayers justifiably feel burdened. On the other hand the payment levels to individuals are low and provide only a minimal safety net. It would probably be impossible, and maybe even undesirable, for SSI to elevate the retired poor to the level of those on OASDI. Our general welfare philosophy, which of course informed the development of the Social Security program is that only those who absolutely cannot provide for themselves should be helped, and even they should only receive enough for a bare subsistence.

Such a system almost guarantees a system of stratification among the elderly based on race and ethnic identity. Immigrants and individuals who never participated in the Social Security program or those who immigrated to the United States in middle or late adulthood face particular problems. Many individuals who are currently receiving OASDI benefits joined the system in adulthood as eligibility for coverage was gradually extended. For many of these recipients Social Security turned out to be an excellent investment: the benefits they receive are far greater than the taxes they paid while they were in the work force, since the Social Security tax rate was lower than it is today. Unfortunately, many individuals did not join the system at all or did not participate for the required ten years. Minority Americans are overrepresented in this population.

Individuals who immigrate to the United States late in life often do not have the time to contribute to the system. Table 3.3 shows that Mexican, Cuban, and Asian immigrants are far more dependent on welfare at all ages than are the native and that fewer of the foreign-born than of the native receive private retirement income. Table 3.4 shows that among Mexican Americans, those who immigrated after age 50 live in households that are far larger than those of native Americans or those who immigrated before age 50. Unfortunately, SSI is highly restrictive when it comes to resident aliens. For aliens

TABLE 3.3
Personal Income Sources, by Age and Nativity

	Mexican American		Cuban American		Asian	
1989	Native	Foreign	Native	Foreign	Native	Foreign
OASDI[1]	75.1	64.2	62.4	58.7	75.5	40.6
SSI/AFDC[2]	19.6	23.3	13.2	27.5	12.6	31.2
Private Retirement Income	21.5	14.1	22.3	15.7	32.9	12.0
N	9,765	6,685	159	4,279	6,148	10,037

SOURCE: U.S. Bureau of the Census. *1990 Census of Population ond Housing: Public Use Microdata Samples, United States* (Washington, DC, 1993).
1. Old-Age Survivor's and Disability Insurance
2. Supplemental Security Income and Aid to Families with Dependent Children

TABLE 3.4
Average Household Size by Age at Immigration and Nativity for Elderly Mexican Americans

	Age at Immigration		
	Before Age 50	After Age 50	Native
Men	3.31	5.05	2.84
Women	2.82	4.73	2.64

SOURCE: U.S. Bureau of the Census. *1990 Census of Population and Housing: Public Use Microdata Samples, United States* (Washington, DC, 1993).

the asset test includes the income and assets of the sponsors, meaning that sponsors are often saddled with the financial responsibility for the immigrants. In addition, the current anti-immigrant climate has serious implications for noncitizens. House Bill 1214 imposes greater restrictions on receipt of SSI by immigrants. Known as the "Personal Responsibility Act," the bill codifies the belief that aliens should be denied welfare and that rather than relying on public funds they should be supported by their families, sponsors, or private organizations (Title IV, sec. 400, para 2a). All of this means that in the future we will see great differences in income among the elderly and that these differences will be determined largely by gender, race and ethnicity, and immigration status. As we illustrate in later chapters, for many individuals the family represents the only refuge.

FOUR

Medicare, Medicaid, and Private Insurance: Group Differences in Health Insurance Coverage

In the last chapter we showed that a private pension is crucial for a comfortable retirement. Having to rely on Social Security alone, especially for those with a limited work history, can leave one scrambling to make ends meet. In this chapter we examine the issue of health insurance coverage and investigate how and why it differs for various groups. Health insurance, like income security, is crucial to a healthy retirement, since age tends to bring with it an accumulation of chronic health problems (Manton, Singer, and Suzmen 1993; Riley and Foner 1968). Although we are living longer and healthier lives today than at any time in the past, the consequences of biological aging cannot be avoided, and the old use more medical care, especially hospital care, than the young (Lubitz, Beebe, and Baker 1995; Rice and Feldman 1983; Waldo et al. 1989; Waldo 1994). Among individuals over fifty-five, physician and hospital use increases with age (Van Nostrand, Furner, and Suzman 1993), although a relatively small fraction of individuals account for a disproportionate amount of the medical care consumed. Such high-volume use is often associated with the treatment and management of fatal diseases (Roos and Shapiro 1981; Verbrugge 1987).

In chapter 2 we showed that a large part of the overall gain in life expectancy that the populations of the developed world have experienced in this century consists of increases in the number of years during which one suffers some health problem. It is useful to remind ourselves that this increase in the number of unhealthy years of life is an inevitable consequence of our medical successes in controlling acute illness and our improved ability to manage chronic illness. If a person does not immediately die of a disease and if a complete cure is not possible, he or she must manage to live with the condition. In the case of chronic conditions such as heart disease, arthritis, and diabetes, a complete elimination of the underlying pathology is not possible, so the medical professionals aim at management rather than cure.

Longer life, therefore, has been purchased at the expense of providing the ongoing medical care that allows the old to live the highest-quality life possible in the face of actual or threatened chronic illness. Adequate management that helps to avoid or delay the onset of complications can make the difference between a high quality of life and one beset by illness and functional decline. For this reason the ability to pay for health care is a major concern among the elderly, and, as we show, the health insurance situation parallels that of Social Security: although Medicare provides a generous health care safety net to the poor, having to rely solely on public financing for medical care can leave one unable to pay for all of the care that one actually needs.

In this chapter we examine group differences in health care coverage both before and during retirement and show that older blacks and Hispanics are less likely than non-Hispanic whites to have private health insurance to supplement Medicare. The reasons for this are complex but relate primarily to a history of employment in jobs that provide neither health insurance in retirement nor enough retirement income to allow an older person to buy a private policy. This situation is particularly disturbing since individuals who do not have private insurance to supplement Medicare face far greater barriers to adequate health care than individuals with such insurance.

Health Insurance in the United States

Our understanding of health insurance coverage and the impact of race and ethnicity on the adequacy of coverage must begin with a review of the way that acute and long-term care are financed in the United States. Unlike other developed nations, the United States does not have a national health insurance scheme that provides coverage to everyone as a citizenship right. Nor do we tend to insure against the risk of the need for long-term care. In the United States, health insurance covers acute care, and for the majority of working-age individuals and their families coverage is provided by employers. Consequently, the key to understanding health insurance coverage in the United States is to appreciate the unique and close association between employment and health care coverage for both the young and the old. In the United States the government provides health care coverage to certain segments of the working-age population who do not have access to private coverage, as well as to certain groups with special needs, such as for kidney dialysis, but most families rely on coverage provided to an employed adult by an employer. For those whose employers do not provide health insurance, but whose earnings are too high to qualify for federal assistance, there are few options other than charity or doing without needed medical care.

For the elderly, though, the situation is very different. Once a person reaches the age of sixty-five, he or she enters a new world, in which all citizens are covered by a national health insurance scheme much like those that provide health care to the entire populations of most other developed nations. Since 1964 Medicare has provided access to physician and hospital services for all Americans over the age of sixty-five, regardless of their ability to pay. Of course, the program has its limitations, and older individuals are required to pay for a substantial portion of the physician and hospital services they receive (Moon 1993). In addition to these charges, Medicare requires that beneficiaries pay the full cost of eyeglasses and a set amount for prescription drugs (Moon 1993). Nor does Medicare pay for nursing home care or custodial home care, both of which can impoverish even a middle class family (Kane and Kane 1990). These expenditures can place a great burden on individuals with limited incomes. As we show, older blacks and Hispanics are particularly vulnerable. Nonetheless, although there are inevitable limits to health care coverage provided to older Americans, in comparison to earlier eras, in which the old received only rudimentary health care, Medicare has made a huge difference. Today the vast majority of Americans over the age of sixty-five are guaranteed the basic medical care they need.

The Health Insurance–Employment Nexus

In the last chapter we showed that blacks and Hispanics are much less likely than non-Hispanic whites to work for employers who provide private pensions. The situation is even more serious when it comes to health insurance. Jobs that do not provide pensions are unlikely to provide any other benefits either. Health care coverage represents a major expense for an employer, and the small firms with low profit margins for which many minority Americans work simply cannot afford to provide it. As a consequence, blacks and Hispanics are seriously underinsured for health care.

Table 4.1 presents information on health insurance coverage from various sources for non-Hispanic whites, blacks, Mexican Americans, and other Hispanics living in households in which the head is between fifty-one and sixty-one. These data are from a newly collected survey of preretirement age individuals carried out by the University of Michigan Survey Research Center (Juster 1993). In this table the data are presented separately for households headed by a single male or by a couple and for those headed by a female. Our previous research shows that, in comparison to male or couple-headed households, female-headed households and families are seriously disadvantaged on every socioeconomic indicator. The table shows that preretirement age blacks and Hispanics are far less likely than non-Hispanic whites to have private health insurance and also illustrates the dramatic difference between households headed by women and those headed by men or married couples. Although the racial and ethnic differentials that are apparent among the male and couple-headed households are reflected also among the female-headed households, among all groups female-headed households are less likely than male or couple-headed households to have private health insurance.

The lack of private health insurance is particularly dramatic among Mexican Americans, among whom only slightly over 40 percent of male or couple-headed households and 30 percent of female-headed households have any form of private health insurance. The table also shows that this lack of private insurance is the result of an absence of employer-sponsored insurance plans. Because they lack private insurance, minority Americans are more dependent on publicly funded programs like Medicare and Medicaid, as the data in table 4.1 clearly show. The differences revealed in this table are huge and demonstrate plainly that in the contemporary United States, race, Hispanic ethnicity, and gender form independent dimensions of disadvantage when it comes to private health insurance coverage.

This lack of insurance has serious implications for the health of blacks and Hispanics, since not owning health insurance means that these groups are much less likely than those with private insurance to get the care they need (U.S. General Accounting Office 1992). The dramatic differences in health insurance coverage between racial and ethnic groups that one sees among younger age groups largely disappear at age sixty-five. Because of Medicare, health insurance coverage among the elderly is nearly universal, and only a small fraction of individuals do not participate in the program. Before the enactment of Medicare the situation among the elderly was even worse than it is among preretirement age individuals today. Prior to Medicare, 50 percent of the elderly had no health insurance. Today over 97 percent of senior citizens are insured by Medicare (Waid 1996).

This universal health care coverage for the old is clearly a major

TABLE 4.1
Health Insurance Coverage of Male-/Couple-Headed and Female-Headed Households, by Race and Hispanic Ethnicity
(weighted percentages)

	Non-Hispanic White	Non-Hispanic Black	Mexican American	Other Hispanic
MALE/COUPLE-HEADED HOUSEHOLDS				
Health insurance				
Private only	81.8	66.2	42.2	59.6
Public only	2.9	10.0	14.0	13.0
Both	6.0	5.8	3.0	3.2
None	9.3	17.9	40.8	24.3
Medicare	7.7	9.6	11.0	11.5
Medicaid	1.6	7.8	7.6	7.8
VA/Champus	5.5	8.6	3.8	3.7
Employee health insurance	76.0	61.1	39.0	54.7
FEMALE-HEADED HOUSEHOLDS				
Health insurance				
Private only	74.9	52.0	31.3	30.4
Public only	8.4	25.2	20.8	30.7
Both	1.2	1.3	1.9	1.1
None	15.4	21.5	46.0	37.8
Medicare	4.0	9.3	7.6	8.1
Medicaid	6.9	19.7	18.1	25.1
VA/Champus	1.8	2.0	0.0	0.6
Employee health insurance	65.2	47.0	27.1	26.3

SOURCE: Thomas F. Juster, "The Health and Retirement Survey," *ICPSR Bulletin* 14 (1993): 1–2.

social and political achievement and reflects the strength of the bond between the generations. As admirable as universal coverage has been, though, it is not the whole story. Although Medicare provides a health care safety net to the vast majority of older individuals, both the quantity and quality of care one receives depends upon whether one has private health insurance to supplement Medicare. The reasons for this require some elaboration. Medicare includes significant deductibles and copayments for hospital and physician services, and it does not pay the full cost of prescription drugs. Nor does it cover long-term nursing home care or devices such as hearing aids. In order to understand health care financing in the United States, therefore, one must understand Medicare in some detail.

Medicare: Universal Health Care Coverage for the Old

From its very inception Medicare has been a great success in providing access to health care to the elderly, including the poor and minority elderly. Most of those eligible immediately enrolled in the new program, and the use of health services expanded rapidly during the 1960s and 1970s—to a point, in fact, at which cost containment measures became necessary (Feder and Scanlon 1982; Moon 1993). The program has clearly benefited the most vulnerable elderly, but as we shall see, for the poor elderly significant cost barriers remain (Davis 1975; Moon 1993). These barriers, in conjunction with the higher lifetime exposures to health risks faced by the poor and minorities, mean that there is probably substantial underutilization of services relative to need among certain groups. As we show below, a significant fraction of older Mexican Americans do not participate in Medicare.

Medicare is the largest health insurance plan in the United States. Over thirty-six million elderly Americans were enrolled in 1994 (Schulz 1995). Medicare helps the elderly with low incomes in two very important ways: it protects the aged from large short-term medical care expenses, and it allows those who might not seek medical care because of its cost to receive it (Davis 1975). Medicare consists of two parts: Part A, which covers hospital expenditures, and Part B, which covers physician and other nonhospital services. Part A, hospital insurance, is funded through a compulsory joint employer-employee payroll tax; Part B, which is known as "supplementary medical insurance," is a voluntary program for which the participant paid a monthly premium of $42.50 in 1996. The participant's premium for Part B is matched by a much larger contribution by the federal government from general revenues.

Although Part A covers postacute care provided by skilled nursing facilities and home health agencies, it does not cover other forms of long-term care. Even with Medicare coverage the costs of hospitalization can be rather high for the individual, especially in the case of multiple hospitalizations, each of which incur deductible and copayment charges. In 1996 the individual was required to pay a $736 deductible for each hospital stay in addition to a co-payment for long stays. After the first sixty days this copayment was $184 per day. After ninety days, instead of paying the actual hospital charges, the individual could choose to pay $368 per day up to sixty lifetime reserve days. Up to twenty days of skilled nursing care are provided for each illness episode at no cost, with an additional eighty days provided at a cost of $92 per day. Unfortunately, after one leaves the hospital only certain services are covered by Medicare. These include postacute nursing home care and home health services provided as part of a care plan supervised by a doctor. Medicare does not pay for the nursing or personal care services that are needed after a serious operation such as hip replacement surgery.

Part B, supplemental medical insurance, primarily covers physician services. After an initial deductible of $100 Medicare pays 80 percent of reasonable charges as determined by the administrators of the program. A major problem arises for older individuals from of the manner in which physicians are reimbursed. A doctor can either choose "assignment," which means accepting the Medicaid reimbursement, which is lower than the usual fee charged in the area, as payment in full, or can bill the patient for the difference between what Medicare covers and his or her usual and customary fee (Schulz 1995). If the physician chooses assignment, he or she is paid directly by Medicare; otherwise the doctor must be reimbursed by the patient or the patient's insurance company. Unfortunately, fewer than half of physicians accept assignment (Schulz 1995). This situation seriously handicaps poor older individuals who are unable to pay the additional amount charged by doctors who do not accept assignment. As a consequence, many of these individuals have great trouble finding a personal physician, especially in areas that are already poorly served.

Medicare has clearly filled a major gap in health care coverage for the old. Yet the program does not cover many areas of need, including long-term care. This omission is particularly serious since as many as 20 percent of the older population will spend five or more years in a nursing home (Rich 1991), at a cost of nearly forty thousand dollars per year (Wiener, Illston, and Hanley 1994). Nor does

Medicare cover the full cost of catastrophic illnesses that require long hospitalizations and nursing home stays. In order to address these shortcomings, in 1988 Congress passed the Medicare Catastrophic Coverage Act (MCCA), which placed a cap on out-of-pocket costs for services covered by Medicare and required only one deductible per year rather than a deductible for each hospitalization (Moon 1993; Schulz 1995). The act also covered short-term nursing home stays, prescription drugs, and a larger spectrum of home health care services. Unfortunately, these expanded services were financed by a monthly surcharge to the Part B premium that fell heaviest on the affluent elderly who already had such coverage through private supplemental insurance plans. Because of their opposition to MCCA Congress repealed the legislation only a year after its passage, and today the poor elderly still have no coverage for many of the services they need, including prescription drugs. Neither do they have protection against catastrophic illness or coverage for long-term care, and the amounts they must pay in deductibles and copayments for each hospital visit can cause serious economic hardship.

Even with these limitations in coverage, though, the cost of Medicare rose steadily from the moment the program was introduced. The rising cost of medical care for the elderly created serious funding problems for the program, and by the 1980s the hospital insurance trust fund (Part A) was threatened with almost immediate depletion. The crisis in Medicare forced Congress to introduce major reforms in the way hospitals are reimbursed for the care of Medicare patients. The major change was the introduction of a prospective payment system (PPS) in which the amount that hospitals are reimbursed for providing services to someone with a particular diagnosis was set in advance (Russell 1989; Schulz 1995; Moon 1993). Prior to the introduction of PPS hospitals had been reimbursed for what they actually spent on an individual patient. The prospective payment system had an immediate and profound effect in reducing the rate of growth in hospital expenditures under Medicare. Limitations in expenditures for physician services under Part B have also been introduced (Schulz 1995), and current proposals in Congress will no doubt reduce physician's reimbursement levels even further.

Because of the gaps in Medicare coverage, the majority of middle-class older individuals have some form of supplemental insurance to make up the difference between what Medicare pays and the actual cost of medical care. In fact, nearly 70 percent of the older population owns such "Medigap" policies (Schulz 1995). There are many forms of supplemental insurance, each with its own terms. Some policies are provided as part of a retirement package by previous employers, others are purchased from organizations such as the American Association of Retired Persons, and yet others are privately purchased on the open market. Some plans pay all of the difference between the Medicare payment and what the doctor or hospital charges, and others pay only a part. The plans differ also in the kinds of services they cover.

Despite their differences, however, most supplemental insurance plans provide coverage that is coordinated with Medicare to ease the burden of excessive medical costs for those on a retirement income. The adequacy of one's health care coverage in old age, then, depends upon whether or not one has such a policy. Even a policy that covers only a portion of the difference between what Medicare pays and the actual cost of medical care places one in a better position than having no supplemental coverage at all. If one's income is not sufficient to allow one to purchase a Medigap supplemental policy, it is certainly not high enough to allow one to pay for expensive medical care out-of-pocket.

Medicaid: Publicly Funded "Medigap" Insurance

Because of the serious burden that these supplemental charges can represent, Medicaid, the federal health care insurance program for the poor, has been extended to provide Medigap coverage for the poor elderly (Angel 1995). For individuals over the age of sixty-five with incomes below the official U.S. government poverty line, Medicaid pays the Part B physician premium and the cost-sharing portion of Part A for hospital coverage. For the impoverished elderly, Medicaid also covers the cost of long-term care, since Medicare does not pay for nursing home stays. Even with its limited coverage, Medicaid provides an important safety net for older Americans.

Each year large numbers of older persons spend down their assets and become destitute paying for nursing home care. Others are poor enough to qualify for assistance from the moment they enter a long-term care facility (Wiener and Hanley 1992b). For both groups, Medicaid assumes the burden of paying for long-term care (Burwell, Adams, and Meiners 1990; Liu, Doty, and Manton 1990; Liu and Manton 1991; Mor, Intrator, and Laliberte 1993; Spence and Wiener 1990a). It is clear that in the absence of the Medigap coverage provided by Medicaid, more individuals would have to do without needed medical care and most poor individuals would have no access to institutional care even if they became seriously disabled.

Falling through the Cracks: Insurance Coverage among Blacks and Hispanics

Although both blacks and Hispanics are disadvantaged in access to health insurance, historically preretirement age Hispanics have had the lowest rates of either public or private health insurance coverage of any racial or ethnic group in the United States (U. S. General Accounting Office 1992; Trevino et al. 1991; Guendelman and Schwalbe 1986; Estrada, Trevino, and Ray 1991; Valdez et al. 1993). In 1990, approximately 32 percent of Hispanics of all ages had no health insurance of any sort, as compared to approximately 13 percent of non-Hispanic whites and 20 percent of blacks (National Council of la Raza 1992). Once again, the core of the problem among blacks and Hispanics consists of low rates of private or employer-based health insurance. The National Council of La Raza (NCLR), an interest group that focuses on Hispanic issues, estimates that in 1990 fewer than half of Hispanics were insured against the costs of serious illness. Only 48 eight percent of Hispanics reported that they had any private health insurance, as compared to 78 percent of non-Hispanic whites and 52 percent of blacks (NCLR, 1992).

What is particularly surprising is that this lack of private insurance among Hispanics is not compensated for by public insurance (U.S. General Accounting Office 1992). Even though they have high fertility rates and low overall family incomes, in 1990 only 18 percent of Hispanics received Medicaid, as compared to 25 percent of blacks (NCLR 1992). Although rates of health insurance coverage are low for Hispanics as a population, there are great differences between the various nationality groups. Among Hispanics in 1990, Central and South Americans and Mexican Americans had the lowest levels of health insurance coverage (approximately 60 percent and 64 precent) and Puerto Ricans the highest (86 percent). Seventy-four percent of Cuban Americans had some form of health insurance, as did 79 percent of the remaining Hispanics (NCLR 1992).

This lack of health insurance among Hispanics is part of a package of disadvantage that includes low levels of education, high rates of unemployment and underemployment, jobs that do not provide health benefits, and residence in states like Florida and Texas which have highly restrictive Medicaid eligibility requirements (Valdez et al. 1993). In combination with poverty and barriers related to language, culture, and location, the lack of insurance has serious implications for the health and well-being of Hispanic Americans, since in the United States a lack of health insurance represents a major barrier to health care (U.S. General Accounting Office 1992). Unfortunately, the situation is only getting worse: while the number of uninsured individuals decreasing among blacks and non-Hispanic whites, it is increasing among Hispanics (NCLR, 1992). If these trends continue—as seems quite possible, given the inability of employers to provide insurance and attempts by the federal and state governments to control the rising cost of medical care—the health and well-being of an ever growing number of both young and older Hispanics may be placed in jeopardy.

Although the problem of inadequate insurance is most serious among young Hispanics, among older individuals Hispanics are also the least likely to be insured. Estimates vary, but it is clear that a substantial fraction of Hispanics over the age of sixty-five do not participate in Medicare. Of those who do, a smaller fraction than of non-Hispanic whites have private health insurance to cover the costs that Medicare does not pay. Data from the 1990 Census and from other specialized surveys indicate that while less than 1 percent of non-Hispanic white elderly and 2 percent of black elderly reported no health insurance, a substantial fraction of Hispanics over the age of sixty-five report no health insurance coverage at all (Angel 1995; Andrews 1989; NCLR 1992). These lower rates of health insurance coverage are largely accounted for by lower participation rates in Social Security by Hispanics. In 1990 only 80 percent of Hispanics over the age of sixty-five reported receiving Social Security, as compared to 88 percent of blacks and 93 percent of non-Hispanic whites (NCLR 1992).

Table 4.2 presents data on health insurance coverage among individuals over the age of sixty-five from a survey sponsored by the Commonwealth Fund in the mid-1980s. In this table we categorize older individuals into four groups: those who report that they have no insurance at all, those who receive Medicaid and own some other form of insurance as well, those who rely on Medicare alone, and those who have private Medigap insurance. Those with private insurance are also eligible for Medicare. The table reveals some rather large differences between groups in their mix of health insurance coverage. A surprising fraction of blacks and Hispanics report that they have no health insurance. Nearly 6 percent of older Mexican Americans report that they have no insurance of any sort.

TABLE 4.2
Health Insurance Coverage of Individuals 65 Years and Over, by Race and Hispanic Ethnicity

Type of Insurance	Non-Hispanic White	Non-Hispanic Black	Mexican American	Cuban American	Puerto Rican
No insurance (%)	1.3	2.9	5.9	2.9	3.1
Any Medicaid (%)	13.3	33.1	37.0	47.9	55.7
Medicare only (%)	18.1	34.5	29.7	19.8	27.2
Private (%)	67.3	29.5	27.5	29.4	14.1
Sample size	(2,016)	(139)	(819)	(653)	(327)
Total (%)	100.0	100.0	100.1	100.0	100.0

SOURCE: Karen Davis, *National Survey of Hispanic Elderly People, 1988* (Ann Arbor, MI: Inter-University Consortium for Political and Social Research, 1990); Karen Davis, *National Survey of Problems Facing Elderly Americans Living Alone* (Ann Arbor, MI: Inter-University Consortium for Political and Social Research, 1992). The 1985–86 survey includes non-Hispanic white and black Americans; the 1988 survey consisted of a sample of Hispanics.

Although blacks and Hispanics report generally lower levels of health insurance coverage than non-Hispanic whites, we must keep in mind that there are large differences within each racial and ethnic group in every aspect of socioeconomic status, including health insurance. Table 4.3 illustrates the point for Mexican Americans using data from our recent study of older Mexican Americans in the southwest (Markides et al. in press). These data show that foreign-born Mexican Americans report particularly low rates of health insurance coverage. As is the case for income, the foreign-born are seriously disadvantaged when it comes to health insurance. The data also show that the foreign-born are particularly dependent on Medicaid.

There are many possible reasons for these lower rates of participation in Medicare among older Mexican Americans and for the lack of private Medigap insurance among Hispanics generally. For Mexican Americans, citizenship status may represent a barrier. Many older Mexican Americans have never become legal residents of the United States. For those who do not speak English—and many older Hispanics do not—access problems may keep them from seeking medical care or participating in Social Security. Among younger age groups, lower rates of participation in Medicaid are largely accounted for by the restrictive participation criteria imposed by states like Texas and Florida. Among the elderly, for whom Medicare is a universal entitlement, state-imposed eligibility barriers are less serious, and other access factors become more salient.

TABLE 4.3
Health Insurance Coverage, for Mexican Americans Aged 65 years and Over, by Nativity

Type of Insurance	Native	Foreign-born
No insurance	2.4	12.4
Any Medicaid	31.4	37.8
Medicare only	34.8	39.2
Private	31.4	10.6
Total (%)	100.0	100.0
Sample size	(1,649)	(1,297)

SOURCE: Kyriakos S. Markides, *A Longitudinal Study of Mexican American Elderly Health* (Washington, DC: National Institute on Aging, 1992).

Health Insurance Coverage in the Years before Retirement

The situation of the elderly is best understood from a life-course perspective, in which an individual's economic and insurance situation in later life is related to the nature and course of his or her working life. A central debate concerning income security among the old is whether or not the inequalities that are apparent among younger age groups persist and perhaps even accumulate as one ages and enters the retirement years, or whether the large differences between the rich and the poor are significantly equalized as a result of Social Security. The answer to this question largely depends on how one defines "significantly." As we noted, Social Security and Medicare have substantially reduced the worst poverty among the elderly and have provided them with basic medical care. Yet, as we have seen, significant differences in income and medical care coverage remain.

In order to better understand the situation of older blacks and Hispanics in retirement, we examine their income and insurance situations in the years before retirement. We employ for this purpose a new data set collected by researchers at the University of Michigan's Survey Research Center in which both groups were oversampled (Juster 1993). These data are from the same survey on which table 4.1 is based. The study collected detailed information on health insurance, as well as other employment, economic, and health information from single individuals between the ages of fifty-one and sixty-one and couples of whom at least one member was between those ages. The researchers attempted to get the most reliable information on health insurance possible from the person in the household who was most knowledgeable about the household's coverage. Unfortunately, among the Hispanics, only the sample of Mexican Americans is large enough for separate analysis. The number of Cuban Americans, Puerto Ricans, and other Hispanics is simply too small to support separate analyses or even the estimation of stable coefficients in pooled analyses. Rather than dropping them from the analysis or pooling them with Mexican Americans, we treat them as a separate category (Other Hispanics).

Let us begin by examining the economic profiles of the groups for which we have information. These data are presented in table 4.4, first for households headed by a single male or a couple, then for those headed by a single female. The data show dramatic differences in home equity and total assets between non-Hispanic whites and the three minority groups and also reveal stark differences in assets between households headed by a single male or a couple and those headed by women. Among single males and couples, blacks and Hispanics have on average half of the home equity of non-Hispanic whites, and none of the three minority groups has anywhere near the total wealth of non-Hispanic whites. Although the same racial and ethnic disparities that we see among male- and couple-headed households emerge among female-headed households, within each racial or ethnic category, female-headed households are far poorer than their couple- or male-headed counterparts. Table 4.4 also shows that the three minority groups have lower household incomes than non-Hispanic whites, and again, single women are particularly disadvantaged.

Overall, then, these data present a bleak picture of the economic

TABLE 4.4
Wealth and Income of Preretirement Age Male-/Couple-Headed and Female-Headed Households, by Race and Hispanic Ethnicity

	Non-Hispanic White	Non-Hispanic Black	Mexican American	Other Hispanic
MALE-/COUPLE-HEADED HOUSEHOLDS				
Mean				
Home equity	$78,708	$36,658	$39,379	$50,696
Total assets	$313,122	$103,922	$91,975	$179,388
Household income	$59,978	$40,541	$30,833	$42,453
Unweighted *N*	(4,390)	(893)	(340)	(203)
FEMALE-HEADED HOUSEHOLDS				
Mean				
Home equity	$51,076	$18,028	$27,443	$13,902
Total assets	$125,657	$49,645	$43,801	$36,339
Household income	$27,635	$21,779	$18,466	$24,584
Unweighted *N*	(877)	(535)	(91)	(85)

SOURCE: Thomas F. Juster, "The Health and Retirement Survey," *ICPSR Bulletin* 14(1993): 1–2.

well-being of preretirement age blacks, Hispanics, and single women. The individuals in this survey are between fifty-one and sixty-one and are not all that far from retirement. It is unlikely that their economic situations will improve dramatically in late middle age, and when they reach their seventies and eighties, many blacks, Hispanics, and single women will have very few assets to draw upon if they need long-term care. Due to the double jeopardy of gender and minority group status, the situation of many single black and Hispanic women is particularly precarious.

Table 4.5 presents information on various aspects of health care coverage for households with health insurance. Again the data are presented separately for the combined category of male- and couple-headed households and for female-headed households. We must keep in mind that the previous tables showed that blacks and Hispanics are less likely than non-Hispanic whites to have employer-based health insurance. This table refers only to the subset of the sample who are employed and who have health insurance, so it is a select sample, representative of the employed population but not of the total population. The first line in each panel presents the percentage of employers that offer a retirement health plan, and we can see that relatively few employed individuals are covered by such a plan. The next section of each panel refers only to those employees with a current health plan. The final group of statistics within each headship panel refers to any private health insurance the household has purchased for itself.

The data reveal certain small differences among groups in various aspects of health insurance coverage, but no really clear pattern emerges. The bottom line in each panel shows that almost no one has long-term care insurance. What is again noticeable is that Hispanics are much less likely than either blacks or non-Hispanic whites to have private health insurance. They are also less likely to report that their retirement plan includes health care coverage. Despite these differences, however, what this table, in conjunction with the previous table, really shows is that although Hispanics may suffer some disadvantage in the type of insurance they have, the real difference between Hispanics and other groups is in the lesser likelihood that

TABLE 4.5
Retirement Health Insurance Coverage of Male-/Couple-Headed and Female-Headed Households, by Race and Hispanic Ethnicity
(Weighted percentages)

	Non-Hispanic White	Non-Hispanic Black	Mexican American	Other Hispanic
MALE-/COUPLE-HEADED HOUSEHOLDS				
Employer offers any retirement health plan	15.3	24.1	16.5	13.2
Premium paid by:				
Respondent/spouse	11.2	12.0	11.9	12.0
Employer	38.0	33.9	39.9	26.9
Respondent/employer	50.4	53.3	47.8	61.0
Other	0.4	0.8	0.4	0.0
Retirement plan includes health coverage	71.2	71.1	63.5	46.5
Employee's contribution				
All	24.0	30.0	16.4	21.9
Some	37.5	40.3	39.9	49.3
None	38.5	29.7	43.7	28.8
Spouse eligible for benefits	89.0	84.9	81.3	79.7
Private insurance	18.9	13.2	5.4	9.0
Basic plan	45.4	48.8	26.6	51.5
Medigap	3.3	0.0	5.5	5.9
Other supplemental policy	29.8	32.6	34.0	22.4
Long-term care insurance	6.8	4.9	4.8	8.3
FEMALE-HEADED HOUSEHOLDS				
Employer offers any retirement health plan	18.7	15.6	0.0	0.0
Premium paid by:				
Respondent	14.7	10.8	22.4	15.7
Employer	39.7	41.4	27.1	34.3
Respondent/employer	44.4	47.0	50.5	50.0
Other	1.2	0.8	0.0	0.0
Retirement plan includes health coverage	58.4	65.6	49.0	31.0
Employee's contribution				
All	22.9	33.2	13.8	30.0
Some	34.9	34.0	49.6	28.3
None	42.2	32.8	36.7	41.7
Private insurance	19.3	12.2	8.2	7.2
Basic plan	54.9	51.7	62.1	41.8
Medigap	0.8	0.0	0.0	0.0
Other supplemental policy	21.6	30.3	26.5	15.6
Long-term care insurance	9.6	8.2	0.0	0.0

SOURCE: Thomas F. Juster, "The Health and Retirement Survey," *ICPSR Bulletin* 14 (1993): 1–2.

they have health insurance at all. Once one enters an employer-based insurance pool, the type of coverage one receives is fairly uniform. The big difference between Hispanics, blacks, and non-Hispanic whites, therefore, is in access to even basic coverage.

Employment, therefore, is clearly a major factor in explaining private health insurance coverage, both before and after retirement. In order to get some idea of the extent to which occupational status accounts for private health insurance coverage in the preretirement years, we used these same data to compare the occupational distribution of blacks, Hispanics, and non-Hispanic whites. Although we do not pressent the data here, they show that a smaller fraction of either blacks or Hispanics than of non-Hispanic whites are employed as managers or professionals. Conversely, a larger fraction of blacks than of non-Hispanic whites are employed as protective, health, and personal service workers, and a larger percentage of blacks and Mexican Americans than of non-Hispanic whites are unemployed. These data, therefore, clearly show significant occupational differences between groups that are associated with differential access to health insurance coverage. Multivariate analyses of these data showed that differences in health insurance coverage between blacks and non-Hispanic whites are largely accounted for by occupational, economic, and sociodemographic variables. For Hispanics, though, this is not the case: their lower rate of insurance coverage persists even after occupational status and other insurance-related sociodemographic and economic factors are controlled (Angel and Angel in press). Occupational status, therefore, explains part of the difference in health insurance coverage between Hispanics and non-Hispanic whites, but not all of it.

The Future of Health Care Financing: Implications for Minority Americans

The health care system of the United States is changing rapidly under the pressures of an aging population and the ever rising cost of providing physician, hospital, and long-term care services to the elderly. Not all that long ago doctors were small-scale entrepreneurs who sold their services to individual consumers. Today groups of doctors contract with large corporations and the federal government to provide capitated care to a burgeoning segment of the population. These changes will affect everyone in some way, but the potential impact of changes in Medicare and Medicaid have particularly serious implications for blacks, Hispanics, and single women, for it is among these groups that dependency on public funding is highest. Already, the Medicare population is being enrolled in health maintenance organizations (HMOs) in the hopes that managed care will reduce the overall cost of providing the services they require. In the future those with few private resources will, in all likelihood, have far more choices in their care than those dependent solely on public financing. The poor and minorities have clearly benefited from Medicare and Medicaid. For the poorest older Americans, Medicaid provides rather generous Medigap coverage. Prior to the introduction of universal health coverage, the elderly poor had to rely on charity for medical care and few could afford to enter a nursing home.

Today that has changed and almost all older Americans are covered by Medicare for acute care and by Medicaid for nursing home care. Because they are so dependent on these programs for health care, the poorest Americans will be most adversely affected by increases in the costs that older individuals must bear. Yet these changes seem inevitable. As we have seen, although Medicare provides a basic health care safety net for the old, the quantity and quality of medical care one receives depends upon one's economic status. The rather substantial deductibles and copayments associated with hospitalization and the cost of prescription drugs, eyeglasses, and hearing aids are serious financial burdens to an older individual on a limited fixed income. Even the rather modest monthly premium for Part B Medicare coverage can constitute a burden to an older individual who must pay for food and shelter as well as medical care out of a small fixed income. Increases in these costs could place much of the care they need out of the reach of many older Americans.

Like the rest of President Johnson's War on Poverty, Medicare was introduced with the great hope that it would eliminate social class differences in access to basic resources. Judged by that criterion it has been a great success. Yet in the course of history one period's success becomes the next period's problem. Increasing expenditures for the acute and long-term care of the elderly have forced us to consider ways of controlling at least the rate of increase in these expenditures, if not their total amount. Those attempts have resulted in reduced reimbursements to hospitals and to physicians and have created a situation in which fewer than half of doctors accept Medicare payments as their total reimbursement for the services they render to the elderly.

Those individuals who have no private Medigap coverage can have a difficult time finding a doctor and the total package of services they receive may not be as complete or of the same quality as those with private Medigap insurance. If, as part of the attempt to control costs, deductibles and copayments are increased at the same time that reimbursements to hospitals and physicians are reduced, both access to care by poor and minority Americans, as well as the quality of care they receive, may suffer. It is even possible that those older individuals who must rely on Medicare alone could suffer stigma if a total reliance on public funding were to become synonymous with welfare. Doctors, hospitals, and other health providers already prefer patients with private insurance, and were Medicare reimbursements to become even less desirable, this trend could accelerate. It is possible, in fact, that we could see the rise of a two-tiered system, in which those with private insurance would receive high-quality care while those reliant on public funding would receive something less. As in other areas, the bottom tier would, in all likelihood, be far more black and Hispanic than the upper tier. Access to private Medigap insurance, then, may come to distinguish the haves from the have-nots in terms of medical care in the future.

Our life-course perspective emphasizes the interdependence of youth and old age: what happens to one during one's working years directly affects one's welfare in the years of retirement. The evidence is overwhelming that among the working-age population low rates of health insurance coverage among minority Americans are largely due to a lack of employer-sponsored plans. Individuals who are inadequately insured prior to retirement are unlikely to be any better off after retirement. A lifetime of employment in jobs that do not provide generous pension plans is not favorable to the accumulation of the assets necessary to purchase private Medigap coverage in retirement. The serious lack of employer-sponsored health insurance among minority Americans in the years prior to retirement, then, means that a large fraction of blacks and Hispanics will have no supplemental Medigap coverage once they retire. In light of the substantial burden that the copayments and deductibles associated with Medicare can represent for individuals on a limited income, this trend suggests that, even though their situation will improve in retirement, a large proportion of older blacks and Hispanics may have only minimal, publicly funded coverage (Rowland and Lyons 1987). Evidence we cited earlier showed that a small but significant fraction of Hispanics do not participate in Medicare, and it may well be that cost is a major reason.

At a very practical level, this lack of private insurance among working-age minority individuals has serious consequences for their health, since the lack of health insurance is a major barrier to obtaining necessary medical care (Aday, Andersen, and Fleming 1980; U.S. General Accounting Office 1992). Again, if we take a life-course perspective, it is clear that the health of many older minority individuals could be compromised if chronic conditions, such as hypertension and diabetes, are not controlled earlier in life. Indeed, the health consequences of a lack of insurance was one of the major reasons that Medicare was enacted.

Our review of the data makes it clear that, although minority Americans face serious barriers to medical care at all ages, specific groups differ substantially both in the particular barriers that they face and the particular health problems from which they suffer. What is perhaps most discouraging about the current health insurance situation among working-age Hispanics is that it is not improving. In recent years the number of uninsured has increased among Hispanics, while it has decreased among blacks and non-Hispanic whites (NCLR 1992). In light of the increasing inability and unwillingness of employers to provide health care coverage, the situation can only get worse in the future with negative health consequences for individuals of all ages. Since we do not have government mandated universal health care coverage in the United States, employment is the major source of health insurance for working-age individuals and their families. For the working poor who hold jobs that do not provide health insurance and who do not qualify for Medicaid, there are few alternatives. For those whose incomes must be used for basic subsistence, medical care is often a luxury or something that is received as charity. When these individuals retire, their situations will improve greatly as they become eligible for Medicare, yet in the years to come the distinctions between those with private insurance and those without it could widen.

The tie between employment and health insurance, then, is a major factor in accounting for low rates of insurance coverage among blacks and Hispanics. Yet employment disadvantages are not the entire story. Other factors that are less well understood contribute to low rates of insurance coverage among certain groups. Even after one takes employment status into account, Hispanics still have lower levels of health insurance coverage than either non-Hispanic blacks or whites. The reasons for this remain unclear. Numerous barriers to health care have been identified among Hispanics, including language difficulties, cultural distance between provider and patient, and a greater reliance on local networks of friends and relatives (Markides, Levin, and Ray 1985; Valdez et al. 1993). To the extent that these factors reduce medical care use, they may also reduce health insurance coverage. The entire medical care system, from its financing components to the actual delivery of services, may remain foreign to certain Hispanics. Future research will have to focus on the specific organizational and personal factors associated with lower health insurance coverage among Hispanics.

Unfortunately, although the amount of data on the health care needs of blacks and Hispanics is increasing, the number of minority Americans in most major studies is limited, and we are only now beginning to understand the health risks and barriers to health care that they face. Information on the health of older minority individuals is even more limited. A deeper understanding of the health risks and barriers to health care that minority Americans face will require a more sophisticated understanding of within-group differences in factors that affect health and medical care. Very often our characterizations of specific groups portray them as homogeneous in social class and cultural orientation. Such characterizations are profoundly incorrect and mask vast differences in income and wealth, residence, education, immigration status, level of acculturation, intermarriage, health beliefs and practices, and much more. These differences translate into wide variations in health risks within the same group sometimes wider than the variations between groups. For example, although blacks as a group suffer high rates of hypertension, risk factors such as obesity operate for them in the same way that they do for everyone else, and being black does not inevitably mean that one will be hypertensive. Mexican Americans have elevated rates of diabetes, yet not all members of this group suffer the most serious consequences of that disease.

One particularly promising avenue of research would be a close examination of nationality differences among Hispanics that would allow us to investigate the impact of such factors as nativity, age at migration, generational status, migration history, and state of residence on specific disease risks, as well as on health insurance coverage and medical care use. Our own analyses have revealed large differences in health and medical care use between Mexican Americans and other Hispanics. A detailed understanding of a specific group's health risks would allow us to target public health initiatives and would be useful in the study of other groups as well. Blacks from the Caribbean, who have a different genetic admixture and social history than blacks who were brought to the United States directly from Africa, may have a very different health risk profile than either blacks in Africa or those whose ancestors were slaves in the United States. They may differ significantly from other groups in health-related behaviors such as diet, sexual behavior, and drug use. Understanding the consequences of these differences for the health of the elderly again requires a life-course perspective that relates health in old age to health and lifestyle in youth and middle age.

The Health and Retirement Survey from which we drew much of our information for this chapter is a longitudinal survey designed to follow respondents from the preretirement years into retirement. Future waves of this survey, in addition to new data that we hope will be collected, will allow us to answer vitally important questions concerning the transition from work to retirement and its association with health and health insurance coverage among blacks, Hispanics, and single women. Such data will make it possible for us to begin to deal with the growing social problem that confronts us. Attempts to contain the rising costs of Medicare and Medicaid can only harm individuals who have very limited resources and who are particularly dependent on publicly financed health care. Given the centrality of health to well-being at any age, promoting health should be one of our central objectives. Although we may not be able to provide all older individuals with the most advanced life-sustaining technologies, we must make sure that all receive the basic health care they need to optimize the quality of their later years.

FIVE

The Role of the Family in the Informal Support of the Elderly

Even as the family comes under increasing pressure and as the number of lifelong marriages declines, it remains the bedrock of our sense of security and belonging in the world. For that reason many observers of contemporary social life fear that the decline of the family represents more than just an innocuous social change, that it bodes ill for our continuation as a society, or at least as a society based on traditional values of interpersonal duty and exchange. For the elderly there can be no doubt that the family is a central source of emotional and instrumental support. By now researchers have dispelled the myth that in the modern world the young have abandoned the old because they no longer serve any useful purpose (Brody, Poulshock, and Masciocchi 1978; Binstock, Chow, and Schulz 1982; Cowgill 1986; Keith 1990; Hanley, Wiener, and Harris 1991; Kendig, Hashimoto, and Coppard 1992; Shanas et al. 1968; Shanas 1979). Yet the greater occupational and geographical mobility, higher female labor force participation, lower fertility, and rising family disruption that characterize our modern world must inevitably affect the family's ability and willingness to provide support to the elderly. All over the world, industrialization and modernization are undermining traditional systems of intergenerational exchange and coresidence, and in years to come the family may find itself increasingly displaced by formal organizations as the primary caregivers to the elderly (Haber and Gratton 1994; Holstein 1995; Quadagno 1982).

In order for family members to provide daily support to an aging parent they must live close enough to the older individual to make it possible to do so. For older individuals with no children, or for those whose children have moved far away, daily assistance is not an option, and for those who are estranged from their sons and daughters there may not be enough of an emotional bond to make the younger individuals want to involve themselves in their parent's lives. As is the case for all other social institutions, then, the profound social and demographic changes that are reshaping the modern world have important implications for the informal social support of the elderly. Since its passage in 1936, Social Security has reduced the family's responsibility for the financial support of the elderly, but it has done much more than that. The entry of the federal government into what was previously a family matter has altered the moral order and radically changed public opinion as to who should be responsible for older individuals' financial security during their retirement years. Parents are no longer dependent on children for economic support, and this fact has led to a change in social mores. Since the 1930s opinion polls clearly reveal in both the young and the old a shift away from the belief that children should provide economic support to their aging parents to the expectation that the government should provide that support (Crystal 1982). Today when money is exchanged between generations, it is usually in the form of gifts from parents to children (Eggebeen and Hogan 1990; Morgan 1983).

This shift in our attitudes concerning financial responsibility for aging parents has clearly been driven by more than just a change in social mores. Changes in mores, after all, usually follow changes in objective circumstances, and during the twentieth century the objective circumstances of the elderly have changed radically. Today life expectancy at sixty-five is at a historical high, and even though the elderly grew up in leaner times, their expectations for material comfort are also high. The greater role of the state in the economic and even day-to-day care of older individuals is an inevitable response to their growing economic and medical needs. Working-age adults today often find themselves squeezed between providing for their children and caring for their aging parents (Oppenheimer 1974). Everyone must live within limited financial and time budgets, and the more time one devotes to the care of elderly parents, the less there is for children or for one's self.

In addition to time, working-age adults face serious economic constraints that make it unrealistic to expect them to assume personal financial responsibility for their aging parents. It is hard enough to save for one's own retirement, and if middle-aged workers were required to help support their aging parents, saving for their own retirements would become only more difficult. Of course, working-age individuals do provide for their parent's care through Social Security and Medicare taxes, but they are less likely to do so on a personal basis. For the most part, the financial support of the elderly, as well as their medical care, has been socialized. When it comes to nonfinancial support, though, the situation is quite different: the family continues to play a major role in providing such services as transportation, food preparation, personal care, bookkeeping, housekeeping, and emotional support to aging family members (Brody, Poulshock, and Masciocchi 1978). Much of this informal help could not be effectively provided by formal organizations, since the need for such services is episodic and unpredictable and family members, if available, are best suited to the task (Litwak 1985).

Yet many cultural, social, demographic, and economic factors influence the family's ability and willingness to provide help to the elderly. Hispanics, for example, have large families and, at least in myth, socialize their children into the expectation that the young should care for their parents when they need help (Markides and Krause 1985; Markides, Boldt, and Ray 1986). We would expect such groups to be more likely to form multigenerational households than groups with lower fertility and weaker norms concerning children's responsibilities for parents. Among cultural groups that value independence, older individuals, unwilling to be a "burden," may continue to live alone and refuse to ask for help from their children even when they suffer serious declines in health (Connidis 1983; Hess and Waring 1978; Worobey and Angel 1990a).

The anthropological literature reveals great cultural variation in living arrangements and exchange relationships, as well as in sources of solidarity and conflict, between age groups (Foner 1986; Keith 1990; Keith et al. 1994). Culture, which is usually operationalized as national origin, affects both the composition and functioning of informal networks (White-Means and Thornton 1990). Why this is so is not entirely clear, although some imaginative theories have been offered. One, for example, relates informal caregiving to the lineal or collateral structure of the family (Woehrer 1978). In lineal families, as the name implies, the primary bonds are based on ties between parents and children, and children and grandchildren assume the role of primary caregivers to older family members. Americans of English and German extraction tend to have families and networks of this sort. In collateral families, on the other hand, bonds are more diffuse and extend to aunts, uncles, and even friends and neighbors. Among these groups individuals other than children provide informal support. Italian, Polish, Irish, and black families tend to be of this sort.

The limited information we have suggests that such a culturally based assignment of caregiving tasks may actually occur. The support networks for blacks, for example, tend to include a wider range of relatives than the networks to which individuals of German, Irish, or English heritage have recourse (Stack 1974; White-Means and Thornton 1990). Ethnicity also affects the number of hours caregivers devote to older, physically impaired individuals. Individuals of German, Irish, or English ethnic origin, for example, are significantly less involved in the care of older family members than are blacks (White-Means and Thornton 1990). These differences persist even after such factors as employment status and other constraints on the caregiver's time are taken into account. Unfortunately, it is not really clear why these ethnic differences persist, or even that they represent substantively important differences. We suspect that the most important group differences are the result of minority group status and poverty, rather than of ethnicity or culture per se.

In this chapter, therefore, we examine the role of informal social support in the care of the elderly and investigate how culture, social class, and minority group status affect the availability of such support. By informal social support we mean material or practical assistance, and even emotional nurturance, that is provided by family members, friends, or neighbors. By contrast, formal support is that assistance provided by governmental or private agencies or organizations. What the literature makes clear is that social class and "culture," or group membership as it is usually operationalized, are intimately interrelated, and that what we often construe to be cultural effects really represent adaptations to poverty (Angel and Tienda 1982). Kinship and family, after all, are based on material exchanges and the need for humans to affiliate in order to survive. The material resources one has at one's disposal, therefore, depend on one's family and living situations, and income and assets, as well as the composition of the household in which one resides, are crucial in determining how much formal or informal support an older person can call upon. With sufficient resources support can be purchased; for the poor it is often necessary that family members and even nonkin pool what little they have so that all may get by. We end the chapter by discussing how the rapid social and demographic change that we will inevitably experience in the years to come may impact the availability of informal support for the elderly and the consequent growing need for formal alternatives.

The Cultural and Social Context of Social Support

Prior to the nineteenth century in many European countries the elderly often attempted to insure that they would be cared for in old age by entering into formal retirement contracts with their children. In the absence of retirement or pensions, these contracts were part of what has been termed the "stepping down" process, a phrase meant to convey the sense of a gradual and often incomplete, rather than an abrupt, withdrawal from economic activity (Plankans 1989; Quadagno 1982). Such contracts transferred estates from parents to children and clearly specified the children's material obligations to their parents, in effect formalizing the duties of the informal support network and, to some degree, insuring that the parents received at least minimal care.

Such formal contracts were never common in America, in which the greater abundance of land and a different history resulted in a unique set of traditions binding parents and children (Vinovskis 1989). Nonetheless, although in America adult children have never entered into formal retirement contracts with their living parents, the informal network was, and remains today, central in providing support to the impaired elderly (Brody 1981; Chapell 1985). In the United States, as in the rest of the world, the informal network is based on kinship, affection, and duty, but like the more formal retirement contacts of premodern Europe, exchanges between parents and children are intimately tied up with the transfer of property.

Informal support is, of course, particularly important when one becomes ill and can no longer function independently. A surprisingly large proportion of the elderly who live alone in the community suffer from serious functional impairments (Worobey and Angel 1990a). Perhaps as many as 10 percent of elderly persons living in the community are as impaired as those in institutions (Callahan et al. 1980). These individuals would have a difficult time surviving in the community were it not for the help of family members and the assistance of extended informal networks. In the absence of assistance with activities of daily living (ADLs) many impaired older individuals would suffer serious deprivation or be forced into nursing homes, a situation that would greatly increase the financial burden on federal, state, and local tax bases. The capacity of the family and the local network to provide that support, therefore, is crucial to the well-being of the elderly, particularly at intermediate and high levels of need, where the presence or absence of family support can make the difference between institutionalization and continued residence in the community.

We begin, therefore, by identifying those factors that influence both the amount and type of informal social support that the elderly receive from family members, and from the local community more generally. Many of these factors are associated with social class and group differences in family size and social mobility. For example, among the working class, support tends to take the form of direct assistance with household chores and activities of daily living, while among the more affluent it consists more often of emotional support and gifts of money or other material goods (Cantor and Little 1985). These contrasting styles of support reflect differences in mobility patterns and economic resources. Working-class individuals are more likely to remain close enough to their parents to provide daily assistance, whereas the highly educated often move far away from their parents in the pursuit of occupational success. All support, though, whether it is emotional or instrumental, serves a useful purpose. Emotional support is important since among the elderly depression often accompanies physical illness and functional incapacity (Berkman et al. 1986), and depression in old age has been shown to be associated with increased mortality (Murphy et al. 1988). Social support at any age is crucial to optimal physical and mental well-being, and those individuals who are well integrated socially enjoy better health than those who are not (House, Landis, and Umberson 1988).

Systems of Social Support

Individual sources of formal and informal support are best thought of as part of a larger system of support that is structured hierarchically. This hierarchy determines whom will be called upon first to provide help and whom later. For example, when an older individual is in need, he or she typically first turns to family, then to friends and the local community, and only when there is no other option, to social and governmental agencies or to long-term care (Shanas 1979; Stone, Cafferata, and Sangl 1987; Taylor 1985). This hierarchy is based both on the physical proximity of more immediate kin as well as the intimate emotional bond between close relatives. Formal sources of support, such as those provided by home health care agencies, are more physically and emotionally distant.

Family members, therefore, are the first to be called on to provide informal care to the elderly. Yet even within the family certain individuals are more likely to provide care than others. Given the nature and meaning of marriage it is not surprising that when one falls ill one turns first to one's spouse for help, especially in the case of more serious illness and disability (Brody 1981; Hess and Soldo 1985). After one's spouse come one's children. Among the widowed, of course, children become the major providers of help, and most older persons tend to live close to at least one of their children (Hanson and Sauer 1985). Daughters are more likely than sons to provide care when both are available, but when there is no daughter, or she is unavailable, sons assume the primary caregiving role (Wolf and Soldo 1988). After spouses and children, other relatives, friends, and neighbors provide help (Cantor 1979; Cantor and Little 1985). This hierarchy reflects the fact that close relatives are more able and willing to provide intensive care and for longer periods than more distant relatives or nonfamily members. Friends and neighbors can be of great help with such tasks as shopping and transportation, but because they are responsible for their own families, they are more limited in what they can do. Regardless of its composition, though, when this informal social support system can no longer provide adequate care, either because the older person's functional status has deteriorated to such a level that the care burden becomes too great or because the network itself is small or does not contain immediate family members, formal community care or institutionalization are the only alternatives.

Cultural and Social Class Differences in Social Support

In reality, of course, one source of support is often substituted for another, and racial and ethnic group membership, as well as social class, can influence who provides help. By now the literature on informal social support among blacks and Hispanics is large and we cannot review it in detail here (see Markides and Black 1996 for a recent review). Instead, we summarize the major findings and point out major unanswered questions. Unfortunately, although we know a great deal about blacks and Hispanics, the same is not true for other groups. Yet it is clear from what we do know that all groups rely on the family for the care of the elderly and that the differences that exist in relations between the generations are more matters of degree than reflections of basic differences in the way the elderly are cared for. What perhaps differs most between groups is the nature of the exchanges that characterize informal support networks, as well as their size and composition (Lockery 1992; Antonucci 1990). Many of these differences reflect economic necessity and social class factors. Some groups concentrate on help with activities of daily living, others on material assistance, and yet others on emotional support.

Of course there is a great deal of overlap in the type of support provided, and actual exchanges depend on material resources as well as residential proximity. Older Mexican Americans and Chinese Americans, for example, are more likely than Anglo or black older persons to live with a child and to receive help from adult children (Lubben and Becerra 1987). This pattern is more pronounced among immigrants and traditional-oriented individuals (Weeks and Cuellar 1981). However, since cultural identity and social class are here confounded, these patterns cannot be taken as evidence that Chinese Americans or Mexican Americans are more familistic than other groups or that they are radically different from non-Hispanic whites or blacks in their norms or preferences concerning living arrangements (Angel et al. in press). At most, the observed differences in living arrangements between ethnic or racial groups are matters of degree only and may reflect larger families, or greater economic need among minority Americans (Angel and Tienda 1982; Lubben and Becerra 1987).

One intriguing question that arises in the study of racial and ethnic differences in household and family structure is whether or not the larger informal networks typical of Hispanics and blacks translate into more or better support. Extended households and the reliance on fictive kin can reflect necessity as much as preference (Angel and Tienda 1982; Mitchell and Register 1984; Mutran 1985). After reviewing the extensive literature on social support and socioeconomic status, Taylor (1985) concludes that, although the data do not warrant a definitive characterization, support is more common among middle-class blacks than among the very poor. A large network, therefore, may not mean that an older individual is receiving adequate support. A large network may, in fact, indicate blocked opportunities and represent a minimal adaptation among several individuals, all of whom are barely getting by.

The Composition of Informal Networks

Informal networks differ in gender composition as well as in size. In every society, and regardless of the age of the care recipient, women are more often the caregivers than men. For certain groups, though, this pattern has been taken to an extreme, and female households with networks composed solely of women and children have become the norm (Angel and Angel 1993; Stack 1974). As a consequence, the number of grandmother-headed households, in which the senior female is responsible for her daughter and her grandchild, has risen. In many of these households the daughter is either physically or functionally absent and cannot carry out the role of mother to her own child (Angel and Angel 1993). Such situations are most often the result of early extramarital pregnancy, and many of the caregiving grandmothers are themselves quite young. Many young women in these situations will never marry, or will be married only temporarily or episodically: hence, they will not spend a large fraction of their lives in the sort of traditional marriage that makes it possible for two individuals to pool their economic and domestic resources. For these women the retirement years will represent a continuation of the poverty they experienced throughout life. As a consequence of this trend, in the future we may witness the rise of a predominantly minority female underclass, characterized by social networks that cannot provide either the old or the young with sufficient help to allow them to escape poverty (Worobey and Angel 1990b).

It is unclear, therefore, just how informal networks operate among the lower classes and how effective they are in alleviating the more negative consequences of poverty. These informal networks are clearly crucial for survival, but they may be less effective in providing high-quality care to the elderly than we imagine. Regardless of one's racial or ethnic group, though, or even one's level of income, if one lives alone and cannot call upon family members for help, some other source of assistance must be found. One adaptation that has evolved among various groups, again often in response to poverty, is the reliance on fictive kin (Stack 1974). Among Mexican Americans fictive kin have historically been a part of a child's parental network (Keefe and Padilla 1987). Such an adaptation was one way of dealing with the uncertainties of life in situations in which the early death of parents was common. A large body of research indicates that among blacks such non-kin are integral members of an older individual's informal support network and are called on in times of crisis (George 1988; Johnson and Barer 1990; Taylor 1985; Taylor and Chatters 1986; Taylor, Chatters, and Mays 1988). For the black elderly, church membership also complements the family-based support network (Taylor and Chatters 1986; Walls and Zarit 1991).

The data, therefore, clearly demonstrate cultural and social class differences in the size and functioning of informal networks. The reasons for these differences are less clear, however. As we noted in the preface, specific European ethnicities have become largely irrelevant as predictors of socioeconomic standing and social interaction. The group differences that remain significant today are those associated with minority group status and its accompanying socioeconomic disadvantage. Most of the significant differences that emerge in informal networks reflect either demography (family size, migration patterns, rural/urban residence) or socioeconomic factors, including education and income. We must be careful, therefore, not to attribute to culture patterns and behaviors that really reflect more concrete and identifiable social class factors. The most useful way of conceiving of the role of culture in social support is to remember that culture, or group membership, provides one with certain social resources that can be mobilized in times of crisis. Such social resources consist of children, other kin, friends and neighbors, churches, and the local community. Depending upon a group's beliefs and practices, this potential network is mobilized or not, and the reliance on the network is affected by one's own and one's family's material resources. It is probably impossible in principle, therefore, to separate the influence of culture and social class since they are so inextricably intertwined.

One other problem that leads to confusion in studies of differences between groups is the failure to adequately deal with the great heterogeneity within specific groups. Much of the literature on Hispanics, for example, either explicitly or implicitly characterizes all Hispanics as familistic. We are aware by now that for most human psychological and social characteristics, within group differences are far greater than between group differences. Many non-Hispanics are as familistic in their behavior as Hispanics. In fact, it would be difficult to find any group that is not to some degree "familistic." To be human is to be part of a family, whether one ever sees them or not. Even within the category of Hispanic one finds large differences in patterns of social interaction and contact with family members. Figure 5.1 is from one of our earlier studies (Angel and Angel 1992) and reveals significant variation among different Hispanic groups in the tendency for individuals over the age of sixty five to have daily contact with their children, to attend church, and to associate with friends (Angel and Angel 1992). Older Mexican Americans are more likely than either Cuban Americans or Puerto Ricans to see their children on a daily basis or to attend church, and Cuban Americans are more likely than other Hispanics to get together with friends. Were we to carry this analysis further and examine differences within each of these nationality groups, we would no doubt find substantial variation in social interaction and support among members of the same group. The same is, no doubt, true for any other racial or ethnic group.

The role of culture in determining the informal support available to the elderly, therefore, remains elusive. It clearly has some impact,

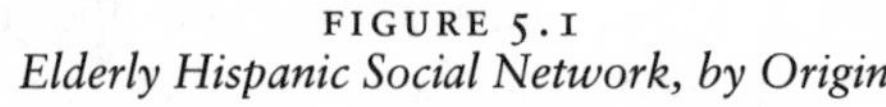

FIGURE 5.1
Elderly Hispanic Social Network, by Origin

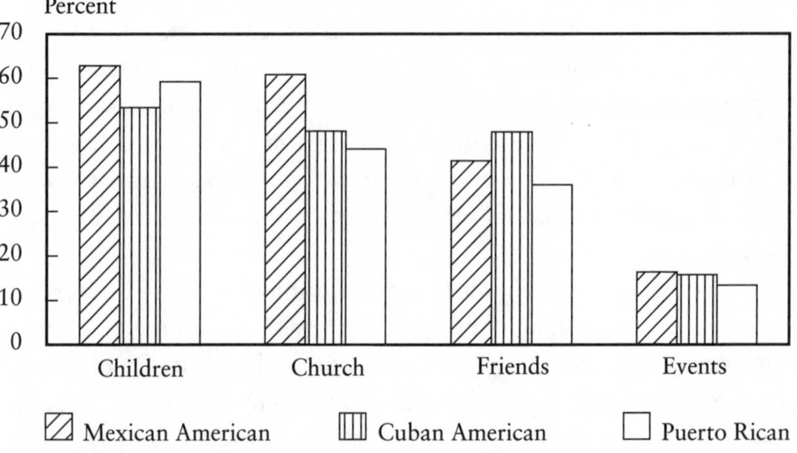

SOURCE: Ronald J. Angel and Jacqueline L. Angel, "Age at Migration, Social Connections, and Well-Being among Elderly Hispanics," *Journal of Aging and Health* 4 (1992): 480–99.

but it is unclear how much, once we take group differences in more mundane socioeconomic characteristics into account. We end our examination of group differences by examining three important factors that influence the informal support of the elderly: living arrangements, rural/urban residence, and immigration status. These factors are possibly among the most important variables affecting the well-being of the ethnic elderly.

Living Arrangements and Social Support

One's living situation is perhaps the major determinant of the amount and type of informal support that one can call upon. Individuals who live alone do not have the kind of immediate help available to someone who lives with a spouse or children. An individual's living arrangement, therefore, tells us a great deal about his or her social world. Unfortunately, knowing the living arrangement tells us nothing about the kind of help he or she receives from individuals outside of the household, and we know that such assistance can make a large difference in the quality of an older person's life. Nonetheless, given the importance of living arrangements in determining most aspects of an older individual's economic and social well-being, knowing how the living arrangements of the elderly are affected by health and informal social resources is crucial in understanding their social support.

Perhaps the major determinant of one's social support is marital status, since marriage provides an immediate source of emotional and instrumental support. People get married and live together, not just for emotional support and affection, but to pool resources and to help one another with the burdens of everyday life. One of the most difficult transitions in later life is the loss of a lifelong companion. Widowhood requires that an older person reorient and restructure his or her local support network. Since women live longer than men, and since they tend to marry men who are older than themselves to begin with, widows greatly outnumber widowers. Today most widows live alone once their husbands are gone (Treas 1995). Since widowhood tends to occur late in life, many of these women are in poor health when they become widowed, and of these a good portion are at high risk of institutionalization. In order to remain in the community they are dependent on formal care, their children, or other family members for assistance with activities of daily living. The vulnerability of older women and the fact that the family may be less able to provide informal support in the years to come has resulted in increased interest in the possibilities of providing more of the kind of formal care that allows seriously incapacitated individuals to remain in the community rather than enter a nursing home.

Although the proportion of older single females who live alone is high among all racial and ethnic groups, as table 5.1 shows, older black and Hispanic women are more likely than others to live with their children (Angel and Angel 1993). These data also reveal differences within the Hispanic population in the tendency of older women to live with their children. Mexican American women are more likely than either Puerto Ricans or Cuban Americans to do so. Again, we do not know what part poverty plays in the decision to live with

TABLE 5.1
Percentage of Unmarried Persons Aged 65 Years and Over Who Live with Their Children

Non-Hispanic White	Non-Hispanic Black	Mexican American	Cuban American	Puerto Rican	Other Hispanic	Asian
WOMEN						
5.8	8.6	16.3	20.9	18.1	21.9	32.5
MEN						
3.9	5.5	11.9	11.9	9.9	14.0	16.9

SOURCE: U.S. Bureau of the Census, *1990 Census of Population and Housing: Public Use Microdata Samples, United States* (Washington, DC, 1993).

one's children, but it is clear that the higher fertility of Hispanics provides these women with a greater opportunity to make such an arrangement if they wish to. Cultural norms that place responsibility for aging parents with children will of course reinforce this trend (Angel et al. in press).

Health is clearly a major influence on an older person's living situation. When an older person's health declines significantly, living alone in the community can become impossible and some other arrangement must be found. In two previous studies we examined factors that determine whether an older person who suffers a loss in functional capacity enters a nursing home or moves in with family members. In the first study we focused on unmarried men and women seventy and older and assessed how changes in their health over a two-year period affected their living arrangements (Worobey and Angel 1990a). What we found was that even though single black elderly persons suffered greater losses in functional capacity than non-Hispanic whites, they were less likely to enter a nursing home but tended instead to move in with family. We also found that women were more likely than men to move in with their children when their health failed. In the second study we examined two more years of data and found that blacks were twice as likely as non-Hispanic whites to continue to suffer declines in functional status and that, once again, the black family mobilized to provide the support that the older person needed (Angel, Angel, and Himes 1992).

Rural/Urban Differences in Social Support

Not all that long ago America was a rural nation, in which the material and social differences between town and country placed them worlds apart. Rural states have historically been poorer than urbanized states, and the isolation and transportation difficulties typical of rural areas made health care and other services difficult to obtain. Even today, rural states have less to spend on providing services to the needy elderly under Title XX of the Social Security Act than do more urbanized states (Nelson 1983). During the second half of the twentieth century, however, the major distinctions between urban and rural areas have diminished. Although the incomes of older persons in rural areas remain lower than those in urban areas (McLaughlin and Jensen 1991), the availability of social and health care services is far more equal today than in the past. Even in the rural South, which was traditionally one of the poorest and least served areas of the country, most elderly individuals have access to health care services (Blazer et al. 1995).

Although there is relatively little information on health and social network differences between the elderly in urban and rural areas, the differences that we know of are neither large nor consistent. In general, older persons in nonmetropolitan areas rate their health as poorer than do metropolitan residents (Van Nostrand 1993). This difference applies to both races; rural blacks rate their health as fair or poor more often than do urban blacks. On more objective measures, such as activity limitations, blood pressure, and obesity, rural/urban differences are less pronounced, nor are there significant differences in health risk behaviors, such as smoking or heavy drinking. On the other hand, elderly rural residents are less likely than their metropolitan counterparts to have seen a dentist in the last year. They also have less access to Medicare home health care services, although these differences have diminished in recent years (Kenney 1993).

The limited data we have, then, indicate that Social Security, Medicare, and the general availability of services have eliminated stark distinctions between older rural and urban residents in both income and health care. The differences that remain appear to result from the greater distances to services that users must traverse in rural areas. We might, however, ask whether informal networks or living arrangements differ significantly between elderly urban and rural residents. The data are again limited but indicate that the differences are largely related to the composition of the informal network. Older rural residents tend to have networks based primarily on nuclear family members, whereas urban residents have more extended networks (Corin 1987). The rural elderly are also more likely to receive help from their informal network than are the urban elderly, who rely more heavily on formal sources of assistance (Lee, Dwyer, and Coward 1990). Our own research corroborates these findings and shows that a larger fraction of rural elderly live with their families than do their urban counterparts. Our findings also show that older rural residents are twice as likely as their urban counterparts to see their children on a daily basis (Angel et al. 1995).

Although these findings suggest that rural elderly may suffer some slight disadvantages in social service and health care delivery, it is clear that the large rural/urban differences of the past have disappeared. Today, because of Medicare and the wider distribution of services, even elderly black rural Americans receive the medical care and other community services they need. We suspect that general rural/urban or metropolitan/nonmetropolitan distinctions are not as revealing today as they once were in understanding the social service and health care needs of the elderly. Rather than focusing our research efforts on attempts to identify general rural/urban differences, then, it would be more useful to focus on specific pockets of need. In rural North Carolina, for example, most residents are within an hour-and-a-half drive of a major medical center, and roads are well maintained; in this region, then, access to high-quality health care is, for the most part, adequate (Blazer et al. 1995). But in the Rio Grande valley of Texas, where many poor elderly Mexican Americans live in inaccessible and poorly served Colonials, social and health services are still hard to come by.

Given the size of the state and the length of the United States/Mexico border, many older rural residents of Texas still have a hard time getting to a major medical center. As of yet, we know almost nothing about the social service or health care needs of these older individuals. Nor do we have a clear understanding of the role of the informal network in their support. A significant number of older Mexican Americans do not participate in Social Security or Medicare; they are completely dependent on their families for support and must rely on charity for whatever medical care they need or simply do without it. The level of unmet need among these elderly individuals is, no doubt, high. Future research should focus less on the identification of large aggregate differences between groups of elderly and more on the needs of particular subgroups within each cultural, social, and economic contexts.

Migration/Age at Immigration

The United States is a nation of immigrants, although that fact really means very little anymore. Most American families have been here for at least a couple of generations, and their ethnic ties are by now little more than symbolic. Immigrants continue to arrive on our shores, but today, unlike the past, they come primarily from Latin America and Asia. Although migrants have historically been young, the reunification of families and migration by entire families means that some individuals come to the United States later in life (Angel and Angel 1992). Such timing poses problems for the immigrant, his or her family, and society at large. Migration is trying at any time of life but is particularly stressful for the old because of the global nature of the changes involved. Moving from one nation and culture to another involves both acute and chronic strains (Angel and Angel 1992). When an individual leaves a familiar environment and travels to a new country, his or her entire world is turned upside down and must be put right again (Evans 1987; Findley 1988; Kasl and Berkman 1983). The immigrant must learn a new language and new norms and practices. He or she must learn to negotiate new bureaucracies and become familiar with a different medical care system (Alston and Aguirre 1987). As part of the process one must sever familiar ties to people and places in the old country and reestablish primary ties in the new (Evans 1987; Portes and Rumbaut 1990; Rogler, Gurak, and Cooney 1987). Clearly, this process is easier the earlier in life it occurs. Children, because they are rapidly changing anyway as a normal part of their development, quickly master the new culture and language. For the old, the task of adapting to an entirely new worldview is much more difficult. Older migrants have less time to rebuild connections, and their networks often remain permanently truncated.

Immigrants naturally tend to retain more of the culture of their country of origin than do second-generation Americans and consequently have a more traditional orientation and outlook. They are more likely than the native-born to live with family members and to rely on them for assistance (Angel and Angel 1992; Biafora and Longino 1990; Weeks and Cuellar 1981; Weeks and Cuellar, 1983). This dependence on family clearly mitigates some of the more practical difficulties involved in migration and can ease some of its emotional trauma as well (Angel and Angel 1992). Immigration, therefore, involves certain common stressors, but it is important to remember that the immigration experience differs greatly from individual to individual, depending on country of origin and age at time of migration. Table 5.2 shows that among Hispanics, the typical age at immigration is very diverse. Of course, Puerto Ricans are U.S. citizens, so migration for them means something different than for immigrants from Mexico or Cuba. The data also reveal a strong association between cohort, listed in the left column, and the age at which they arrived in the United States. Older Puerto Ricans are far more likely than older Mexican Americans to have immigrated to the U.S. mainland later in life. The same is true for Cuban Americans over the age of seventy. In fact, almost no Puerto Ricans or Cuban Americans in any age group were born on the U.S. mainland. On the other hand, most of the Mexican Americans were born in the United States or moved here in early childhood. This varied immigration history is one reason for the great heterogeneity within the Hispanic population of the United States. Some Mexican Americans have been residents of what is now the southwestern region of the United States

TABLE 5.2

Life-Course Stage at Migration, by Birth Cohort

Group	In Years (Birth Cohort)	Youth or U.S.-born[1] 0–11 Years	Adolescence[2] 12–21 Years	Early Adulthood[3] 22–40 Years	Middle Adulthood[4] 41–50 Years	Late Adulthood[5] 51 Years or Over
Mexican American	65–70 (1918–23)	69.1%	6.7%	15.1%	3.4%	5.7%
	71–79 (1909–17)	78.8%	6.3%	8.1%	2.5%	4.4%
	80+ (before 1908)	58.8%	23.2%	3.5%	2.3%	12.2%
	N = 937					
Cuban American	65–70 (1918–23)	2.2%	3.5%	28.1%	44.2%	22.1%
	71–79 (1909–17)	3.7%	3.2%	7.2%	25.5%	60.4%
	80+ (before 1908)	2.7%	8.0%	3.3%	3.1%	82.9%
	N = 714					
Puerto Rican	65–70 (1918–23)	12.7%	14.5%	57.1%	5.5%	10.2%
	71–79 (1909–17)	13.2%	18.8%	34.3%	18.7%	14.9%
	80+ (before 1908)	15.1%	7.2%	32.2%	15.7%	29.7%
	N = 368					

SOURCE: Ronald J. Angel and Jacqueline L. Angel, "Age at Migration, Social Connections and Well-Being among Elderly Hispanics," *Journal of Aging and Health* 4 (1992): 480–99.

NOTES: Percentages may not sum to 100% due to rounding.

1. Chi-square not significant between groups.
2. Chi-square significant between groups.
3. Chi-square not significant between groups.
4. Chi-square significant between groups.
5. Chi-square significant between groups.

since colonial times, while others immigrated from Mexico only after these territories had become part of the Union.

In a recent study of Mexican Americans over the age of sixty-five we examined the consequences of late-life migration on an older individual's living arrangements and sources of income (Angel and Angel 1992). The data clearly show that individuals who migrated after the age of fifty are more dependent on family members for support. Many of these late-life immigrants do not have the time to contribute the required ten years to Social Security in order to qualify for benefits, and under current law they do not qualify for SSI for a period of five years. Their dependency on family is exacerbated by the fact that the income and asset eligibility criteria for SSI are quite stringent, and for immigrants the sponsor's income and assets are taken into account. An older immigrant may well, therefore, find him- or herself permanently dependent on family, since neither employment nor public support are realistic options. The results of our study suggest that this may, in fact, be the case. Table 5.3, which presents data on income sources for women who immigrated at different ages, shows that over 16 percent of those who arrived in the United States after age fifty receive money from children. Proportionately fewer of these women receive Social Security, pension income, or SSI than do those who immigrated at earlier ages, and proportionately more receive public assistance. This economic dependency, in

TABLE 5.3
Income Sources for Women, by Age at Immigration and Nativity

	Age at Immigration				Native
	1–19	20–39	40–49	50+	
Percent receiving $50 or more from:					
Social Security	82.9	83.5	84.0	53.6	89.1
Private Pension	8.8	9.5	9.5	3.2	13.0
SSI	35.1	31.5	31.1	21.8	29.7
Children	3.5	8.5	5.1	16.2	9.0
RR or Military Pension	1.2	1.7	0.6	0.5	3.8
General assistance	3.5	2.4	3.5	4.3	4.1
Stocks, bonds, rent	0.6	4.4	2.1	0.2	4.3
Unweighted N	(195)	(264)	(94)	(165)	(990)

SOURCE: Kyriakos S. Markides, *A Longitudinal Study of Mexican American Elderly Health* (Washington, DC: National Institute on Aging, 1992).

TABLE 5.4
Depression, by Age at Immigration and Nativity

	Immigrant				Native
	Age at Immigration				
	1–19	20–39	40–49	50+	
Percentage Depressed	29.7	24.8	23.2	34.6	22.8
Unweighted *N*	(351)	(474)	(162)	(274)	(1,704)

SOURCE: Kyriakos S. Markides, *A Longitudinal Study of Mexican American Elderly Health* (Washington, DC: National Institute on Aging, 1992).

conjunction with the other stresses involved in migration, can be quite demoralizing and can result in poorer functioning and elevated levels of depressive affect. Table 5.4 reports the proportion of individuals who received scores of over sixteen on the Center for Epidemiologic Studies Depression Scale (CES-D), a score which is often interpreted as indicating potential clinical depression. The data show that a larger fraction of those individuals who migrated after age fifty have scores over sixteen, reflecting poorer overall life satisfaction.

These data clearly demonstrate, then, that among Mexican Americans the age at which an individual immigrates to the United States has a large impact on his or her economic welfare and living arrangements, as well as on his or her subjective well-being. Those individuals who migrated before the age of fifty may suffer some disadvantage, but their socioeconomic profiles are much closer to those of native-born individuals than are those of individuals who migrated late in life. Late-life immigrants face particularly serious problems in reestablishing themselves in the United States, and proposed changes in the immigration laws and tighter restrictions on SSI can only make the situation of such immigrants worse. Of course, if family reunification ceases to be a policy objective, older individuals may simply be barred from immigrating. On the other hand, even if they are allowed to come, the economic burden on their children who are already here will be great. Unlike longer-term residents, such families will find it necessary to provide for both the young and the old. For a group that is struggling to survive and to move into the economic mainstream, such a burden may prove excessive and hinder the social mobility of all concerned.

Race, Ethnicity, and the Future of the Family in the Care of the Elderly

For all groups, therefore, the family forms the core of the informal network, particularly in rural areas, where distances between friends and neighbors are great and isolation is more of a problem than in the city. For poor blacks and Hispanics, as for poor non-Hispanic whites, the family serves as a refuge in which at least minimal material and emotional support are available. For the elderly whose families are not available, the loss of functional capacity can mean institutionalization and dependence on formal systems of support. As important as the family is in the care of the elderly, though, recent demographic trends raise concerns about its continuing ability to provide such care. In the future the trends toward single parenthood, fewer children, employment of women outside the home, and long-distance migration may make it more difficult for the family to serve as the primary support system for the elderly. As we noted earlier, norms and expectations evolve with changing objective circumstances, and even groups that have been regarded as highly familistic may find their values changing as all groups adapt to the more mobile and dynamic society of the twenty-first century.

Hispanics and Asians have traditionally been characterized as more familistic than other groups. We suspect that this characterization is based as much on myth as on reality (Lockery 1992). Almost all immigrant groups appear to be familistic upon arrival in the United States. In a foreign environment new arrivals must band together in order to survive economically and counter the hostility with which they are often greeted. After a few generations, though, the grandchildren of these immigrants move into the American mainstream and, if they are economically successful, become indistinguishable from the majority population. Those who do not succeed economically stay at the bottom of the socioeconomic hierarchy, and for these individuals reliance on the extended family and the informal network may continue to be necessary in order to insure a minimal standard of living. Unfortunately, because they are formed specifically to compensate for the economic and social vulnerability of their members, such networks may be less adaptive and supportive than the structurally looser networks of the middle class.

Our proposal to optimize the role of the family in the community care of the elderly must, therefore, be tempered by an appreciation of the changing social reality in which the family will operate in the twenty-first century. In the modern world formal organizations are intruding ever more deeply into areas that at one time were the exclusive domain of the family. This process is occurring in the care of the elderly as well as in such areas as education and child care. As much as we might like to reinvent the family and foster the helpful interaction of kin, the smaller more mobile families of the future may simply be unable to provide support services to the elderly. If the family were able and willing to accept the burden, the state might well find it possible to shift responsibility for aging parents back to family members. If, however, the family is no longer available to provide care, cutting services at a time of increasing need simply means that many elderly people in the community will suffer serious privation and, ultimately, find that they have no alternative but to enter a nursing home.

The scale of modern life demands adaptations from all social institutions, including the family. From here on out the state will inevitably play an even larger role in our lives, despite the objections of some traditionalists who wish to scale back big government and return to a simpler time. The social and economic progress upon which our material wealth is based, as well as the political freedom that most Americans value highly, insure that the future will be ever more fluid and changing and will require even greater adaptations on the part of families. What is particularly worrisome, as we mentioned earlier, is the possibility that a concentration of poverty among minority Americans, and increasingly among unmarried women, could lead to a two-tiered system of care for the elderly. The poor may find themselves thrown back on the family, who, because of their own blocked opportunities, may find the burden onerous. The affluent, on the other hand, will be able to take advantage of the more desirable long-term care options that we discuss in the next two chapters.

The ethnographic literature clearly shows that extended networks of kin and fictive kin can be an adaptive response to poverty that improves the lives of both the young and the old (Stack 1974). On the other hand, although pooling physical and economic resources may be a necessity, it may well interfere with the ability of the family to accumulate resources that would allow its younger members to acquire a first-rate education and escape poverty. Again we see that the welfare of the elderly is intimately intertwined with the welfare of the young. As we discuss further in our final chapter, such a situation, in which poverty blocks opportunities for education and asset accumulation, can be passed on from one generation to the next, impeding the social mobility of groups as a whole.

Despite the strains the family has come under, though, our human need for an intimate haven and the necessity of pooling our efforts and resources in order to survive both physically and emotionally leads us to continually reaffirm the family even in the face of rapid and extensive social change. Given the centrality of the family to the care of the elderly, every effort should be made to enhance its ability to provide it. In the future the family will change in ways that are, as yet, impossible to predict. The practice of relying on fictive kin may grow beyond the traditional communities in which it is now confined, and we may see the rise of a world in which individuals seek emotional and instrumental support in families they create, rather than those into which they are born or are committed to by marriage. Whatever its form, though, some form of the family will probably continue to define us as social beings and members of the human species. Policy directed toward the care of the elderly must, therefore, be informed by an understanding of the wide variety of families that may come into being and the great variation in the cultural and social class contexts in which they will operate. The only alternative is an increasing reliance on formal support, the subject to which we turn in the next chapter.

SIX

A Refuge of Last Resort: Culture, Social Class, and the Use of Institutional Long-Term Care

As we pointed out in the last chapter, although families have in general not abandoned their elderly, some disturbing trends are at work that increasingly threaten the family's ability to provide support to older members. Despite a nearly universal desire among policy makers to maintain the family in the caregiving role, the large-scale social and economic changes that are shaping the modern world have altered the family and its economic and social context to such an extent that in the future a larger proportion of families may find that they simply cannot serve as the primary caregivers for the elderly (Kendig, Hashimoto, and Coppard 1992; World Bank 1994). Single mothers who must raise their children alone, couples in which both husband and wife work, and children who have moved away from their parent's community or who have no siblings to help share the burden of caring for aging parents are severely limited in what they can do.

If current social and demographic trends continue, and there seems to be little reason to imagine that they will not, more and more families will find themselves in this situation. Even Hispanics, for whom the family plays a central role in the care of the elderly, will find their ability to care for aging parents increasingly strained as their families are affected by the same social, economic, and demographic forces that have loosened family bonds among other groups. For better or worse, then, a growing number of older individuals will have no alternative but to turn to formal sources of support. One of the most consistent predictors of institutionalization among the elderly is the lack of an informal network, and more and more older individuals will find that their informal networks are inadequate to allow them to remain in the community (Cantor 1983; Shanas 1979). In order to address the growing demand for formal services that will inevitably accompany population aging, such services will have to be not only available but designed in such a manner as to satisfy the needs of individuals from different racial and ethnic backgrounds, if they are to adequately complement or, if necessary, replace the family in the daily care of the infirm elderly.

Does Formal Support Replace the Family?

As a prelude to this discussion, we wish to emphasize that the expansion of formal support services, whether institutional or community-based, may be a mixed blessing. Well-designed programs for providing care to elderly individuals in need clearly have the potential to improve the quality of their lives and allow them to remain in the community for as long as possible. Unfortunately, as many concerned observers have noted, there is also a potential down side to formal state-sponsored programs: the very availability of such programs may accelerate the decline in the role of the family in caring for older parents (Chappell 1990; Tennstedt, Crawford, and McKinlay 1993). Today children no longer expect to assume the responsibility for their parents' financial needs. Social Security has given rise to the universal expectation that the federal government should provide financial support to the elderly. A similar shift in expectations concerning long-term care might remove the family from its active care-giving role, or at least reduce its involvement substantially. If the family collapses as a support system, services that are currently provided at no cost by family members will have to be paid for and will place even greater strains on already burdened state and federal treasuries. Our national experience with other social programs, such as Medicare and Medicaid, clearly demonstrates that the availability of services can generate its own demand and lead to the sort of spiraling increases in costs that, sooner or later, trigger taxpayer revolts and generate cynicism concerning the role of government generally.

The concern over the potential harm to informal support systems that might unintentionally result from governmental attempts to deal with the growing needs of aging populations is not confined to the United States. In developing nations the family is increasingly stressed by forces associated with social and economic change. A decline in the family's capacity to provide care could spell disaster for the elderly in situations in which there are no formal alternatives. A recent report published by the World Bank admonishes developing nations not to undermine the family's role in the care of the elderly as they create the state-sponsored systems that will be necessary to provide basic support to their older citizens in the years to come (World Bank 1994). Unfortunately, although such admonitions alert us to the potential danger of such unintended consequences, the introduction of new programs invariably alters the ground rules that people live by, and norms governing the family's role are bound to follow suit. In the United States it is clearly impossible to predict how the mix of informal and formal support will change in the future, since the increasing demand for long-term care will alter both the ways in which it is provided and the way in which it is viewed. All that we can be certain of is that nothing will remain the same and that the role of the family in caring for the elderly will be very different from what it has been in the past. We would be wise, therefore, to attempt to understand the forces that are likely to influence the evolution of formal long-term care options as we enter the twenty-first century and begin to think about how they may affect the family's role in the care of the elderly for various groups.

As of yet, it appears that the availability of formal alternatives has not significantly reduced the family's commitment to the care of the elderly. Several studies indicate that even when they use home health care services, family members do not significantly reduce the amount of time they devote to the care of older infirm parents (Moscovice, Davidson, and McCaffrey 1988; Hanley, Wiener, and Harris 1991; Wiener and Hanley 1992a). Such findings give us hope that it might be possible to create a system in which numerous alternatives in long-term care complement the family's contribution, rather than replace it altogether. The substitution of formal for informal care, though, is probably much more complex in its effects than these preliminary, and rather broad, findings can indicate. Substitution of formal for informal care does occur in certain situations, primarily when one's informal support network ceases to function or when its structure changes, as when a spouse dies or a person who lives alone suffers a serious decline in functional capacity (Kemper 1992; Tennstedt, Crawford, and McKinlay 1993). The number of older individuals with inadequate informal support will become more common in the future and research must begin to identify the factors that lead to the replacement of informal support by formal support in specific situations.

Our experience with formal long-term care programs, and the public's knowledge of them, is fairly recent and limited (Holmes, Teresi, and Holmes 1983). Neither institutional nor community-based options were common until very recently, and to the man or woman on the street long-term care is still probably synonymous with nursing homes. After all, until very recently in human history old folks lived and died at home; if they left home, it was to go to an institution that provided skilled full-time care that the family could no longer provide. As the population ages, though, both institutional and community-based long-term care alternatives are evolving and expanding at a rapid rate, and as they become more common, they will gain wider acceptance. For better or worse, as expectations concerning the duty of the family to care for its older members change, and as both children and the old turn to the state as the main source of support for an ever growing fraction of the elderly, those informal systems, based in the family, that for millennia have knit us together in networks of mutual support may atrophy. Unfortunately, in its ability to provide care to the elderly in times of serious economic downturns, the state may prove to be far less adaptable and resilient than the family.

Options in Institutional Long-Term Care

Let us review the various options in long-term care and compare the most intensive arrangement, the skilled-care nursing home, to less intensive institutional options, in order to better understand the cultural, social, and economic barriers to the use of such facilities that minority group members and the poor face, as well as the potential for more imaginative and culturally appropriate alternatives. Given the growing need for institutional care, even among groups that have historically avoided nursing homes, it is imperative that we begin to understand how best to provide it. The skilled-care nursing home is not only the most comprehensive form of long-term care but also the most expensive. The care provided in such facilities is designed for individuals who need postacute care for short periods after they are released from a hospital or for the most seriously debilitated individuals, those who are in the final stages of physical and mental decline. Although many individuals enter nursing homes at some time during their lives, most are discharged after a relatively short period (Wiener and Harris 1990). As many as 20 percent of those who enter nursing homes, though, remain for five years or more (Rich 1991).

The predictors of admission to nursing homes include, among other things, poor health, old age, functional and cognitive impairment, the need for such devices as walkers and other aids, living alone, being confined to bed, high physician use, and living in areas with a large nursing home supply (Branch and Jette 1982; Cohen, Tell, and Wallack 1986; Greene and Ondrich 1990; Nocks et al. 1986). The distribution of these risk factors varies for different racial and ethnic groups. For example, blacks have generally poorer health than whites and Hispanics tend to live in areas with few nursing homes available. But in any particular case, it is these factors, working together, that determine the probability that an older individual will enter a nursing home.

Continuing Care Retirement Communities (CCRCs)

Nursing home residents with serious illnesses represent the greatest need in terms of intensity of care, but a far greater number of individuals could benefit from less intensive assistance. As the life span increases, so do the number of years during which one could use some help with activities of daily living. Even if one is functioning fairly well, there comes a time when one may find the responsibilities of keeping up a home too difficult or when, because of minor physical problems, one would welcome some help with personal care tasks. It would make little sense to place an older person in a skilled nursing home facility when all that he or she needs is some assistance in maintaining his or her usual life-style in the community. Usually, such assistance can easily be provided by family members, but if they are not available, intermediate care alternatives fill the void. Several forms of this less intensive care are becoming increasingly common (Cohen et al. 1987; Somers and Spears 1992). They range from what are little more than old-age communities, in which functionally healthy older persons can affiliate with others of their own age, to facilities that are just short of nursing homes and provide medical care as well as assistance with activities of daily living.

Like Health Maintenance Organizations (HMOs), long-term care options have developed so rapidly that it is impossible to exhaustively list all of the alternatives. We will simply summarize the basic types, to illustrate the growing number of options in the long-term care of the elderly. Some of the less intensive, community-based options may prove to be more appealing to minority elderly (who tend to be younger, on average, than majority group elderly) especially if such alternatives were designed with a sensitivity to the client's cultural preferences. The basic characteristic of most of the institutional alternatives we cover in this chapter is that they are based on a common residential location, although not necessarily in the same building. They are also based on an the pooling of risk and, as with insurance schemes generally, they spread the costs of providing services over the enrolled population (Cohen et al. 1987; Schulz 1995). Many have entrance fees, which can be non-refundable, completely refundable, or refundable on a prorated basis (Somers and Spears 1992). All impose some monthly charge, paid either by the individual him- or herself or by the state. Some cover medical expenses and provide more intensive care for short periods; others do not.

The most typical residential arrangement has the formal title of continuing care retirement communities (CCRCs) or assisted living plans. CCRCs are one example of a long-term care arrangement that combines housing, health insurance, and social support in a managed care environment (Cohen et al. 1987; Somers and Spears 1992). Continuing care retirement communities are similar to health maintenance organizations, except that they also offer long-term care for the frail elderly. Typically, an older person or a couple pays an entrance fee and then rents an apartment at a central facility for a monthly fee. In return, they receive assistance with activities of daily living and medical care when they need it (Somers and Spears 1992). Both the entrance fee and the monthly payment can be rather large. In 1994, for example, the average median entrance fee for a one-bedroom unit ranged from a low of $59,010 to a high of $85,868 and the monthly fee ranged from $1,046 to $1,399 (Scruggs 1995). Clearly, such costs place the CCRC option out of the reach of many older individuals.

Variations on the CCRC

One variation on the CCRC is the life-care-at-home option developed by researchers at Brandeis University (Cohen et al. 1987). This plan is similar to the CCRC except that individuals remain in their own homes and are fully covered for medical care and other services in a managed care environment. Because it is not based on aggregate residential facilities, though, this option is more like the community-based alternatives we discuss in the next chapter. Other options for the care of the elderly differ from the CCRC in their basic medical and long-term care coverage, as well as in the other services they provide. Building on the concept of the health maintenance organization (HMO), social health maintenance organizations (SHMOs) deliver a package of services for a fixed premium (Cohen et al. 1987). Typically, though, the SHMO provides only limited coverage for long-term care.

All of the variations on continuing care communities, therefore, involve a centralized residential location. For individuals who are no longer able to maintain a household or for those who no longer care to, such facilities offer an alternative to the nursing home or dependence on family members for assistance. Although such arrangements require that one leave one's home, they offer some aspects of community living and allow a considerable degree of autonomy. Intermediate-care residential arrangements are appealing to many elderly for another reason: they allow one to interact with people of one's own age. Old people often feel stigmatized and left out when they live in communities with younger individuals. Living with one's age peers not only reduces such perceived stigma but puts one in contact with those who have shared the same historical experiences and who, consequently, often hold similar values. Members of the same cohort remember a world that is lost, and, regardless of one's age, it is easier to communicate with those who share one's worldview than with those who, in a certain sense, inhabit a different world and whose values and behavior go against one's cherished beliefs.

Such common worldviews, of course, are based on more than generational membership. They are based on a common culture and social class. Individuals who speak different languages and who belong to different social classes experience the same historical period in very different ways. Those who have immigrated recently who have experienced discrimination, or who, for whatever reason, remain alienated from the mainstream culture will clearly have a hard time adjusting to an institutional environment designed for middle-class non-Hispanic white elderly. The age difference between majority and minority elderly also contributes to the disparity in interests. All of these differences, in addition to poverty and the cultural "foreignness" which institutional life itself represents, no doubt contributes to the low use of nursing homes by blacks and Hispanics. Were institutional arrangements that included more blacks and Hispanics available, these groups would, no doubt, use them in greater numbers. Of course, grouping individuals on the basis of race or ethnicity might appear little more than segregation and result in inferior, publicly funded facilities for minority group elderly and higher-quality facilities for the affluent middle-class majority. Although differences in personal wealth inevitably lead to differences in the quality of long-term care the elderly receive, the challenge we face is to provide high-quality, culturally appropriate long-term care to everyone who needs it.

Paying for Long-Term Care: The Role of Private Insurance

Long-term care has been one of the most challenging aspects of health care policy reform. Federal and state governments have hesitated to take on the potentially massive burden of providing such care, and the private insurance system has, until recently, not found long-term care to be a potentially profitable market. The basic problem is that people are not usually motivated to purchase long-term care insurance until they are old enough to imagine themselves needing it. For younger adults the education of children, saving for retirement, and life and health insurance are more pressing needs. But by the time the purchaser is old enough to be at risk for needing long-term care, insurance premiums must be high and benefits limited if the insurer is to make a profit. The insurer also faces a serious moral hazard problem. In insurance theory, moral hazard refers to the likelihood that one will elicit a behavior by insuring against it. If an older person has insurance that will pay for care, the chances that he or she will use such care are greatly increased. This moral hazard problem is akin to the more general problem we mentioned above, in which the very availability of services paid for by the state, or in this case a private insurer, runs the risk of shifting responsibility for the care of the elderly to some third party and thus increasing use. These actuarial realities mean that premiums must remain high and coverage limited. In consequence, most current long-term care policies remain out of reach for many older individuals because of the cost, and because of the limited coverage they are often unappealing even to those who can afford them.

Once the government intervenes to more closely regulate the industry and help standardize the products, and as tax and inheritance laws are changed to make private long-term care insurance more attractive, coverage will inevitably increase. As of yet, though, long-term care policies are owned by only a small fraction of the elderly (*Consumer Reports* 1991; Schulz 1995; Somers and Spears 1992; Wilson and Weissert 1989). An economically rational insurer is, of course, motivated to exclude those individuals who represent an excessive risk of financial loss. In the case of long-term care, as with other forms of insurance, the insurer must exclude specifically those individuals who are in greatest need of coverage or, at least, must charge them a higher premium. Older applicants are frequently denied long-term care coverage, and as many as 40 percent of those who apply are turned down because of preexisting conditions such as cancer and heart disease. If an individual with such a condition is offered coverage, he or she must pay even higher premiums. An individual with Alzheimer's disease, for example, would have to pay more than two and a half times as much as someone without the condition in order to purchase even limited coverage (*Consumer Reports* 1991).

There are other shortcomings to current long-term care insurance. Often the home care components of such policies do not include personal care or assistance with basic activities of daily living. Current policies typically cover only skilled nursing care performed by licensed registered nurses and health care professionals. In light of the great need for basic home health care, such limitations in coverage are a major drawback. Perhaps the most serious problem with long-term care insurance, though, is the financial instability of many long-term care insurance companies. Until the industry evolves further and is regulated by the federal government, it is hard to know whether an older person should risk what may be a large portion of his or her life savings for a product that may not be delivered when he or she eventually needs it.

Private long-term care insurance, therefore, will necessarily remain expensive and provide only limited coverage. Studies based on typical economic assumptions and techniques for estimating the cash value of in-kind transfers and illiquid assets suggest that perhaps as many as 30 to 50 percent of older persons could afford some form of long-term care insurance (Cohen et al. 1987; Cohen et al. 1992). Unfortunately, these optimistic figures include the less comprehensive forms of coverage and, in reality, it is unlikely than even 10 percent of older persons are likely to be able and willing to pay the cost of the more expensive forms of long-term care (Cohen et al. 1987). Private long-term care insurance, then, will not address the needs of low-income elderly or those over the age of seventy-five (Cohen et al. 1992). The poor simply cannot afford the premiums, and those over seventy-five have become uninsurable because of their elevated risk of catastrophic illness and the need for intensive nursing home care. These individuals will continue to rely on Medicaid for support. The best hope for the poor and the very old, therefore, is an improved Medicaid program (Cohen et al. 1992).

Despite the potential problems with long-term care insurance, though, the number of policies sold has increased in recent years, from fewer than one hundred thousand in 1986 to nearly two million in 1991 (Health Insurance Association of America 1995). As the industry matures and as people find that they are able to protect at least a portion of their estates by purchasing such policies, the popularity of long-term care insurance will increase. This trend is fueled by people's growing awareness that the chances are very high that they will spend some time in long-term care. An estimated 40 percent of the population will enter a nursing home at some time during their lifetimes. What makes long-term care potentially desirable both to individuals and to insurers is that most of those who enter nursing homes are released within one year of admission (Spence and Wiener 1990b). Given the high cost of nursing home care and the limited duration of most stays, even limited coverage can substantially reduce an older person's out-of-pocket expenses and may represent a good buy. For the insurer, the risks of major losses through protracted nursing home stays are eliminated by limitations on coverage. This means that coverage can be offered at a cost that is within the scope of at least a segment of the older population (Cohen et al. 1992). Insuring against the risk of limited nursing home stays, therefore, may become as common in the future as is major medical insurance today.

Because of all of these problems in both public and private financing, then, the long-term care delivery system of the United States has remained underdeveloped, expensive, and fragmented (Atkins 1990; Somers and Spears 1992). The situation, however, is changing rapidly, in response to the increasing demand from an aging population, especially at the older ages (Somers and Spears 1992). The need for long-term care and the potential market it represents is huge, and both private and public providers will introduce many more options in the years to come. As we showed in chapter 4, despite this growth in options, certain segments of the older population, including the poor, minorities, and the very old, will never be insurable in the private market because of the cost of private insurance or excessive risk to the insurer. These individuals will continue to depend on public funding for long-term care, and they are particularly vulnerable to any potential reductions in funding for long-term care under Medicaid.

Medicaid and Long-Term Care

In 1992 Americans spent more than sixty billion dollars on long-term care (Cohen et al. 1992). The majority of the cost of this care is paid for by the elderly themselves; the rest, largely by the joint federal and state Medicaid program. The lion's share of the cost of long-term care is for nursing home stays, the most expensive form of long-term care (Wiener, Illston, and Hanley 1994). Yet only about 1 percent of nursing home expenditures are covered by private insurance (Cohen et al. 1992; Wiener and Harris 1990). Unfortunately, many older individuals and their families erroneously believe that Medicare or their Medicare supplemental policies will pay for long-term care (Cohen et al. 1987). Medicare pays for postacute nursing home stays, but neither Medicare itself nor the typical supplemental Medigap policy cover long-term custodial care. Many older individuals, therefore, are at risk of losing everything they have if they become seriously ill.

In the absence of private long-term care insurance, older individuals must pay out-of-pocket for whatever care they receive, and this appears to be what most people do (Short et al. 1992). When their assets are depleted, Medicaid takes over, but to qualify for Medicaid one must liquidate nearly all of one's estate and "spend down" to Medicaid eligibility (Moon 1993). Medicaid eligibility criteria are highly restrictive and allow the older person or his or her spouse to retain very few assets. For example, since 1990 a spouse could keep up to $856 dollars per month of the nursing home resident's income plus $62,550 of their joint assets. However, in 1993 Congress passed new legislation that requires the state to recover the costs of long-term care from the estates of individuals receiving Medicaid (Schulz 1995). In addition, even after older persons have depleted most of their assets, they are required to spend most of their current income for care before Medicaid kicks in. Medicaid eligibility criteria are particularly hard on spouses who remain in the community. The spouses of older individuals on Medicaid are allowed to keep only a modest amount of assets and income (Moon 1993; Schulz 1995). In any one period, though, only a small fraction of individuals actually spend down to become eligible for Medicaid. The majority of individuals who qualify for Medicaid have relatively few assets or income to begin with and are eligible from the time of admission (Wiener and Harris 1990). As we showed in chapter 3, blacks and Hispanics on average have very few assets by the time they retire, and many have no personal resources to call upon to pay for long-term care. They are, consequently, dependent on Medicaid from the start if they need nursing home care, and the care provided to Medicaid patients is frequently not of the same quality as the care provided to those who can afford to pay the higher cost of private facilities (Diamond 1992).

Group Differences in the Use of Nursing Home Care

Historically, older blacks and Hispanics have entered nursing homes at lower rates than non-Hispanic whites (Angel 1991; Burr 1990; Eribes and Bradley-Rawls 1978; Espino et al. 1988; Greene and Ondrich 1990; Morrison 1983; Torres-Gil and Fielder 1987; Worobey and Angel 1990a). Data from the 1990 Census on the living arrangements of individuals over the age of sixty-five show that on any one day 3 percent of Mexican Americans and Puerto Ricans, and less than 2 percent of Cuban or Asian Americans, are resident in nursing homes. On the other hand, almost 5 percent of older blacks and nearly 6 percent of elderly non-Hispanic whites are living in nursing homes. Even when they experience serious declines in health, black and Hispanic older persons are less likely than non-Hispanic whites to be institutionalized. Rather, they continue to live in the community or move in with family (Angel 1991; Angel, Angel, and Himes 1992; Worobey and Angel 1990a). Although data from the 1990 Census indicate that the proportion of blacks in nursing homes is nearly as high as that for non-Hispanic whites, the generally lower levels of health and functional capacity among older blacks suggests that a large fraction of black elders with significant health problems are managing in the community with the help of their informal networks (Angel, Angel, and Himes 1992).

Several reasons for the lower rates of nursing home use by Hispanics have been offered, including the lack of long-term care facilities in minority communities, cultural differences between the providers of care and minority group members, more powerful cultural norms among Hispanics concerning children's responsibility for the care of aging parents, and cultural differences in preferences in living arrangements (Angel et al. in press). In a recent survey of Mexican Americans over the age of sixty-five, we asked respondents where they would expect to live if their health deteriorated to the point where they could no longer care for themselves. As table 6.1 shows, relatively few said that they would expect to enter a nursing home. The high cost of long-term care that we documented earlier represents a clear barrier to the use of nursing homes for populations that

TABLE 6.1
Where Older Mexican Americans Would Care to Live if They Became Incapacitated

	Percent
With spouse	46.0
With children	34.2
In a nursing home	5.7
Somewhere else[1]	14.1

SOURCE: Kyriakos S. Markides, *A Longitudinal Study of Mexican American Elderly Health* (Washington, DC: National Institute on Aging, 1992).

1. This response covers those persons indicating "my house," "retirement community," and "alone."

have generally low incomes and live in areas that are not well served by long-term care facilities. The answers to our question concerning preferences in living arrangements may reflect a realistic assessment on the part of older Mexican Americans of their inability to pay for nursing home care. In one study researchers found that poverty was the largest predictor of nursing home use among older Hispanics in the Southwest (Eribes and Bradley-Rawls 1978). Poor Mexican Americans simply have no choice but to keep their aging parents at home and, consequently, because there is such low demand for nursing homes in Hispanic areas, potential providers are discouraged from providing nursing home services.

Although there has been a great deal of speculation about the extent to which culturally conditioned norms governing children's obligations to care for their aging parents explain the lower use of nursing homes by older Hispanics, it is still not clear how much of a role culture, independently of income, plays (Gratton 1987; Oriol 1994; Weeks and Cuellar 1981; Williams 1990). In one study, older minority respondents reported that they believed that formal services were meant only for persons who did not have family to whom they might turn for support. These older individuals evidently felt that it was the family's obligation to provide care (Holmes, Teresi, and Holmes 1983).

Of course, in order for an older person to enter a nursing home one must be available. In places like the Rio Grande valley of Texas, an area with a high concentration of individuals of Mexican origin, there are few nursing homes. The closest long-term care facilities are hundreds of miles away, near large metropolitan areas. Were the family to place an aging parent in such a facility, they would have to travel long distances in order to visit and, in all likelihood, would only see the older individual infrequently. Such abandonment would be hard on individuals of any race or ethnicity and clearly discourages the use of nursing homes, even by very frail individuals who might be better off in a skilled care facility.

Even if the older individual and his or her family were receptive to nursing home care, the typical nursing home environment, as we noted earlier, is usually culturally foreign to members of minority racial and ethnic groups who have spent a lifetime in their own cultural enclaves. An unfamiliar physical and cultural environment, unpalatable food, difficulty with English, and staff whose behavior is governed by an alien set of norms can make the nursing home a truly terrifying place for an older person. The decision to enter a nursing home, then, is a complex one, and a great number of factors, including nursing home availability and affordability, the older person's preferences, and the family's capacity and desire to keep an aging parent in the community ultimately determine the decision for or against institutionalization (Groger 1994). As of yet we know relatively little about the decision-making process involved in institutionalizing an older parent. Yet the data make it clear that it is influenced by numerous cultural and social class factors, as well as family preferences. As the institutional environment matures and changes in years to come, it will be necessary to understand more about how such decisions are made and how they are affected by cultural and social context.

Whatever the reason for the relatively low rate of nursing home use by blacks and Hispanics, though, it is certainly not because they are in better health than non-Hispanic whites. The evidence we presented in chapter 2 clearly reveals a great deal of unmet need for medical and social services among older individuals in the community (Cox 1993; Barusch 1994). As we noted, even when they suffer serious declines in health, the elderly of all racial and ethnic groups apparently prefer to live alone rather than to enter nursing homes (Worobey and Angel 1990a). As we showed in chapter 5, whether they can indulge their preference depends to a great degree on the availability of family support, and this availability varies widely from group to group. Black and Hispanic older persons have more children on average than non-Hispanic white elders, and individuals with larger families are better able to remain in the community.

The evidence we have reviewed up to this point certainly suggests that for blacks and Hispanics the family functions as an alternative to institutional care. Much of the evidence is inferential, but it clearly points to the family's role in keeping older individuals out of nursing homes. Certain evidence suggests that the desire or the need to keep older parents in declining health at home is, in fact, so strong that the family avoids institutionalization until the older person is severely disabled. In one study of a nursing home in New York City, researchers found that, although Puerto Rican nursing home residents were much younger than non-Hispanics, they were also much more impaired (Espino et al. 1988). The authors of the study speculated that the higher disability rates among Puerto Ricans were the result of the tendency for Puerto Ricans to keep functionally impaired older persons at home until their health has deteriorated to a degree beyond that which, typically, would have prompted a non-Hispanic family to institutionalize an aging parent.

With the data available such possibilities are only speculation, but they are intriguing nonetheless. A similar hypothesis has been put forward to explain the relatively low use of nursing homes by blacks. In one study researchers found that even after taking into account the risk factors for institutionalization we mentioned above, Hispanics and blacks were still less likely to enter a nursing home than non-Hispanic whites (Greene and Ondrich 1990). However, the authors also report that once older blacks are admitted to nursing homes, they are less likely than whites to be discharged. The authors speculate that the lower discharge rates for blacks result from the tendency for black families to keep aging parents home until they are very seriously impaired, often resulting in the exhaustion of the support capacity of the informal network. In effect, the informal network is simply worn out, and, as a consequence, once the older person enters the nursing home, he or she is less likely to be discharged.

Institutional Alternatives or Alternatives to Institutionalization?

We know, then, that neither black nor Hispanic elderly individuals enter nursing homes in large numbers, even when their health deteriorates significantly. Because of this we, the authors, have spent several years investigating the alternatives that minority Americans resort to when they suffer serious declines in functional capacity, and we have found that for black and Hispanic elderly there are really only two options: moving in with family or making do on one's own (Angel 1991; Worobey and Angel 1990a). Single black women face particular hardship in the community, and even though they suffer on average more serious losses in functional capacity than non-Hispanic white women, they rarely make use of nursing homes. For all groups, women are more likely than men to live with family in the event of a serious deterioration in health.

These findings suggest useful avenues for innovation in providing institutional care to the minority elderly as well as potentially fruitful avenues of research. The data show that blacks and Hispanics are more likely than non-Hispanic whites to keep their aging and incapacitated parents at home, but they do not tell us why. The tendency may simply reflect poorer health among minority Americans, who are, after all, at higher risk of poverty and its associated threats to health. Nursing home care is expensive even when it is available, and high-quality institutional care is simply out of reach for many minority Americans. Nursing home residents who must rely on Medicaid to pay for such care do not receive the same amenities and attention that residents who pay their own way enjoy (Diamond 1992). In addition, a reliance on Medicaid, even for nursing home care, is stigmatizing, since it is based on means tests that require an older person to be virtually destitute. Such a situation is one that most individuals, and especially those who might find the nursing home culturally and socially foreign, would wish to avoid.

Institutionalization, though, will always be a part of the package of long-term care options. Although community-based arrangements are clearly preferable for those who are functioning at a moderate level, some individuals will find that life in the community is impossible. Providing the care that these individuals need at a reasonable cost will require imaginative and culturally appropriate options in institutional care or noninstitutional alternatives. Although the nursing home will always lack the vitality and engagement of life in the community, homes that provide pleasant environments and the company of people who understand one's culture and speak one's language offer the best hope for seriously impaired older individuals whose families cannot care for them. Unfortunately, there have been few incentives for providing high-quality institutional care to older individuals who are almost exclusively dependent on Medicaid financing. However this situation is changing rapidly because of an increased demand for services among the minority elderly and the movement to managed care. With the proper incentives even Medicaid dependent individuals could be offered reasonable care.

Nursing home care is clearly a business in which labor constitutes a large fraction of the cost. In the United States high-quality labor is expensive and often difficult to find. One intriguing suggestion that has been offered for the Hispanic elderly is to allow older persons to collect Medicare and Medicaid in Mexico (Warner and Reed 1993). High-quality labor is available in Mexico at a very reasonable price, and facilities can be built at much lower cost than in the United States. For some members of the Mexican American population, and even for some non-Hispanics, life across the border could be more pleasant, and their limited incomes stretched much further, than in the States. The infusion of dollars into the Mexican border economy would be a boon to the area and could perhaps ameliorate some of the glaring poverty that forces people to enter into the United States illegally. Such a suggestion, of course, seems a little visionary at present, but may seem less farfetched in the future, as the problem of caring for the elderly reaches a critical juncture.

Since nursing homes are a business, there is simply a limit to what they can do for individuals on Medicaid. As was the case for retirement income and health insurance, then, we find that the reliance on public funding for long-term care places one at a distinct disadvantage in terms of the options available. For the poor, reliance on Medicaid for long-term care means that they have little choice in the type of care they receive. Were the number of long-term care options for Medicaid clients to increase, the number of choices for minority elders and the poor could also grow. If, on the other hand, in the attempt to contain rapidly rising expenditures under Medicaid, reimbursements to nursing homes and the number of services covered are reduced, those options may become even more limited.

As long as relatives, fictive kin, friends, and neighbors are available and willing to assist the older person, and as long as his or her physical or mental condition is not too deteriorated, staying at home is clearly preferable. As we show in the next chapter, recent experiments in community-based care prove that even seriously impaired older people can be kept in the community. The best possibility for accomplishing that objective is a well-managed and coordinated combination of formal and informal care sources. As we noted at the beginning of the chapter, though, in the future, black and Hispanic families and communities will come under increasing pressure that may limit their ability to care for the elderly.

The current political mood is one of disillusionment with big government and a desire to return to local responsibility and control, including the responsibility of families for their own members. For better or worse, though, because of the changes that families of all racial and ethnic groups are undergoing, it is unlikely that the role of the state in the care of the elderly will decrease substantially. Even when family members are available to provide assistance to an elderly parent, there often comes a point at which the older person's functioning is so compromised that caring for them becomes an unbearable burden. Individuals with advanced Alzheimer's disease, those who are incontinent, those with cancer or serious heart disease, or those who break a hip often require round-the-clock supervision that is far too demanding for family members alone to provide. When the family cannot deal with the burden, the only alternative is institutionalization and the only way of paying for such care is, for most institutionalized individuals, Medicaid. The efficient use of public funds and the assumption of responsibility for oneself and one's relatives are laudable ideals, but the reality of change cannot be ignored, even if it is seen as decline by some. Formal support systems for the elderly will only become more important in years to come, and our only hope is to design the best and most cost-effective systems possible—which of course will mean making the best use of whatever family support resources are still available.

In the fairly near future, the rapid and extensive aging of the population will force society into experiments with new forms of long-term care. Although the most debilitated individuals will always require intensive and skilled nursing home care, our increased desire to insure the highest quality life at the lowest cost will result in many new experiments in the community support of the elderly. The need for new alternatives is made even more imperative because of the racial and ethnic diversity among the older population. A one-size-fits-all approach to long-term care will not address the needs of many of the most disadvantaged elderly individuals, and cost effectiveness considerations alone will require that we develop a much more sophisticated understanding of the diversity among the older population, not only in terms of mental and physical capacity but in terms of culturally conditioned desires and preferences in living arrangements. In the next chapter we examine options in long-term care that keep individuals in the community and closer to home.

SEVEN

Staying at Home: New Options in the Community Care of the Elderly

The data we have presented so far leave little doubt that most older persons prefer to stay at home even when they suffer serious declines in health. For most older individuals and their families the nursing home is the last resort, to which they turn only when the informal network can no longer cope with the burden of caring for a seriously disabled older person (Doty 1986; Rivlin and Wiener 1988a). Such negative attitudes toward nursing homes are neither surprising nor irrational, since the stereotype of the nursing home, if not necessarily the reality, is of a place where one goes when one's productive life is over. Most people see it as essentially a holding facility, where very old and feeble people, completely incapable of attending to their own basic needs, go to spend their final months or years, in the company of others who are also awaiting death. Who would wish to leave one's home and familiar surroundings for something not only unfamiliar but associated with senescence and the end of life? Yet, despite the emergence of the institutional alternatives we outlined in the last chapter, the nursing home remains at the core of the long-term care system for the seriously impaired elderly and is still the option with the greatest visibility.

The consequences of the most serious declines in health are probably unavoidable, and there will always be many individuals spending months or even years in highly dependent states in which their quality of life is low. Common experience and the data clearly show that the risk of disability increases with age (Branch et al. 1984; National Center for Health Statistics 1983). Since we, as a society, do not condone euthanasia, the most seriously impaired individuals will always require intensive care in institutions. But for the majority of elderly individuals, life in the community, with all of its boisterousness, commitment, and joy is possible almost to the very end of life. Some of the experiments in community care that we discuss below demonstrate that with sufficient help even seriously disabled individuals can be kept in the community. The most important practical problem we face, then, is designing affordable long-term care options that make productive activity and normal community life possible for the elderly. Clearly, the family, insofar as it continues to provide the vast majority of practical care to older individuals, must form the basis of any community care initiatives. Programs that supplement and enhance the family's ability to care for the elderly hold the greatest promise.

As we showed in the last chapter, elderly and infirm Hispanic and black individuals are less likely than non-Hispanic whites with similar impairments to enter nursing homes. Yet many seriously impaired older minority individuals, as well as many non-Hispanic white older persons, are in need of both medical and practical assistance. A large fraction of these individuals make do in the community, relying on the help of family and friends or simply going without the assistance that they need. The functional incapacity of an aging parent places great strains on the family even when it is able and willing to provide care. Because they lack the resources to buy formal assistance, many black and Hispanic families simply have no choice but to assume the entire burden of caring for an infirm older parent themselves. But as marriage and the family change and as women increasingly find it necessary to work, without some formal assistance that burden may become unbearable. One of the greatest promises of community-based long-term care is that it might ease some of the burden upon the family, thus lowering the probability that the infirm parent will have to be institutionalized, and perhaps even reducing strains that lead to family disruption. With this hope in mind we examine the range of possibilities in community-based care and call for new experiments designed to determine how it can be provided efficiently and in a culturally appropriate and cost-effective manner.

The Nursing Home or Community Care?

As we showed in chapter 2, the increase in the number of years in which one experiences some disability is an almost inevitable consequence of our longer life spans, and it means that there is an ever growing number of individuals in the community who need some help in order to live rich and fulfilling lives. The vast majority of such individuals do not need institutionalization, nor do they necessarily need a great deal of help. Most would benefit from some help with specific tasks like transportation to the doctor or the grocery store; some need ongoing assistance with light housework or personal care tasks. After all, it does not take much impairment to make such tasks difficult. Currently, the majority of older individuals with such needs either make do on their own or rely on family members for the help they need (Rivlin and Wiener 1988). Studies of the elderly in the community clearly show that most chronically disabled individuals receive no formal in-home help (Hanley and Wiener 1991).

The rapid growth in the number of disabled elderly and the potential skyrocketing costs of institutional care have generated great interest in home and community-based care among legislators and others concerned with the welfare of the elderly. The elderly clearly prefer home care to institutionalization, since it allows them to live independently in familiar environments (McAuley and Blieszner 1985; Cetron 1985; Meiners and Tave 1984). Home health care also holds the promise of assisting family caregivers cope with what can be onerous burdens associated with the care of frail elderly parents. It is not difficult to imagine that it would be much easier to keep one's mother in her own home if someone else could prepare meals, help with housekeeping, or assist with dressing, bathing, and other basic activities. An adult child could still provide help, but at a level more compatible with his or her own job, household, and child-rearing responsibilities.

To provide older individuals with the richest and most fulfilling lives possible for them, we must design a community care system with five basic characteristics. First, it must offer the older individual and his family a wide variety of options in living arrangements, from group housing to remaining at home. Second, it must offer family members a wide variety of options in the extent of their personal involvement, so that they are not faced with either an impossible caregiving burden or the necessity of institutionalizing an aging parent. Third, it must integrate the older person into the community to the greatest degree possible, so that he or she is not isolated. Fourth, it must be designed in every way to complement rather than to replace the family and the informal support network. Fifth, and finally, it must provide these services at a cost that is no greater, or only marginally greater, than that of placing the older person in a nursing home.

Clearly, for such a system to operate it must be based on a sophisticated understanding of its clientele's needs and preferences. A system that is based on the assumption that all older individuals are identical is doomed to failure. Cultural differences, as well as differences in life experiences and personality, mean that older people will always have very different needs and preferences. Although a great deal more research and experience will be necessary before we can determine the best mix of services and the best method of providing those services to various groups, it is clear that race and ethnicity must be taken into account in designing any community-based system of support for the elderly. Among poor and minority Americans the family and the church have always played an important role in the care of the elderly. That experience provides a rich basis for the development of more formal community-based options. In areas in which the church and other community organizations are already providing assistance to the elderly, our public-policy objective should be to design a formal system that works with those community organizations and furthers their efforts.

What Is Community Care?

"Institutionalization" is a ponderous term that carries with it a great number of negative connotations. To be institutionalized implies the loss of one's freedom and autonomy, which in the case of Erving Goffman's "total institution" is nearly complete (Goffman 1961). Although nursing homes and skilled-care facilities are not prisons, they share many of the characteristics of "total institutions." They are places in which, because of physical and mental decline rather than the judgments of civil authorities, one must give up much of one's freedom and autonomy. Clearly, nursing homes need not be horrible places, yet even the nicest is not like a home. One's home, after all, is where one lived one's life; it is full of the memories that give the past and the present their meaning (Redfoot 1987). The desire to stay at home is strong, and a familiar environment is central to an older person's well-being. A familiar environment is even more important to an older minority group individual, who may view the larger external world as hostile and foreign. Much of the justification for community-based care, therefore, is based on its potential for enhancing the quality of an older person's life.

Community-based long-term care, then, is any formally provided package of services that allows a person to stay at home, or as close to home as possible. Many of the institutional arrangements we reviewed in the last chapter share aspects of community-based care, but they still require the transfer of the older person to some central residential facility. Community-based care self-consciously attempts to keep older individuals out of such facilities for as long as possible. Although some community-based options place older individuals in group quarters, the options we deal with in this chapter are less institutional than those we previously outlined.

Since the family is so central to this objective and to the well-being of the elderly, the best community-based options will attempt to involve the family in the care of the aging parent while at the same time acknowledging that the family cannot go it alone. A seriously disabled older person requires intensive care twenty-four hours a day, and it is usually the relentlessness and magnitude of that burden that leads to the collapse of the informal network's ability to cope. Yet the informal network need not be placed under unbearable strain, and the old person need not be institutionalized. Families that can call upon some supplemental assistance to give them respite from ongoing caregiving duties are better able to cope with the burden of caring for an older person than those without such help. Today's smaller families, in which both husband and wife must work, are more limited in the care they can provide to an incapacitated parent than were the larger and less geographically mobile families of the past and are therefore more dependent on outside aid. Such supplementary help in providing daily care to older parents is so important, in fact, that family members prefer it to cash payments (Horwitz and Shindelman 1983).

Community-based options, therefore, are a necessary complement to institutional care in our total package of long-term care arrangements. As in the case of institutional care, though, we are just now beginning to seriously experiment with alternatives in community-based long-term care. Since levels of need vary greatly among the elderly, these options must be tailored both to preferences and to need. Some individuals can make do with only limited assistance, such as help with preparing meals and getting to and from places outside the home. Others need much more comprehensive care if they are to avoid institutionalization. In both cases, and for those who fall between these extremes, community-based care promises to ease the care-giving burden of families and improve the quality of older people's lives.

The Potential of Induced Demand for Home-Based Care

Unfortunately, despite all of the obvious advantages of community-based care, there are a number of possible problems with it that cause policy makers serious concern. This concern is fueled by the potential extent of unmet need for services among the elderly in the community and the potential demand that providing such services might induce. In addition, many fear that were government-sponsored, home-based formal care to become available it would take the place of informal care. Formal home-based care programs could potentially undermine the role of the family and give rise to the general expectation that the state should provide daily care to the elderly. As we have seen, there are a great number of individuals who live alone in the community and who might benefit from home-based services (Barusch 1994; Harris and Associates 1986). Were such services to become available, a great number of these individuals would, no doubt, use them. Such a substitution of formal for informal support could greatly increase the public cost of long-term care. Studies show that millions of days of informal support are provided to the disabled by family members each week (Liu, Manton, and Liu 1985). Were even a fraction of this burden transferred from the informal sector, where it is provided as a free good, to the formal sector, where it must be paid for, the costs could be staggering.

Social programs that address clear areas of need, as in the case of Medicare and Medicaid, usually experience program and budgetary growth that greatly outstrips initial projections. Reducing the danger of rapidly growing induced demand for community-based services would require limitations in the services provided and stringent eligibility requirements that might penalize certain groups. It might even be necessary to base eligibility for participation on need. Unfortunately, any program based on means or assets tests would inevitably suffer the stigma and political vulnerability of other programs for the poor.

Initial hopes for community-based care were that it could be provided at a lower cost than institutional care. As we will later discuss, this has not been the case, and it was probably naive to imagine that one could provide transportation to medical facilities, food, assistance with physical and instrumental activities of daily living, and the rest of what an impaired older person needs on an individual basis at a lower cost than is possible in a centralized facility. In the absence of proven cost-effectiveness, then, community-based care must be justified on the ground that the elderly and their families prefer it and that life in a normal community is richer than life in an age-segregated facility (see Weissert and Hedrick 1994 for a recent review of the literature). Yet, since such care must be paid for largely out of increasingly strained state and federal budgets, better and less expensive ways of providing community-based care must be developed if it is to prove a viable option to institutionalization. Several models of community-based long-term care have been tried, and these form the basis for our speculations about what might be possible in the future. In what follows we examine these options and propose a model of community-based long-term care that makes the best use of the informal network and views formal care as a supplement to, rather than a replacement of, the family. Such a model increases the options available to older individuals and their families.

National Policy and Program Options in Community-Based Long-Term Care

In presenting community-based long-term care options, we begin with the least intensive alternatives and move to the most ambitious and comprehensive. Our objective is to examine how community-based options operate, how their financing affects access by minority Americans, and how they might be adapted for use in specific communities. Certain community-based options, like some of the institutional options we summarized in the last chapter, are intermediate between institutional and community care. What distinguishes the approaches we deal with in this chapter from more institutionally focused care is the desire to keep the individual as close to home as possible and the purely temporary nature of any institutionalization that is involved. In long-term care, as in managed care and health care delivery generally, alternative forms are evolving so rapidly that one cannot definitively summarize or characterize all of them. What we can do is to broadly outline the various options and discuss their general characteristics of each one.

The Older Americans Act (OAA) and Other Federal Community-Based Programs for the Elderly

Although almost everyone is familiar with Social Security and Medicare, other federal programs also provide services and support to older individuals in the community. The most important of these was created by the Older Americans Act (OAA), which was signed into law on July 14, 1965 by President Lyndon B. Johnson. This act established the Administration on Aging (AOA), whose mission is to address the unmet social service needs of the noninstitutionalized elderly in areas such as income, health, housing, long-term care, nutrition, and transportation (Hudson 1995). Today the AOA puts special emphasis on the needs of poor and minority elderly.

The mission of the Administration on Aging—to provide the services that permit elderly individuals to remain in their own homes and avoid institutionalization—is carried out by a network of state and local area agencies. The objectives of the Administration on Aging are broad and include, among many others, providing information about services available in the community and assistance in obtaining such services, transportation, case management, homemaker assistance, home health aides, telephones, and legal services. The Administration on Aging also supports senior centers, trains those who care for the elderly, offers counseling and referrals for mental health and financial issues, assists in finding housing and in adapting existing homes, screens for health problems and provides nutrition services and supportive services for caretakers.

The local agencies that implement the Administration on Aging's objectives serve as advocates for needy Americans sixty and over, and in 1991 approximately 68 percent of the Administration on Aging's budget was devoted to the support of this network. Funds are distributed to state agencies on aging based primarily on the proportion of the state's population aged sixty and over, and the state agencies, in turn, award funds to local agencies, to be disbursed in each planning and service area (PSA) designated by the state agency (Chiplin 1989). Each state area agency operates an access and assistance program that seeks to inform older persons about available services from which they might benefit. These services are targeted to those older persons with the greatest economic or social needs, with particular attention to low-income minority elderly (Leutz et al. 1995).

As one can see, like most War on Poverty programs, the OAA was very ambitious in its intent and its funding is clearly inadequate to accomplish all of its objectives. Although the appropriations have risen since the program's inception, from seven million dollars in 1966 to nearly one and a half billion dollars today, the demand for services has increased even more rapidly, and a wider scope of planned services are now offered (National Academy on Aging 1995). In 1995, Congress appropriated a total of seventeen million dollars for the Administration on Aging, the agency which implements the Older Americans Act, and the Federal Council on Aging, an advisory body to the Administration and Congress on matters related to the elderly (National Academy on Aging 1995). Since 1970 the OAA has targeted disadvantaged elderly groups, such as ethnic minorities and, like all programs geared toward the poor and disadvantaged, it is politically vulnerable. In these times of serious federal budgetary cutbacks, one cannot be optimistic about its future funding. The services sponsored by Administration on Aging, at least in principle, are very important to poor and minority Americans, and it would be useful to examine some of the more serious areas of need that OAA and other federal programs address.

Table 7.1 presents data on the use of community-based services by various racial and ethnic groups. Like other studies (cf. Miller et al. 1996), they show that only a small fraction of elderly individuals of any racial or ethnic background use any service. Elderly Puerto Ricans, however, are twice as likely as other groups to use home health aides and three times as likely to use transportation and homemaker services. Let us take a closer look at some of these community-based services.

Transportation

Without transportation one's life is seriously circumscribed. An older person must have access to dependable private or public transportation in order to get to the grocery store, the doctor, or the homes of friends. A disproportionate number of minority group members do not drive, either because they cannot afford to maintain a car, are too physically impaired, or never learned to drive. A rather large fraction of older Mexican American women have never learned to drive and are consequently dependent on family members or on public transportation to get to where they need to go. Mexican American families provide a great deal of support to their older members, but family members work and are often unavailable when the older parent needs a ride. Yet public transportation systems, especially in rural areas, are often inadequate or nonexistent (Fuguitt, Brown, and Beale 1989). The lack of transportation, therefore, reduces access to health care facilities and even to shopping malls, in which a great deal of health-related information is available (Espino, Moreno, and Talamantes 1993). In addition to providing access to services, transportation is necessary for social health. Maintaining relationships in the community, attending church, and participating in recreational activities all require transportation.

Because of the importance of transportation, since the 1960s, the federal government has enacted several programs to improve older people's access to public transportation. The 1974 OAA reauthorization designated transportation as a priority area and the 1979 amendments to the Urban Mass Transit Act of 1964 increased access to public transportation for the frail elderly. The National Mass

TABLE 7.1
Percentage of Persons 65 and Over Using Social Services in the Last Year

	All Elderly[a]	Mexican American[b]	Cuban American[b]	Puerto Rican[b]	Other Hispanic[b]
Transportation	5	9	18	21	19
Senior center	15	12	8	19	13
Meals delivered	2	8	4	5	3
Congregate meals	9	15	9	12	9
Homemaker	2	6	9	14	4
Home health aide[1]	4	14	17	23	11

SOURCE: [a]E. Hing, and B. Bloom. "Long-Term Care for the Functionally Dependent Elderly." *Vital and Health Statistics.* Series 13, 104, p. 31, 1990.

[b]Westat Inc., *Final Report to the Commonwealth Fund Commission on Elderly People Living Alone* (Rockville, MD: Westat, 1989), table 25.

1. Includes health aide and visiting nursing services.

Transportation Assistance Act of 1974 and the 1978 Surface Transportation Assistance Act reduced fares for elderly persons and the handicapped as well as for individuals in rural areas (Cox 1993). All of these initiatives were motivated by the realization that without transportation an older person is at great risk of isolation and of poor physical and emotional health.

Case Management

Case management is perhaps as important as transportation in assuring the rational community care of the elderly, and it is becoming an integral part of managed care programs. For elders living in the community, case management is offered by various private and public organizations and as part of many OAA sponsored programs. Case managers help the older person and his or her family negotiate the complex social service and health care delivery systems (Zawadski and Eng 1988). The case manager makes sure that the client's needs are adequately assessed, that he or she applies for the entire range of services necessary, and that those services are used. Case management is, therefore, a vital access service and a crucial component of the service package that enables the frail elder to remain in the community (Kane and Kane 1987). A recent evaluation of the effectiveness of the case management model in the delivery of long-term care identified several advantages, including increased client and caregiver life satisfaction and greater confidence in the health care system (Kemper 1990). This evaluation also found that case management does not appear to reduce the amount of informal caregiving by the family. Because of improved service coordination, the number of case management programs is increasing and are now mandated under Medicaid (Cox 1993).

Nutrition

Adequate nutrition is, of course, vital to good health at any age. Because of a lack of transportation and the difficulty they often have in preparing meals, many elderly do not have an adequate diet. To address this problem the 1972 reauthorization of the Older American's Act established a national nutrition program that provides congregate meal services to meet the nutritional needs of older persons. The 1978 OAA reauthorization added appropriations for home-delivered nutrition services and gave preference to older persons with the greatest economic or social needs. Between 1987 and 1991 the OAA was expanded to provide nutrition services to frail elderly living at home; to residents of long-term care facilities; to persons at risk of abuse, neglect, or exploitation; and to low income elderly who are eligible for, but not receiving, benefits under other federal programs. Older individuals who receive SSI are also eligible for food stamps which allow them to buy food at a subsidized rate (Social Security Administration 1994). In 1987, the OAA reauthorization liberalized eligibility requirements and benefit levels for federal housing and food stamp programs for certain needy elderly.

Respite Care

While transportation, case management, and nutrition services directly benefit the older person, respite care is designed to give the family temporary relief from the burdens of caring for the older person (Kane and Kane 1987). Respite care is not unlike day care in that it allows the caregiver time to rest and to attend to other duties. It can involve institutionalizing the older person for a few days so that the caregiver can go on a vacation, simply relax, or deal with the complexities of her or his own life. The caregivers who are most likely to use respite services are those who are themselves in poor health (Kosloski and Montgomery 1992). Respite care is very helpful to families who wish to provide the majority of care for older parents themselves but who need periodic relief. Nonstop caregiving can quickly wear down even an energetic and dedicated person and lead to the premature collapse of the informal network's ability to function. With some help the network might function at a higher level of efficiency for a longer period.

Adult Day Care

Adult day care is similar to respite care but, as the name implies, it is not designed to provide services on a twenty-four hour basis (Kane et al. 1991). Such adult day care facilities are usually either health-oriented programs, typically affiliated with a nursing home or rehabilitation hospital, or social service programs sponsored by a church, a local social service agency, or a Special Purpose Center (SPC) that serves a particular clientele, such as veterans or persons with physical impairments or mental illnesses (Weissert, Cready, and Pawelak 1988). Of course there are several variations and combinations of these types of services. Adult day care is particularly useful since isolation and neglect are major problems among the infirm elderly. Because of physical and cognitive impairments many are unable to get out or even care for themselves adequately. Adult day care, therefore, addresses both the needs of the older person for care and social interaction and the needs of the family for relief from the daily tasks of caregiving.

Medicaid pays for adult day care under a program created by Congress in 1981 (Section 2176 of the Omnibus Budget Reconciliation Act of 1981, P.L. 97–35) that allows states to waive standard Medicaid procedures and provide the full range of home- and community-based services for those frail elderly who would otherwise require institutionalization (Burke, Hudson, and Eubanks 1990). Adult day care services include physical therapy, health maintenance programs, and help with activities of daily living, as well as social and recreational opportunities (Kane and Kane 1987; Kaye and Kirwin 1990; Kirwin 1991; Weissert et al. 1989).

Other Residential Options

Other arrangements for the care of the elderly combine aspects of nursing home and community care. The label "board and care" refers to a large number of arrangements with various names, including domiciliary care homes, adult foster care, sheltered care, and halfway houses (Kane and Kane 1987). Some facilities are almost indistinguishable from nursing homes, while others are more like bed and breakfast arrangements. The main difference between board and care and nursing homes is that the former provide no medical or nursing care (McCoy and Conley 1990). Some programs are covered by Medicaid; others are paid for privately, sometimes with the aid of supplements from social service agencies. In general, the concept of board and care involves the services of someone other than a family member (National Association of State Units on Aging 1992). The services provided are typically nonmedical and include food, shelter, and various other forms of assistance, such as linking residents to community services. Board and care homes can be licensed by the state, although many are not (Kane and Kane 1987).

Housing Programs and Services

In order to remain in the community one must, of course, have a place to live and some means of maintaining it. Numerous programs make it possible for an older person to stay at home or at least in the community, including (in addition to many others) low-rent public housing that is financed by the federal government and operated by local nonprofit housing administrations and subsidized housing for those with low incomes. Subsidies are provided to older persons to make up the difference between what he or she can afford and what the Department of Housing and Urban Development determines to be a fair market rent. Section 202 of the Housing Act of 1959, which was revised in 1974, provides funds to private, nonprofit organizations to develop low-cost housing for needy elderly persons. The Low-Income Home Emergency Program and the Weatherization Assistance Program provides financial assistance to states to enable nonprofit organizations to help poor older persons with emergency maintenance and with the materials and labor to weatherize their homes.

Other programs offer residential options that, again, are intermediate between staying at home and entering a nursing home. The demonstration projects provided for by the Congregate Housing Act of 1978 consist of dormitories in which the older residents of a community can live with others of the same age. Variations on this approach involve shared housing, in which two or more older persons live together, and life care communities, which are similar to continuing care retirement communities but include medical and nursing services as well as residential and social services (Cohen et al. 1989). For that reason they are more similar to the nursing homes we discussed in the last chapter.

Reverse Equity Mortgages: Gaining Access to One's Home Equity

Whatever alternative one chooses, however, it must be paid for. Most of the programs for poor older individuals are paid for by the federal government, sometimes supplemented by the state or private nonprofit organizations. In many cases eligibility is tied to the receipt of SSI. For individuals who do not qualify for SSI or for other housing assistance, life in the community must be paid for by a combination of current income (usually Social Security) and accumulated assets. For most older individuals their major asset is the equity they have in their home. Although some can draw on income from stocks, bonds, and rents, for most minority individuals and for many widows home equity is pretty much all they have. But home equity can only be liquidated by selling the house. This poses a serious dilemma: the only way to remain in one's own home is to get rid of it!

An innovative and promising solution that, as yet, has not caught on widely is home equity conversions, or reverse annuity mortgages (RAMs). These allow an older individual to draw upon the equity in his or her home by selling the house to a mortgage company or bank while retaining the option of remaining in the house and receiving monthly payments until he or she dies, until the home is sold, or until an agreed-upon period of time has elapsed (Fannie Mae 1995). A variation on RAMs are sale/leaseback arrangements, in which the older person sells the house to the mortgager, who immediately leases it back to the seller (Kane and Kane 1990).

Such plans allow older individuals to stay in their homes in circumstances in which it might not otherwise be possible. Few would enter into such an arrangement if they had any other recourse, since, for most, the estate they leave to their children consists primarily of their home. As when an older person must spend-down and impoverish him- or herself in order to qualify for Medicaid, home equity conversions can mean that one has nothing to leave to one's heirs. As we discussed in chapter 4, the pact between the generations is symbolized and sealed by material exchanges, and most individuals' sense of self-worth is enhanced by the knowledge that they are leaving something to future generations. As we discuss more fully in the next chapter, the rich and the poor differ not only in what they can afford during life but in what they can leave to their children after death.

On Lok: The Ultimate Community-Based Model

The alternative forms of community-based care, therefore, span a broad range from simple help with home maintenance and personal assistance to what is almost institutional care. For any individual or couple the choice of a care arrangement obviously depends on their ability to pay, their preferences for group or solitary living, their health, and the availability of the various options. We have saved for last the most comprehensive and ambitious model of community-based long-term care, the On Lok program in San Francisco's Chinatown. This program, which provides the complete range of medical and social services to older individuals in an attempt to keep them in their own homes, has given rise to several spinoffs in other parts of the country (Lewin 1994). It is particularly intriguing because it makes maximum use of local community resources and the informal network and has demonstrated that, with sufficient help, even the most seriously impaired older individuals can be kept in the community. On Lok is a paradigm of the sort of coordinated program that combines the formal and informal support system to make the best use of family, community, and health care system resources and hence to improve the quality of life for the older person and his or her family.

On Lok Senior Health Services is a consolidated model of community-based long-term care that integrates the full range of primary, acute, and long-term care services for frail elderly people eligible for nursing home care in San Francisco's Chinatown. Several features of the On Lok program distinguish it from other community-based long-term care approaches (Ansak 1990). First, it focuses on highly impaired, frail individuals who need intensive care and who would otherwise require institutionalization. Second, it emphasizes community residence and community involvement in the older person's care. Third, it aims at providing comprehensive medical, social, and other supportive services. Since the program operates under a Medicaid waiver, it is able to integrate funding from private insurance, Medicare, and Medicaid and provide preventive care, which is usually not covered by Medicare. Fourth, it relies on a multidisciplinary team approach to identify and address the older person's needs. Finally, it is a fully capitated and cost-conscious care model, since it requires that the provider of care assume financial risk.

On Lok operates adult day care centers and clinics as well as On Lok House, a housing facility for low-income seniors, and a second, single-room occupancy residential facility (Ansak 1990). The unique aspect of On Lok is that the multidisciplinary assessment team, which includes a physician or nurse practitioner, occupational and physical therapists, a dietician, a day health center supervisor, a recreation therapist, a social worker, a health worker, and a driver, among others, consolidates service delivery. This means that the team assumes responsibility for all of the care that the older person receives. They assess the client's needs, develop a treatment plan, directly provide most services, manage contracted services, monitor the client's progress, and adjust the care plan as required (Ansak 1990; Zawadski and Eng 1988). In other, less comprehensive programs, supervision of the various components of service delivery is the responsibility of different teams or individuals, and care is therefore provided in a less consolidated and coordinated manner.

Controlling costs while providing high-quality care is a central objective of On Lok. Since the clientele are all nursing-home–eligible, they represent a high-risk population, and the program receives a higher per capita Medicaid payment to reflect this increased risk.

Nonetheless, cost control is a major concern and is accomplished through several mechanisms. A focus on preserving and even enhancing the participant's health minimizes hospital and nursing home use. The continual monitoring of the client's health reduces the number of acute illness episodes he or she experiences. A concern with the participant's psychosocial well-being and the maximization of his or her functional capacity also reduce the need for costly services. Providing low-cost services in the least restrictive settings, including the participant's own home, again reduces costs.

The On Lok model, then, promises to keep even highly impaired older individuals in the community. Because of this promise the model has been replicated in other parts of the country as part of the Program of All-Inclusive Care for the Elderly (PACE). Unfortunately, recent cost-efficiency studies that compared the overall success of the On Lok and PACE programs yield mixed results (Kane, Illston, and Miller 1992). On Lok has been clearly successful in reducing hospital and nursing home use and their associated costs (Yordi and Waldman 1985). In 1992, On Lok spent approximately $32,400 per client, which is between 5 and 40 percent lower than the cost of taking care of a person with similar medical care needs in a nursing home (Menagh 1993). On the other hand, a study that compared seven PACE sites to On Lok found large differences in the implementation of the PACE program and in combined monthly Medicare and Medicaid costs, as well as in the number of services used (Branch, Coulam, and Zimmerman 1995). This study also found that eligible individuals did not enroll in the program at the rate initially expected, suggesting that it may not be as appealing to prospective participants as the designers think. The study also found evidence that some of the more potentially expensive individuals were excluded from the program, suggesting that any cost saving may be more the result of selective enrollment than of actual program success in reducing per-capita costs.

In terms of cost, therefore, the jury is still out on the PACE program generally. Successful programs of this sort depend greatly on the energy and commitment of their founders, and this is certainly a major advantage of the On Lok experiment in San Francisco. We are particularly enthusiastic about On Lok because it calls on unique community resources to assist in the care of the frail elderly and provides services in a familiar environment and in a manner appropriate to its ethnically homogeneous clientele. Similar programs can be established elsewhere, but in each case they will have to be adapted to the needs of the local community. An "On Lok" program for older Mexican Americans in the Rio Grande valley will look very different from the one in San Francisco's Chinatown, because the differences between San Francisco and South Texas, in both the health care delivery environment and the local culture, are enormous. Local adaptation will also be necessary for programs that provide services to older blacks in rural North Carolina. Wherever the model is tried, intensive interaction between program designers and the community is the key element.

Can We Afford Community-Based Long-Term Care?

According to one description, an economist is someone who knows the price of everything and the value of nothing. Much of what gives meaning to life is inherently nonquantifiable, and many human choices seem far less rational than economic theory would hold. Yet when all is said and done, the economist conveys a profound message. However our preferences are formed, we cannot have everything that we might want, and both individuals and societies must operate within real budgets that require choices among what are often equally meritorious objectives. For the rational-choice economist the cultural and social forces that give rise to an individual's preferences in living arrangements may be of less interest than the factors that constrain his or her ability to act on those preferences. For others with different perspectives, the inherently nonquantifiable aspects of life that give rise to one's sense of self-worth and social connectedness are of equivalent or even greater interest. Both sets of considerations are relevant in assessing the long-term care needs of the elderly, and we must begin to understand how an individual's culturally and socially influenced preferences can be satisfied so that the quality of his or her life can be maximized within the very real budgetary constraints that limit what we can do.

The formal economic procedures for determining this are called cost-effectiveness or cost-benefit analysis. In a strict sense cost-effectiveness analysis involves choosing between two or more ways of arriving at similar outcomes, while cost-benefit analysis involves comparisons of the relative costs of arriving at different objectives (Greene, Lovely, and Ondrich 1993a). In trying to choose between community-based care or institutionalization, one could assume that staying at home or entering a nursing home are equivalent outcomes, although such an assumption would strike most knowledgeable observers as ridiculous. The data we have reviewed make it abundantly clear that individuals prefer to stay at home for as long as possible and that for most older individuals staying in the community or going to the nursing home are in no way equivalent outcomes.

Most cost-effectiveness studies come to the conclusion that community-based care is not cheaper than institutionalization and that it does not significantly reduce the risk that an older person will eventually enter a nursing home (Weissert, Cready, and Pawelak 1988; Greene, Lovely, and Ondrich 1993a, 1993b; Vertrees, Manton, and Adler 1989). Weissert and Hedrick (1994), for example, reviewed a total of thirty-two studies of programs that provide home health care, adult day care, and coordinated packages of services. Despite differences in study designs, locations, populations, or services provided, the results showed little variation. In almost all cases, community-based long-term care did not increase survival, nor did it slow the rate of deterioration in functional status. In some studies the older individual's life satisfaction, as well as that of his or her caregiver, increased, but these benefits tended to disappear after a few months, despite continued program participation. These and other studies suggest that in order to achieve cost-effectiveness community-based programs will have to improve their risk prediction so that they can better target patients who are likely to benefit from the services.

On a strict cost basis, then, community-based care is not cost-effective, but such a conclusion ignores all of the nonquantifiable and subjective factors that affect one's quality of life as well as one's subjective well-being. In the end it is not very surprising that studies that simply compare the cost of institutional and community-based long-term care find that keeping an older person in the community is not cost-effective. How could one provide nutrition, medical care, transportation to hospital, and other supportive services inexpensively to a highly impaired older person living at home? Manufacturers discovered early on in the industrial revolution that bringing workers together in factories was much more efficient than having them work at home, and today we produce goods, educate children, and treat the seriously ill in centralized locations where the process can benefit from economies of scale.

Nursing homes make it easier for physicians to deal with their patients and for older person's needs to be attended to by a staff of professionals. There are clear economies of scale in such arrangements, but the price that the older person pays is the often traumatic loss of familiar surroundings and the entry into a strange institutional environment. Much of what is lost in this process is as real a part of an older individual's utility as factors that can be expressed in terms of dollars. The cost-benefit tradeoff between community-based care and institutionalization, therefore, is far more difficult to assess than the simple cost of either. The choice of long-term care options is invariably value-laden and political in nature. It would be convenient if some impartial accounting or statistical technique would allow us to arrive at an objective assessment of how best to care for the frail elderly. Unfortunately, there are no such techniques, and any useful debate on the tradeoff between the costs and benefits of various long-term care options requires that we be continually aware of the moral and political nature of the choices we make. How we choose to care for the elderly reflects as much who we are and what we believe as it does concrete financial constraints.

We end this chapter by returning to the observation that, although physical or mental decline are necessary conditions for institutionalization, functional incapacity alone is not the sole determinant. The presence or absence of family support is every bit as important

(Cantor 1983; Shanas 1979). Those individuals who have no one to provide help have few alternatives but to enter a nursing home. We also know that racial and ethnic groups differ in the extent to which family members are available and willing to help. Many of these families are in poverty, and the caregiving burdens they bear are as much the result of necessity as of choice. Yet the patterns of intergenerational assistance that have evolved in the community provide an opportunity for more effectively caring for the infirm elderly. For this reason it is imperative that our attempts to assist the family care for elderly be informed by a much more sophisticated understanding of specific needs associated with specific health conditions, as well as of the coping resources of different families and groups (Jette, Tennstedt, and Crawford 1995). In many neighborhoods churches and community organizations are already involved in assisting older persons by providing meals, social support, and transportation. These efforts deserve encouragement and assistance and could form the basis of even more comprehensive systems of care that employ both formal and informal sources of support. The On Lok and PACE models are only the most recent and ambitious attempts at the community care of the frail elderly. Many more will follow. From these efforts we will learn what works and what does not in particular cultural and social class contexts. We will also learn how to adapt comprehensive support programs to the needs and resources of specific local communities and neighborhoods. To the extent that such programs succeed, they promise to limit the burden on families at the same time that they improve the quality of older person's lives.

As promising as community-based programs are, though, there is a danger in relying entirely on the family and community for the care of the elderly. As we develop long-term care options, it is imperative that we avoid penalizing groups with large families in which older persons live with their children out of necessity. From a purely financial perspective it would be rational to target community-based services to those with no other source of support, particularly those living alone. Were such programs to target services only to those individuals with no available family, they could potentially favor the non-Hispanic white and middle-class elderly, who tend to have fewer and more mobile children than minority group elderly. Black and Hispanic elderly older persons have more children on average, and those children are more likely to stay closer to home because of fewer opportunities for occupational advancement.

It is possible to envision a two-tiered system in which non-Hispanic white elders receive high-quality institutional or community care and poorer black and Hispanic elders find themselves thrown back on family simply because family is all that is available. What we advocate is a system that optimizes the choices available to all older individuals and their families regardless of racial or ethnic classification. Unfortunately, given the realities of the distribution of wealth in this country, it is highly likely that in years to come a great deal of racial and ethnic stratification in the quality of long-term care for the elderly will persist.

EIGHT

The New Pact between the Generations: Intergenerational Exchanges in a Multicultural Society

As we move into the twenty-first century, we find that the pact between the generations is, from one point of view, as simple as it has always been and, from another, far more complex. The good news is that, so far, the family has not abandoned the elderly and, despite the tremendous strains it has come under, the informal network still provides the majority of care that infirm older parents need. Today, as always, parents care for their children and furnish them with the opportunities for a rich and rewarding adulthood. Adult children, in turn, through the taxes they pay and the direct services they provide, care for their aging parents and assure them the opportunity for a rich and rewarding retirement. Humans are dependent both at the beginning of life and at its end, and our survival, both as individuals and as a species, depends upon our mutual assistance throughout life. For the most part, the material and emotional exchanges that take place between age groups are based on genuine affection, as well as the clear understanding that, just as we are all at one time young, unless we die prematurely, we will all one day be old. To be an adult is to accept the responsibility both for those who are younger than oneself and for those who are older, and most of us accept that responsibility willingly. There seems to be very little disagreement that the contribution of the old to building our world deserves respect and reward.

Yet it would be foolish not to recognize that there are now serious threats to the pact between the generations and to the family's ability to provide the care that the old need. The aging of the population, in combination with slower economic growth, rapid increases in the cost of managing chronic disease, and growing opposition to taxation generally, could cause serious strains in the relationships between age groups. One of the greatest threats arises from the potential divisiveness of the very heterogeneity that we have dealt with in this book. If differences between the young and the old, between minority and majority Americans, and between men and women become the basis of self-serving interest groups, then there is indeed much potential for conflict. It is entirely natural, and even desirable, for people to join together to further their common interests, but if those interests are construed too narrowly, nobody wins.

The potential for intergenerational conflict clearly exists in the United States today. The rise of what has been termed an "old-age politics" hints at the potential for serious conflict between age groups (Torres-Gil 1993). From relative political powerlessness at the turn of the century, the elderly have emerged as one of the most powerful political constituencies in the nation. They are represented by such organizations as the American Association of Retired Persons (AARP), the National Council on Aging (NCOA), the National Council of Senior Citizens (NCSC), the National Association of Retired Federal Employees (NARFE), and the National Committee to Preserve Social Security and Medicare (NCPSSM). These organizations are well financed, have professional leadership and staffs, and are among the most effective lobbying groups in Washington (Day 1990; Longman 1985).

These groups have been remarkably influential in protecting the rights of middle-class older persons (Binstock 1983; Heclo 1988; Longman 1985). The defeat of the Medicare Catastrophic Coverage Act (MCCA) of 1988 and the inability of the Reagan administration to greatly curtail Social Security clearly demonstrate the political power of the elderly (Torres-Gil 1993; Moon 1993). Yet this power has been a mixed blessing. Although its exercise has resulted in gains for the elderly, it has also led to the growing suspicion that the old are benefiting unfairly at the expense of the young. The repeal of the Medicare Catastrophic Coverage Act (MCCA) demonstrated the ability of the old to shape public policy to their own end. The act was an attempt to extend Medicare coverage to include such services (primarily to the poor elderly) as long-term care, prescription drugs, and rehabilitative treatment and, thereby, address serious gaps in the program, but unlike most other social welfare programs, the financing was to come from the old themselves in the form of a surcharge that fell heaviest on affluent elderly (Moon 1993). This fact spelled doom for the act since the middle-class elderly were already adequately covered by private insurance for services that Medicare does not cover, and they had relatively little to gain from reforms that primarily benefited the poor. Organizations like AARP effectively lobbied against the MCCA and, except for a few provisions, the legislation was repealed only a year after its passage.

The Medicare Catastrophic Coverage Act has the unique distinction of being the only major piece of social welfare legislation that has been repealed by Congress and clearly demonstrates the organized power of the middle-class elderly. The success of organizations like AARP in lobbying against MCCA, however, added to the growing perception that the old care only about their own welfare, are unwilling to contribute to the reduction of our massive federal budget deficit, and are quite ready to saddle future generations with the bill for their current support. The old, on the other hand, justifiably see their benefits as earned rights, and few see themselves as particularly affluent. Most do, in fact, live off fairly modest incomes. Yet the rise in poverty among children, the increase in taxation among the working-age population at a time when real wages are dropping, and the sheer magnitude of the cost of programs that benefit the elderly have led many to question the basic equity of the current arrangements.

In his presidential address to the Population Association of America in 1984, Samuel Preston framed the question of generational equity in terms of the trade-off between programs that benefit the old and those that benefit children (Preston 1984). Preston pointed out that because of Social Security and other programs that benefit the elderly, the rate of poverty among the old has dropped while increasing dramatically among families with children. Preston's address alerted us to the potential disaster looming if a large fraction of children grow up in poverty and are denied an adequate education and the opportunity to lead full and productive lives, and it reminded us of the hard choices that finite budgets force upon us. We simply cannot provide everything to everyone, and when economic growth is slow, the economy approximates a zero-sum game in which the gains of one group are won at the expense of another.

The growing resentment that some younger individuals feel toward the old was embodied in the philosophy of the short-lived Americans for Generational Equality (AGE), founded by Senator David Durenberger in 1984. AGE was founded to oppose the legislative objectives of organizations like AARP and the other lobbying groups that further the interests of the old; namely (and understandably), to increase benefits to the elderly from all of the major income support and health programs that apply to them. Members of AGE disagreed profoundly with the basic philosophy underlying the old-age welfare state and questioned the very assumption that the young are responsible for the old (Battin 1994; Quadagno, Achenbaum, and Bengston 1993; Quadagno 1990). They felt that, as it is currently funded, Social Security represents an unfair subsidy of the old by the young. Although AGE has disbanded, it has been replaced by many other groups, and the sentiment which motivated the founders of the organization will always be felt by some younger individuals, because Social Security is a pay-as-you-go program and not a true annuity. Retirees are supported by the current contributions of working-age individuals. Were our economic or employment situations to worsen, the burden on working-age taxpayers could grow and the potential for conflict between the old and the young could increase.

The Old-Age Welfare State and the Possibility of Intergenerational Conflict

David Thompson, employing data primarily from New Zealand and the United Kingdom, predicts that generational tensions will rise throughout the developed world in the years to come and could emerge into serious conflicts between age groups (Thompson 1991; Thompson 1993). Thompson locates the source of such tensions in the age-based welfare policies of the developed nations. Until the 1960s state policies concerning taxation and income supports favored young families and the working-age population. Since then, however, funding priorities have shifted to benefit the old. This shift has led to a situation in which those individuals who are currently retired will benefit economically far more than the young can ever hope to. Retired individuals, who are now in their late sixties and seventies, reaped the rewards of the postwar prosperity and the tax and income policies that favored working-age families when they were young, and now benefit from the expansion of programs for the elderly. Because of a changing ratio of retirees to working-age individuals, lower rates of economic growth in the developed world, and the tax burden required to support the elderly today, those workers who will retire at the beginning of the next century cannot hope to reap such rewards.

Those individuals who are currently working will pay far more in taxes over their lifetimes than did those who are currently retired, and they will enjoy far lower returns on their contributions to Social Security (Thompson 1993). Such a situation has profound social and political implications, since it undermines people's sense of continuity, reciprocity, and equity between the generations. A situation in which younger generations benefit less from their lifetime contributions to the system than older generations renders the notion of a "right" to comfort and security meaningless, since the right belongs only to older cohorts. Such a system is inherently unfair, and it is hard to see how conflict could be avoided, since it is unlikely that the old will voluntarily settle for less than they feel they have earned, or that working-age individuals will bear, without protest, increasingly burdensome taxation from which they themselves will not benefit. The old, like everyone else, have fought for a larger piece of what was until recently, a growing economic pie. Unfortunately, the pie is no longer growing at the same rate as in the past, and we cannot predict what struggles may erupt over its division and how those struggles will affect generational politics. Thompson's well-reasoned cautionary note, though, is a sobering message that should be carefully heeded.

Other observers are not as pessimistic as Thompson. Richard Easterlin has spent decades demonstrating that the size of birth cohorts influences their relative economic success in life (Easterlin 1980). Baby boomers, who faced serious competition in the labor market due to their numbers, have not fared as well as previous, smaller cohorts. In order to match the economic well-being of these smaller cohorts, baby boomers have had to make substantial life-style adjustments, such as curtailing fertility and postponing the purchase of a home. Easterlin notes, though, that the baby boomers' experience may not signal a continual decline in the overall well-being of future generations. The relative economic situation of younger cohorts may well improve because of the labor shortages that will accompany the arrival of the "baby bust," as the smaller postboom cohorts are referred to (Easterlin 1990a; Easterlin 1990b). But even if their relative wages increase, it is hard to imagine that individuals born during the baby bust will not in any way suffer from the huge burden of supporting the retired baby boom generation.

The Consequences of Heterogeneity among the Elderly

Easterlin's otherwise optimistic projections contain a disturbing downside. Although the overall economic situation of the baby boomers is at least as favorable as that of previous cohorts, largely because of the life-style adjustments they have made, the degree of inequality among those born between 1946 and 1964 has increased (Easterlin et al. 1993). This means that in retirement the disparity between the poor and the more affluent will widen, and it is not difficult to imagine who the most disadvantaged will be. Blacks,

Hispanics, and single women will find themselves in a situation no better, and perhaps even worse, than they are in today, and this fact has serious implications for the possibility of conflict between age groups. The dangers of an age-based politics are grave enough, since they could profoundly alienate segments of our society from one another, but what makes the possibility of age-based conflicts even more worrisome is the fact that they could be exacerbated by a racial and ethnic overlay (Hayes-Bautista 1992). As we have demonstrated throughout the preceding chapters, race and Hispanic ethnicity greatly affect economic and social well-being throughout life. Because of higher fertility and migration rates among minority Americans, the working-age population of the future will be heavily black and Hispanic, while the retired population will be overwhelmingly non-Hispanic and white. This fact, in itself, poses no particular threat, but if Thompson's scenario plays out, and a largely white and politically powerful retired population draws excessively on the earnings of an increasingly minority working-age population with generally lower levels of education and productivity, the strain could give rise to conflicts that are based both on age and racial and ethnic identity. The more the dimensions of difference that enter into a conflict the harder it is to resolve, and we face the danger that fellow citizens will come to look upon each other as strangers and enemies.

The political power of the old is legendary and the political impotence of minority groups well documented. If organizations that represent the old pursue only the interests of their constituents and ignore the plight of those upon whom they depend, it is hard to imagine that serious conflict can be avoided or a general sense of community maintained. The old deserve their fair share of our aggregate wealth, but any society that does not make children and the young its highest priority is doomed to senescence and cannot remain productively competitive for long. What is necessary is a public policy based on a life-course perspective that recognizes the interdependence of all ages, and in particular the close connection between the prosperity of the young and their willingness and ability to care for the old (Longman 1985).

Fernando Torres-Gil, who has served as director of the Administration on Aging, is a social scientist and gerontologist who fully appreciates the implications of the great cultural, economic, and social heterogeneity among the elderly for all aspects of our social existence. He points out that most discussions of the pact between the generations and of generational equity implicitly assume that the old are a monolithic group whose common interests are represented by organizations like AARP (Torres-Gil 1993). Although it is true that the majority of the old are white and that organizations like AARP have lobbied primarily for legislation that benefits middle-class non-Hispanic white elderly, the older population includes an ever growing proportion of blacks, Hispanics, single women, and poor. Torres-Gil points out that in the years to come these differences may become the foci of organized political action groups that could trigger serious conflicts among the elderly. In conjunction with the delegitimation of the old-age agenda that resentment of the old could bring about, such fragmentation among the elderly themselves along racial, ethnic, and income lines could reduce the political power of the old and result in a very different political landscape.

The potential for intracohort conflicts is also increased by the relative age differences among the various racial and ethnic groups. Although the proportion of older persons is increasing for all groups, among those over the age of sixty-five blacks and Hispanics are younger than non-Hispanic whites. While relatively affluent white elderly might be interested in increasing the availability of long-term care options and in protecting their estates and pensions, younger black and Hispanic elderly may be more interested in basic housing and support services, as well as increases in SSI and other income and in-kind supports (Torres-Gil 1993). All of these possibilities make for an interesting future, and there is simply no way of knowing what will happen. All that we can be certain of is that things cannot go on the way they are and that when they retire, today's young workers cannot expect to receive the same benefits that current retirees get. Baby boomers will have to liquidate assets in order to pay for long-term care. Many will have no assets or effective informal networks and will find themselves as dependent on the state as are current retirees. It remains to be seen just how much support the state will be willing or able to provide. If the family retains its role as primary caregiver to the old, it will be as much the result of necessity as of choice. Unfortunately, for the reasons we have elaborated throughout this book, the family may be seriously compromised in its ability to fulfill that role.

Is The Modern Welfare State Equitable?

The major source of the potential for age-based political conflict in the United States, therefore, is the very age-based nature of our welfare state. Although Thompson's prediction is that all developed nations will experience growing intergenerational tensions, such tensions are emerging more rapidly in the United States than elsewhere. In fact, no organization like Americans for Generational Equity has emerged in any other nation, nor has the issue of unequal exchanges between age groups become as much a matter of concern as in this country. One reason for the lack of resentment toward the elderly in other developed nations is that the more universal nature of most welfare states diffuses resentment toward any one group (Kamerman and Kahn 1978; Kane and Kane 1990; Pierson and Smith 1994). In Canada, for example, Medicare applies to all citizens, not just those over a certain age (Marshall, Cook, and Marshall 1993).

Well aware of the age-old wisdom that programs for the poor are poor programs, the designers of Social Security and Medicare adamantly insisted that they be universal and not targeted to the poor (Quadagno 1990; Achenbaum 1986; Marmor, Smeeding, and Greene 1994). Means-tested programs are viewed negatively and tend to be politically vulnerable. This is hardly surprising, since those who do not benefit directly are unlikely to be strong supporters. Unlike welfare, Social Security and Medicare are universal programs, and a program that guarantees benefits to everyone at a certain age avoids many, but not all, of the negative aspects of programs geared mainly to the poor. But from another point of view, Social Security and Medicare are not truly universal, since they are age-based and not everyone can hope to benefit to the same degree.

Resentment toward age-based programs like Social Security and

Medicare is tempered by the fact that no one is excluded in principle; if one lives long enough, one will benefit at least to some degree. The more serious problem that compounds the age-based nature of our old-age welfare state is that it is not only age-based but racially and ethnically biased. Blacks face a higher risk of death at younger ages and have a shorter life expectancy at age sixty-five than whites. A black person, therefore, is likely to receive less of a return on his or her contribution to Social Security than a white person. If we were to operate Social Security like an insurance pool, blacks would pay lower Social Security taxes during their working lives than whites or receive higher benefits during retirement to compensate for the shorter time they will, on average, collect benefits. This inequitable distribution of benefits is compounded by the fact that, because of more limited labor market opportunities and lower average earnings, blacks and Hispanics receive lower benefits on average than non-Hispanic whites and are more likely to depend on minimal OASDI or Supplemental Security Income. The increasing inequality that Easterlin predicts among retiring baby boom cohorts will only exacerbate whatever feelings of inequity exist and could result in a highly stratified older population, in which race and Hispanic ethnicity place older men and women at increased risk of poverty.

Inequalities in Health Care

Even with universal Medicare coverage, we may see a worsening of inequalities in access to health care. As we showed in chapter 3, older blacks and Hispanics are much less likely than non-Hispanic white elderly to have supplemental health insurance to pay for services that Medicare does not cover. Given the rate of increase in both hospital and physician costs, as well as in the cost of long-term care, serious cutbacks and limitations in Medicare coverage are unavoidable. The problem that will arise, of course, is that attempts to control mushrooming costs will hit the most vulnerable elderly hardest, including blacks, Hispanics, and single women. The affluent will always be able to afford supplemental coverage, and the quality of care they receive will remain high.

For perfectly understandable reasons, physicians and hospitals prefer patients with private insurance or those who can pay their own way to those with only Medicare or Medicaid. The rapid expansion of managed care may change this, but it is still the case that individuals with only Medicare can have trouble finding a physician. If, as the result of attempts to control costs, these patients become even more undesirable to providers or insurers, the health of black and Hispanic elderly individuals may suffer. The poor would clearly be the greatest beneficiaries of a national health insurance scheme, just as they would have been the biggest winners had the Medicare Catastrophic Coverage Act not been repealed. But the clear fact of the matter is that in the United States universal programs for the old tend to be less than universal in the extent of coverage and in the quality of care. The poor fare far worse than the affluent, and since being black or Hispanic increases one's chances of being poor, these groups are relegated to second-class status.

As we have seen, therefore, race and Hispanic ethnicity, as well as gender, seriously complicate considerations of equity in the support of the elderly. Because of lifelong labor force disadvantages, a greater prevalence of family disruption and single motherhood, higher rates of poverty, and fewer assets, many minority elderly find themselves dependent on SSI in old age. These elderly are clearly far better off today than they would have been in the era before Social Security, Medicare, and the other programs from which they benefit. Yet as we grapple with the financial problems of an aging population in the years to come, inequality between those who must make do with what the state provides and those who can draw upon private resources will widen. Among the elderly, as among the young, the difference between the poor and those who are better off will depend largely on race and Hispanic ethnicity.

Intergenerational Exchanges and the Rise of the "Third Age"

As we have shown, then, the combination of Social Security, private pensions, and income from assets has made retirement a potentially rich and rewarding time of life for an ever growing fraction of the population. For those with sufficient resources, rather than signifying the approach of death and the end of one's productive years, retirement today brings with it the opportunity to engage fully in life, freed from the more burdensome aspects of full-time work. Peter Laslett (1989) points out that in the study of aging the categorization of the life course is a commonplace, and he calls upon one such categorization that people have found useful in recent years to help illustrate the profound personal and social implications of increasing life spans. In this categorization the life course is divided into four ages, much like the seasons, and includes a period that has emerged only since the middle of the twentieth century: the "third age."

In this four-part categorization, the first age includes childhood and that stage of life during which one is preparing for the responsibilities of adulthood. The second age includes the period of young and mature adulthood, in which one assumes those responsibilities. In this second age one scrambles to get ahead, to earn a living, to educate one's children, and to save for retirement. Until this century this second age was quickly followed by decline and death, largely because of the low quality of life, onerous working conditions, and the rudimentary state of medical knowledge. But by the second half of the twentieth century all that changed, and what used to be the third and final age, characterized by decline and dependency, has been pushed out into the late seventies, eighties, and nineties and is now more appropriately thought of as the fourth age. The new third age consists of those years, following the midlife scramble and preceding mental and physical decline, in which one can focus on personal fulfillment. The third age represents the true reward of our improved standards of living.

The concept of the third age, though, sensitizes us to the importance of accumulated resources and income in our lengthening life spans. Fulfillment may be a state of mind, but it requires adequate resources to attain. As we documented in our discussion of active life expectancy in chapter 2, a large fraction of the greater life span that is typical of recent cohorts consists of years in which one is likely to suffer some physical impairment. To make the third age last for as long as possible, one must have an adequate income and access to good medical care. Because of the importance of material resources in determining both the length and quality of the third age, factors like minority group status and gender, which influence not only one's health but one's material situation at every age, must be taken into account. Without an adequate retirement income one can expect to spend many years unable to purchase the medical and personal care services that would enhance the quality of one's life.

The research we have reviewed makes it clear that income from assets and accumulated wealth are major factors separating those who are well off in retirement from those who are not, and we showed in chapter 3 that blacks, Hispanics, and single women have very few assets either to draw upon in times of need or to leave to their children. Because of the importance of accumulated wealth in determining the overall welfare of any group, it is necessary that we emphasize the role of inheritances and bequests in structuring the pact between the generations, and for this purpose a life-course and intergenerational perspective focused on asset accumulation and group social mobility is most useful. Such a perspective helps direct our attention to the economic interdependence of generations as well as upon the impact of minority group status and gender on the ability of the young and the old to provide mutual support. What we propose is a new way of thinking about the pact between the generations that emphasizes the material basis of that pact. Families are clearly held together by bonds of affection, but that affection has a solid material and practical foundation. In every society the basic reason for the existence of marriage and kinship is to formalize rules of reciprocity between generations that not only define lineage but also govern the transfer of wealth from one generation to the next.

In the United States, inheritances and bequests account for the largest fraction of aggregate personal wealth (Kotlikoff 1989). For most individuals, the vast majority of what they earn over the life course is consumed, and large, and even moderate, estates are usually the result of property that is passed down from one generation to the next. Of course, the opportunities for educational and occupational advancement that children receive from their parents are also bequests, additions to young people's human capital that are as real as money. A lack of education and material resources of the sort that keeps one from accumulating even a modest estate during one's lifetime not only places one at risk of poverty in old age but keeps one from passing material wealth or opportunities for economic and social advancement on to one's children. In the long run, this lack of intergenerational asset accumulation affects the ability of the group as a whole to care for its elderly. Most middle-class parents attempt to preserve their estates for their children, since such bequests serve to define families and cement the bond between the generations. For a large fraction of lower-class minority Americans, passing on either material wealth or the opportunities to earn it is very difficult. Black and Hispanic parents, as well as single mothers, invest less in their children's education than do non-Hispanic whites, primarily because they cannot afford to do so (Goldscheider and Goldscheider 1991).

For these groups, then, the inability to acquire wealth is passed on from one generation to the next in the form of lower productivity and few material resources. In such a regime, expectations of reciprocity between generations, as well as the practical potential to provide help, may be undermined. In order for groups to progress socially, economic exchanges must move forward from older to younger generations, and we should remain continually aware of the very real possibility that the loss of that tie between the old and the young could lead to resentment and an increasing reluctance on the part of working-age adults to provide for the elderly. Although some may object to the materialistic basis on which we ground the pact between the generations, it would be naive to imagine that human motivations are solely altruistic or that we possess an unlimited capacity for self-sacrifice. A more materialistic view leads us to the realization that a system in which the accumulation of assets ties one generation to the next is one in which bonds of generational reciprocity and affection are maximized. Conversely, a system in which the material ties between children and their parents are weak faces the risk of turning the young and the old into strangers.

As we enter the twenty-first century, we are leaving behind a time that was ruled more by tradition and inherited norms concerning both the material and affective aspects of life than will be the uncertain period that lies before us. Such norms will, therefore, play less of a role in exchanges between age groups in the future. For minority Americans (as for many majority Americans also), family life is far different today than it was either in their countries of origin or in this country only a few decades ago. The traditional pact between the generations has been irretrievably weakened, and a new one will have to be negotiated, based on the new material, as well as social, realities that characterize the developed nations at the turn of the century.

A New and Informed Public Discourse

Public debate over issues related to aging has increased dramatically in just a few years. The parents of the baby boomers have reached retirement age, and the issue of how to take care of them has become highly salient to a large number of people. At the same time, it has become clearer that dealing with the massive federal budget deficit will be impossible without controlling the growth of the entitlement programs that benefit the middle class. Many individuals would rather keep Social Security off the table in budget discussions and balance the budget without reducing funding for programs that benefit the old. Increasingly, though, it is clear that attempts to deal with the budget deficit without dealing with Social Security and Medicare are doomed to failure.

Yet the consequences of cuts in entitlement programs, or even reduction in their rates of increase, are very real, and unfortunately, by definition, will fall hardest on those individuals and groups who are most dependent on the federal safety net. The middle class will certainly feel the pinch as Social Security is fully taxed and as higher deductibles and copayments are required for Medicare. Individuals with assets will almost certainly be forced to liquidate at least a large fraction of those assets to pay for long-term care, and the middle-class tradition of preserving one's estate for one's children will be in jeopardy.

Current proposals in Congress go even further and would require that adult children pay at least a portion of their parent's long-term care (U.S. Senate 1995). It is fairly easy to see what the consequences of such a requirement would be. It is hard enough to save for one's own retirement, often while paying for one's children's education. If, instead of inheriting a parent's estate, an adult child inherits the debt associated with their parent's long-term care, their own dependency on their children is insured, and if the children's education and life chances were to be compromised as a result, the consequences would be an overall decline in productivity and material well-being.

Although proposals that would require adult children to contribute financially to the care of their infirm parents are greeted with dismay by many, they remind us of the fact that someone must pay. In this nation we have chosen to socialize the costs of medical care for the elderly through Medicare and of their long-term care through Medicaid. The choice to do so reflects the strength of the pact between the generations, as well as our basic belief that everyone should be cared for. Such a socialized system clearly benefits the poor and minorities, for whom financial support from children would be meager and seriously strain the younger individuals.

The problems that an aging population poses and the magnitude of the inequalities among the elderly are more obvious than the answers. The old-age welfare state in the United States is barely seventy years old, and Medicare and Medicaid are even younger. Yet even at this point in their evolution it is clear that our ability to provide all of the help that those in need require is limited by very real resource limitations and the zero-sum nature of our national budget. Because rates of economic growth will be modest in the future, programs that benefit the elderly will have to be financed at the expense of other causes and the need to make difficult choices will be unavoidable.

The Consequences of Various Proposed Reforms of Social Security for the Poor, Minorities, and Women

The growing sense of crisis associated with the aging of the population has resulted in a number of recommendations for controlling the costs of programs for their support. Most of these recommendations would seriously penalize the poor, yet it is clear that reforms of some sort will be necessary in order to control runaway costs. Very few informed observers would disagree that programs devised during periods in which the proportion of elderly was relatively small will have to be revised for an era in which they represent a far larger fraction of the population. But any reforms that we institute must be equitable and not take unfairly from those who can least afford it.

It is important to keep in mind that there are several different programs that benefit the elderly and some are in greater fiscal danger than others (Kingson and Quadagno 1995). It is also important to realize that the various proposed solutions to the fiscal problems of Social Security, Medicare, and Medicaid reflect basic philosophical differences concerning the role of the welfare state as much as they do strictly financial considerations. Many conservatives wish to reduce the size and role of government in general and limit its responsibility for the care of vulnerable and disadvantaged groups.

Several specific proposals have been offered to deal with the fiscal crisis of the major entitlement programs for the old. Let us here examine the major recommendations and reflect upon their potential consequences for various groups. One of the most radical solutions, and one that on the face of it appears to favor the poor, is to means-test Social Security (Concord Coalition 1993). Such a means or affluence test would reduce benefits to high-income beneficiaries. Were such a radical reform enacted, households in the highest income brackets could lose up to 85 percent of benefits from federally sponsored programs. The result would be substantial savings without penalizing low-income Americans. Yet as Kingson and Quadagno (1995) point out, an affluence test would very likely undermine public support for Social Security and, ultimately, undermine the program. The architects of Social Security were well aware of the dangers of means-testing benefits. Members of organizations like AGE and other affluent individuals already feel that they are not getting their money's worth from the system (Kingson and Quadagno 1995). Moving to a system in which the middle class receives even less would only increase their resentment and have immediate negative consequences for everyone who depends on Social Security. Those who received benefits—the poor, single women, and minorities—would be stigmatized much as are welfare recipients today. The long-term outcome would be a politically vulnerable Social Security program, viewed by many as just one more subsidy of the poor by the middle class.

Such a radical solution to the supposed Social Security crisis is not only ill-conceived but unnecessary (Kingson and Quadagno 1995). The increases in Social Security taxes and adjustments in benefits that were introduced during the early 1980s have eased the fiscal crisis in the program, and the Social Security Trust Fund is projected to be solvent well into the next century. Further adjustments will, of course, be necessary and will result in higher taxes and lower benefits, but with only modest adjustments the solvency of Social Security can be assured. If we want evidence that the supposed crisis in Social Security is being overstated, we need only look to other developed nations, like Austria and Sweden, which devote over twice as much of their gross domestic product to public pensions as does the United States (Kingson and Quadagno 1995).

The situations of Medicare and Medicaid, on the other hand, are more precarious. The most immediate concern is with the Medicare Hospital Insurance Trust Fund, which is projected to be depleted in less than ten years. Of course, such an outcome is unacceptable, and the changes needed to avert a crisis will, no doubt, be made (Moon 1995; Kutza 1995). Unfortunately, the necessary reforms will inevitably penalize the poor, single women, and minorities. Despite the attempts of liberal Democrats to spare the poor, even they concede that there is really no alternative to cost-saving measures like increasing the premiums for doctor's visits and the fair-share components of hospital charges that recipients must pay. Cost-saving measures may include greater restrictions in physician and hospital payments and fewer options in providers. These changes will increase the cost to the elderly and, potentially, make it more difficult for those without private supplementary insurance to find a physician. The debate between liberals and conservatives on Medicare and Medicaid does not really focus on the need for cuts, but rather on the timing for the introduction of cost-saving reforms.

Other proposals that could seriously penalize the poor include increasing the age of eligibility for Social Security to seventy and lowering the fraction of lifetime earnings that Social Security replaces (Kingson and Quadagno 1995). Since blacks have lower life expectancies than whites, though, increasing the age of eligibility would unfairly penalize older blacks, who on average receive benefits for a shorter period. Proposals to increase the age of eligibility also decrease the benefits of those who retire at sixty-two. For low-income recipients who retired early because they could not find work or were in poor heath, such a decrease could mean real hardship, and again, minority Americans would suffer the most.

Currently, Social Security replaces a larger fraction of the total lifetime earnings of low-income workers than of higher-income workers. One set of proposals for reducing the cost of Social Security would be to adjust the formula by which benefits are computed to lower the fraction of earnings that are replaced at the higher replacement rates. Such proposals would seriously penalize individuals with low lifetime earnings, since a smaller fraction of their earnings would be replaced at high rates and a larger fraction at the lower rates currently applied to the highest income categories. Again, given their lower lifetime earnings and more sporadic labor force involvement, the poor, women, and minorities would bear the greatest burden.

Other proposals involve the elimination of Social Security altogether and its replacement by personal savings or individual retirement accounts, similar to those of the defined contribution retirement plans we discussed in chapter 3. How such plans would work, who would choose the instruments in which contributions would be invested, and whether the program would be mandatory or optional are all, as of yet, questions to which no one has proposed an answer. Regardless of how such a privatized program would operate though, it is likely that the poor, women, and minorities would fare worse than they do in the current system, in which at least minimal benefits are guaranteed.

The Moral Foundation of Our Interdependence: A Policy Agenda

Looking to the future we have a series of recommendations for developing an intergenerational public policy. It is clearly imperative that we attempt to preserve the social welfare safety net that is so crucial to the well-being of poor and minority elderly. To that end we might make specific recommendations concerning the programs we have discussed in this book. But it seems to us that our greatest need as a society is to understand the fit between various forms of long-term care and the potential consumers of it. Only then can we make informed decisions about how existing and proposed programs could become more cost-effective without undermining their capacity to address the needs of minorities and the poor. As we have seen, long-term care is a complicated issue for everyone involved, including federal, state, and local governments, public agencies, private organizations, families, and the elderly themselves. The number of public and private options is growing daily, and the task of comparing them, in terms of cost, coverage, entry requirements, types of services offered, administration, case management objectives, overall care plan, and daily routines, are daunting (Capitman and Sciegaj 1995). Selecting the best option for each individual requires an informed clientele.

Rather than proposing specific changes in programs that will already have changed by the time this book is published, we offer a series of recommendations for better understanding the needs of elderly of all racial and ethnic groups and for developing an intergenerational policy agenda that recognizes the interdependence of all age groups. We present these recommendations at two levels. The first set consists of general recommendations for an ongoing public discourse focused on the moral foundation of the pact between the generations. The second consists of more specific recommendations for facilitating that discourse. Public discussions surrounding long-term care tend to be very practical and focused on immediate instrumental ends. This is quite understandable, since it is, after all, easy to see what has happened to one's gross salary after Social Security and other taxes have been withheld, and the consequences of even modest increases in the amount of Social Security that is taxed or the part of Medicare that one must pay out of pocket are painfully obvious to those with only modest incomes. Yet the entire system is based on fundamental assumptions about who we are, what we owe to one another, and what constitutes equitable exchanges between the generations. In our opinion this moral foundation of the pact between the generations must be made explicit.

Our first general recommendation, therefore, is for an ongoing, broadly based, public discourse focused on the life course and the interdependence of age groups. In our age-graded society the old and the young often have little contact with one another, and it is easy for individuals of different ages to come to the conclusion that their interests are fundamentally different. Nothing could be further from the truth. Although we base our conception of the family in material exchanges, material considerations alone cannot give meaning to life. Eric Erikson's theory of generativity gives us insight into how different age groups cooperate to create a just and meaningful world (Erikson 1963). The old need the young, not merely as providers of material and instrumental assistance, but as a tie to the future and as a way of giving meaning to their life's work. The young, in turn, need the old, to provide a link with the past. Without such ties we are all in danger of becoming anomic and rootless strangers to one another and to ourselves.

As Thompson warns, the feeling of inequity that arises when certain cohorts benefit more from their contributions to the system than others can have pernicious effects. Such sentiments can pit one age group against another and, what is worse, lead to a decline in civic consciousness and an obsessive concern with one's immediate personal interests. In the years to come everyone will be called upon to sacrifice in some way to preserve the common good, and it will be necessary to maintain an ongoing discussion concerning, among many other things, the tradeoffs between the common good and individual rights, between the justice of allowing individuals to enjoy the fruits of their labors and the need to care for the poor, and between confiscatory estate taxes and the maintenance of family property. Such questions can only be answered through an informed public debate. Does, for example, the individual right of an aging professor to stay on the faculty take precedence over the need of a new Ph.D. to begin a career? How do we provide high-quality education to young people at a time when tax-strapped voters may reject school bonds routinely? How do we insure an adequate safety net for the poor, minorities, and single women in a time of slower economic growth?

Our second general recommendation is that in our public discourse we begin to devise ways of understanding and dealing with the consequences of the unbelievable pace of change that characterizes modern life. As we approach the end of the twentieth century, we are finally coming to terms with the passage of the institutions of the nineteenth. As much as some may lament it, for a large proportion of our society traditional marriage and family patterns are a thing of the past. As we showed in chapter 3, the current Social Security system is based on outmoded assumptions of lifelong marriages and a traditional gender-based division of labor and consequently penalizes women with limited work histories, as well as minorities among whom family patterns have fundamentally changed.

Until fairly recently, children's lives tended to closely mirror those of their parents. Marriage, the family, and all of the larger social institutions they are connected to remained very much the same for generations, and the slow rate of social change gave people and institutions an opportunity to adapt. The industrial revolution brought that continuity to an end, and each generation's life began to diverge from that of its predecessors at an ever increasing rate. Social change during the twentieth century has proceeded at an astonishing pace, with implications for every one of our social institutions and even our psychological sense of who we are (Giddens 1991). Those who are currently retired were born at the beginning of the twentieth century, and even though their lives were already very different from those of their parents, the change that has reshaped the world of their children is immense, and parents today are often estranged from their children, primarily because of immense differences in worldviews. The old lived through the depression and World War II, when divorce rates were low and marriage and the family were based on fairly traditional patterns. During their lifetimes traditional gender roles have been abandoned, marriage and fertility have become uncoupled, and the very meaning of social continuity has changed. A true discourse between the old and the young is made all the more difficult by such large differences in the moral foundations upon which people build their lives. Compounded by the differences between majority and minority, and between racial and ethnic groups, these generational differences make our task of maintaining a discourse all the more difficult. Yet we must make the effort.

An Opportunity for Imaginative Experimentation: Specific Recommendations

A greater awareness of the moral grounding of the pact between the generations can also help us appreciate the more general interdependence between racial and ethnic groups and between the poor and the more affluent. As Arthur Schlesinger Jr. warns us, we simply cannot allow ourselves to become a nation of strangers if we hope to survive (Schlesinger 1992). In the world of the future the poor, as always, will be in great danger of coming up short if the more radical proposals for dealing with the fiscal crisis of the old-age welfare state are implemented. Economic and political power are concentrated in the middle class, and it is unrealistic to imagine that they would tolerate serious threats to their life-styles. Reductions in funding, limitations in coverage under Social Security, Medicare, and Medicaid, and a general need to make less go further seem an inevitable fact with which we will have to come to terms in the years ahead. In such a world of limited budgets, the potential for age-based conflicts, compounded by racial and ethnic strains, is very real. Avoiding serious and damaging clashes will require the imaginative deployment of those options in the support of the elderly that make the best use of the family and informal support networks. We must begin now to experiment with these options, in order to find the best ways to provide care to the elderly at a reasonable cost.

After seventy years of experience with the old-age welfare state we have come to the realization that there are very real economic and political limits to what we can do, and it is also clear that the welfare of the elderly depends on far more than just funding. The quality of one's life at any age depends upon one's social connectedness and one's ability to engage in useful and productive activity. The community care of the elderly requires new experiments in providing culturally appropriate services that maximize the ability of the family and community to care for aging parents. One of the most frequent observations in the vast gerontological literature is that the family and the informal network are central to the care of the elderly. Even when formal services are available, families use them only to supplement their own efforts, or for temporary respite. The family's commitment to the elderly is as yet strong and resilient. Even so, the demographic and social changes that have so deeply affected the family will inevitably make it far harder for the family to provide these services in the future, and if both the young and the old come to expect the state to take care of the elderly, the family's role may shift dramatically.

Our first specific recommendation, then, is that the family be given as many options as possible to provide care for infirm elderly parents. Both aging parents and their adult children prefer a situation in which the older individual can remain in the community. For the smaller, more mobile families of today, in which both husband and wife must work, some formal assistance is often necessary if the burden of elder care is not to become overwhelming. The On Lok model and the other experiments in community care that we reviewed in chapter 7 show that it is possible to intimately involve the family in the care of the elderly without forcing them to shoulder the entire burden. Respite care, adult day care, and home health care services can make the difference between having to institutionalize an infirm older parent and being able to keep him or her in the community. To succeed, such programs will have to be tailored to the specific clientele they serve and informed by an understanding of their culture.

This leads us to our second recommendation, which focuses on the tremendous racial, ethnic, and class heterogeneity that we have documented among the elderly. Our old-age social welfare state is based not only on the traditional concept of the family but also on the assumption that everyone is basically similar in terms of needs and preferences in living arrangements, the desire for social interaction, medical care, and much more. Yet even casual observation makes it clear that the elderly population is hardly homogeneous. In certain states, like California, Florida, and Texas, the number of Hispanics and Asians is growing rapidly and will represent a substantial segment of the population in years to come. Many of these individuals are first-generation immigrants, who cling more closely to their culture of origin than longer-term residents. Their long-term care needs and the possibility of employing the informal network in their care will be different than for other groups. Long-term care will have to be provided in their native language by professionals who understand their cultural beliefs and practices concerning health and illness, intergenerational relations, diet, and the protocols of death and dying. Such an approach may offend individuals who wish to make English the official language of the United States, but it is the only way that the quality of older people's lives can be maximized in a cost-effective manner.

Most older people and their families are unfamiliar with the various options in long-term care and begin to educate themselves about these options only when an older parent's health has seriously declined. It is disturbing to contemplate physical decline and death, and many people persist in a state of denial until the illusion of permanent health and vitality is shattered. Such denial was harmless, and maybe even beneficial, at a time when there were few decisions to be made concerning long-term care but is most certainly counterproductive today, when a large proportion of the old will need some form of long-term care sometime in their later years. In the future pre-need decisions concerning long-term care insurance, the passing on of assets, and how long one wishes to be kept alive in the event of serious illness will be unavoidable.

Our third specific proposal is for regional and local forums and focus groups designed to identify important policy issues affecting the health and income security of older Americans, with a special emphasis on subgroups of the population, including minorities and women. Such forums could be sponsored by governmental or private agencies and would be aimed at increasing mutual understanding between the generations and between racial and ethnic groups. Currently, much public debate is based on stereotypes, and both the young and the old view the problems inherent in dividing up our economic pie only from their own perspective. Focused discussions could increase mutual understanding between the young and the old and between majority and minority group members, and inform social policy as well. As we showed in chapters 2 and 3, many of the problems associated with aging fall heaviest on women, especially minority group women with low incomes. Our public discourse must pay particular attention to the long-term care needs of these women. It must also be informed by a sophisticated understanding of the great heterogeneity within age groups and within racial and ethnic groups. Stereotypes of blacks or Hispanics often portray them as uniformly poor and uneducated when, in fact, there are rather striking disparities within all groups in such health-related risk factors as education, work history, and income.

Other within-group differences potentially affect the needs and preferences of older individuals, and these can only be fully understood through open communication. As we showed in earlier chapters, Hispanics differ greatly from one another in their needs and problems, depending on how long they have been in the United States and how old they were when they arrived. Recent immigrants are culturally closer to their roots than are longer-term residents, and are more likely to depend on family for both material and instrumental support than are longer-term residents. Those who come to the United States later in life face particularly daunting problems in adapting. Focus groups could begin to shed light on issues related to the housing and health care needs of infirm minority group elderly men and women in the community and allow us to develop more cost-effective ways of addressing those needs. Subsequent forums could cover specific topics such as the assessment of housing needs, sources of instrumental assistance with activities of daily living, sources of payment for home health care, estate planning, and relieving the burden on full-time family caregivers (National Council on the Aging 1988).

These public forums could serve to educate individuals and their families, as well as to encourage greater responsiveness on the part of local, state, and national policy makers to the needs of various groups. They could also serve to motivate and inform private organizations on how best to become involved in designing long-term care options for all racial and ethnic groups. The insights gained from this series of forums could provide baseline data for the design of a national intergenerational awareness campaign (Minkler 1992). Joint funding could be obtained through private foundations and public agencies for a campaign to educate the elderly and their families on long-term care options and bring home the need for both society and the family to plan ahead for meeting long-term care needs.

Local organizations that deal with the elderly could organize forums to help older individuals and their adult children understand important elements of long-term care financing and provision and thus increase their capacity to make intelligent decisions about their options in long-term care. Such an educational approach could help alleviate much of the confusion that typically accompanies the onset of declining health and the realization that an older parent has become dependent. As in the case of other problems, information and communication greatly reduce uncertainty and help people deal both emotionally and practically with difficult situations. As much as we like to avoid the topic, it will become necessary to discuss the issue of death openly. Advances in medical technology that make it possible to prolong life long after its quality has deteriorated to very low levels place the decision as to when life is over in the hands of older individuals themselves, and already living wills are common.

An important part of our proposed public discourse is the dissemination of information on long-term care options to potential consumers in a way that makes those options, and their real cost, clear. One possibility is a computer-assisted interview that would inform potential clients of the various options available and help them make more informed decisions about what sort of long-term care arrangement best fits their needs and desires. Such interviews, tailored to the needs of specific groups, could be made available on the Internet or through the Area Agency on Aging's network of information dissemination services. As individuals become more familiar with long-term care options and as our public discourse evolves, much of the sense of crisis surrounding the care of the elderly, and the concomitant potential for generational conflict, will abate. The hard decisions that must be made can be faced more calmly and rationally in an environment in which information is more available and stereotypes are reduced. As the public sees that well-designed and cost-effective community-based programs are possible they will be willing and even eager to fund them (Hudson 1995, 36). As we enter the twenty-first century, program planners involved in developing models of long-term care will have to take the consumer's point of view and preferences in living arrangements into account in designing home and community-based alternatives.

Everywhere one looks imaginative approaches to the care of the elderly that recognize the reality of generational interdependence are being introduced. Those that are informed by a clear understanding of the culture of the target populations hold the greatest promise. Private-public partnerships that promote intergenerational relationships and facilitate service provision are one such innovation. In Austin, Texas, for example, former state representative Wilhelmina Delco has proposed a creative project entitled "Vision Village." This planned program would bring elderly individuals, academically troubled adolescents, and unmarried teenage mothers and their children together in a mutually supportive, mixed-income residential community on the grounds of a recently closed state school. If such a program were well designed, adequately funded, and wisely administered, it could offer the younger individuals stable role models and the older individuals a vital part to play in solving some of our more serious social problems.

In the years to come both the elderly and their families must seize the initiative and create an effective intergenerational public advocacy agenda that addresses the future needs of the nation as a whole. The Third Millennium, an example of such an effort, is a national nonprofit and nonpartisan organization established by young Americans whose primary objective is to redirect the country's attention away from a myopic obsession with the next presidential election toward a broader concern with longer-term issues (Third Millennium n.d.). The organization's mission is to find or build solutions to America's problems—the national debt, the crises in Social Security and health care financing, the deteriorating environment, the failure of our schools, the tensions between races—that satisfy all groups. The leaders of the Third Millennium believe that Americans of all ages must work together to inspire changes that will benefit future generations as well as those alive today. Toward this end, the organization offers a variety of educational programs which help inform the public about the long-term challenges facing the United States.

There is obviously no way of knowing in detail what the future holds. We must always remain open to new possibilities and changing realities. The one thing that we can be certain of, however, is that the world of the future will be much more diverse than the one we are used to. We end our journey by returning to the observation that the only way of preserving the welfare of the old is to insure the health and welfare of the young. Renewal is the very definition of life, and the health of any population, society, or organization depends on its success in bringing new members to responsible and productive adulthood. Insuring the health and education of our youth and providing them real opportunities for occupational and social advancement are the best insurance we can have against the moral and cultural decline that has led to the collapse of so many societies in the past.

Christopher Lasch has characterized modern society as a "culture of narcissism" in which civic consciousness has declined and individuals have become obsessed with their own fulfillment and satisfaction (Lasch 1979). Even the language we use to refer to the aging process reflects this obsession with self. The commonly used term "life course" emphasizes the historical and personal uniqueness of each life and rejects the notion that the dead hand of the past constrains our choices. "Life cycle," on the other hand, implies renewal and the ties that bind individuals to both the past and the future. There is hardly any point in arguing over labels, but Lasch's criticism once again reminds us of the dangers that accompany the dissolution of the pact between generations and the loss of a sense of connection to those who came before us and those who will come after. Without a generational consciousness and a deeper understanding of the world-views of different ages, cultures, and social classes, we are doomed to a moral solitude that bodes ill for our continued survival as a society.

BIBLIOGRAPHY

Abbott, Julian. 1977. "Socioeconomic Characteristics of the Elderly: Some Black-White Differences." *Social Security Bulletin* 40: 16–42.

Achenbaum, W. Andrew. 1986. *Social Security.* New York: Cambridge University Press.

Aday, Lu Ann, Ronald Andersen, and Gretchen Fleming. 1980. *Health Care in the United States: Equitable for Whom?* Beverly Hills, CA: Sage.

Alba, Richard D. 1990. *Ethnic Identity: The Transformation of White America.* New Haven: Yale University Press.

Alston, Leticia T., and Benigno E. Aguirre. 1987. "Elderly Mexican Americans: Nativity and Health Access." *International Migration Review* 21: 626–42.

Amaro, Hortensia, Rupert Whitaker, Gerald Coffman, and Timothy Heeren. 1990. "Acculturation and Marijuana and Cocaine Use: Findings from HHANES 1982–84." *American Journal of Public Health* 80 (supplement): 54–60.

Andersen, Ronald, Sandra Zelman Lewis, Aida L. Giachello, Lu Ann Aday, and Grace Chiu. 1981. "Access to Medical Care among the Hispanic Population of the Southwestern United States." *Journal of Health and Social Behavior* 22: 78–89.

Andrews, Jane. 1989. "Poverty and Poor Health among Elderly Hispanic Americans." *A Report of the Commonwealth Fund Commission on Elderly People Living Alone.* 624 North Broadway, Room 492, Baltimore, MD.

Angel, Jacqueline L. 1991. *Health and Living Arrangements of the Elderly.* New York: Garland.

Angel, Jacqueline L. and Ronald J. Angel. 1992. "Age at Migration, Social Connections, and Well-Being among Elderly Hispanics." *Journal of Aging and Health* 4: 480–99.

Angel, Jacqueline L., Ronald J. Angel, Judi L. McClellan, and Kyriakos S. Markides. In press. "Nativity, Declining Health, and Preferences in Living Arrangements among Elderly Mexican-Americans." *Gerontologist.*

Angel, Jacqueline L., Gordon F. DeJong, Gretchen T. Cornwell, and Janet M. Wilmoth. 1995."Diminished Health and Living Arrangements of Rural Elderly Americans." *National Journal of Sociology* 9.1: 31–57.

Angel, Jacqueline L., and Dennis P. Hogan. 1992. "The Demography of Minority Aging Populations." *Journal of Family History* 17: 95–114.

Angel, Ronald J. 1995. "Health and the Extent of Private and Public Health Insurance Coverage among Adult Hispanics." Paper presented at the 1995 Health and Retirement Survey Minority Perspectives Workshop, University of Michigan, Ann Arbor, May 26–27.

Angel, Ronald J., and Jacqueline L. Angel. 1993. *Painful Inheritance: Health and the New Generation of Fatherless Families.* Madison: University of Wisconsin Press.

———. 1995. "Mental and Physical Comorbidity among the Elderly: The Role of Culture and Social Class." In *Handbook on Ethnicity, Aging, and Mental Health,* ed. Deborah Padgett, 47–70. Westport, CT: Greenwood.

———. 1996. "The Extent of Private and Public Health Insurance Coverage among Adult Hispanics." *Gerontologist* 36: 332–40.

Angel, Ronald J., Jacqueline L. Angel, and Christine L. Himes. 1992. "Minority Group Status, Health Transitions, and Community Living Arrangements among the Elderly." *Research on Aging* 14: 496–521.

Angel, Ronald J., and P. J. Guarnaccia. 1989. "Mind, Body, and Culture: Somatization among Hispanics." *Social Science and Medicine* 28: 1229–38.

Angel, Ronald J., and Ellen Idler. 1992. "Somatization and Hypochondriasis: Sociocultural Factors in Subjective Experience." In *Research In Community and Mental Health,* ed. James R. Greenley and Philip J. Leaf, vol. 7, 75–97. Greenwich, CT: JAI.

Angel, Ronald, and Peggy Thoits. 1987. "The Impact of Culture on the Cognitive Structure of Illness." *Culture, Medicine, and Psychiatry* 11: 23–52.

Angel, Ronald J., and Marta Tienda. 1982. "Determinants of Extended Household Structure: Cultural Pattern or Economic Need?" *American Journal of Sociology* 87: 1360–83.

Ansak, Marie-Louise. 1990. "The On Lok Model: Consolidating Care and Financing." *Generations* 14: 73–74.

Antonucci, Toni C. 1990. "Social Supports and Social Relationships." In *Handbook of Aging and the Social Sciences,* ed. Robert H. Binstock and Linda K. George, 205–20. San Diego, CA: Academic.

Applebaum, R. A., M. Harrigan, and P. Kemper. 1987. "Community Care Demonstrations: What Have We Learned?" *Health Care Financing Review* 8: 87–100.

Atchley, Robert C., and Judith L. Robinson. 1982. "Attitudes toward Retirement and Distance from the Event." *Research on Aging* 4: 299–313.

Atkins, G. L. 1990. "Politics of Financing Long-Term Care." *Generations* 14: 19–23.

Bagley, Shirley P., Ronald J. Angel, Peggye Dilworth-Anderson, William Lui, and Steven Schinke. 1996. "Panel V Adaptive Behaviors among Ethnic Minorities." *Health Psychology* 14: 632–60.

Ballard, Edna L., Florence Nash, Katherine Raiford, and Lindy E. Harrell. 1993.

"Recruitment of Black Elderly for Clinical Research Studies in Dementia: The CERAD Experience." *Gerontologist* 33: 561–65.

Barusch, Amanda S. 1994. *Older Women in Poverty: Private Lives and Public Policies.* New York: Springer.

Bass, David M., and Linda S. Noelker. 1987. "The Influence of Family Caregivers on Elders' Use of In-Home Services: An Expanded Conceptual Framework." *Journal of Health and Social Behavior* 28: 184–96.

Battin, Margaret Pabst. 1994. "A Truce in the Age Wars? Intergenerational Justice and the Prudential Lifespan Solution in Health Care." In *Economic Security and Intergenerational Justice: A Look at North America,* ed. Theodore R. Marmor, Timothy M. Smeeding, and Vernon L. Greene, 133–53. Washington, DC: Urban Institute.

Baydar, Nazli, and Jeanne Brooks-Gunn. 1991. "Profiles of America's Grandmothers: Those Who Provide Care for Their Grandchildren and Those Who Do Not." Working Paper 92-11, Seattle Population Research Center, University of Washington.

Bean, Frank D., and Ruth R. Berg. 1993. "Cultural and Structural Assimilation and Marital Disruption among Mexican Americans." Paper presented at the annual meeting of the Population Association of America, Cincinnati, OH. April.

Bean, Frank D., Jorge Chapa, Ruth Berg, and Kathryn Sowards. 1994. "Educational and Sociodemographic Incorporation among Hispanic Immigrants to the United States." In *Immigration and Ethnicity: The Integration of America's Newest Immigrants,* ed. by Barry Edmonston and Jeffrey Passel, 73–100. Washington, DC: Urban Institute.

Bean, Frank D., and M. Fix. 1992. "The Significance of Recent Immigration Policy Reforms in the United States." In *Nations of Immigrants: Australia and the United States in a Changing World,* ed. G. Freeman and J. Jupp, 41–55. New York and Sydney: Oxford University Press.

Bean, Frank D., C. Gray Swicegood, and Ruth R. Berg. 1991. "Assimilationist and Ethnic Resilience Factors in Mexican Origin Fertility: A Three Generational Study." Paper presented at the annual meeting of the Population Association of America, Washington DC. March.

Bean, Frank D., and Marta Tienda. 1987. *The Hispanic Population of the United States.* New York: Russell Sage.

Becerra, R. 1983. "The Mexican American Aging in a Changing Culture." In *Aging in Minority Groups,* ed. R. McNeely and J. Cohen, 108–118. Beverly Hills, CA: Sage.

Berkman, Lisa F., C. S. Berkman, S. Kasl, et al. 1986. "Depressive Symptoms in Relation to Physical Health and Functioning in the Elderly." *American Journal of Epidemiology* 124: 372–88.

Berkman, Burton Singer, and Kenneth Manton. 1989. "Black/White Differences in Health Status and Mortality among the Elderly." *Demography* 26: 661–78.

Bernstein, M. C., and J. B. Bernstein. 1988. *Social Security: The System That Works.* New York: Basic.

Biafora, Frank A., and Charles F. Longino. 1990. "Elderly Hispanic Migration in the United States." *Journal of Gerontology* 45: 5212–19.

Binstock, Robert H. 1983. "The Aged as Scapegoat." *The Gerontologist* 23: 136–43.

Binstock, R. H., Chow, W. S., and Schulz, J., eds. 1982. *International Perspectives on Aging: Population and Policy Challenges.* United Nations Fund for Population Activities, Policy Development Studies no. 7. New York: UNFPA.

Blazer, D. G., et al. 1995. "Health Services Access and Use among Older Adults in North Carolina: Urban vs. Rural Residents." *American Journal of Public Health* 85: 1384–90.

Borjas, George. 1990. *Friends or Strangers: The Impact of Immigrants on the U.S. Economy.* New York: Basic.

Borjas, George, and M. Tienda. 1987. "The Economic Consequences of Immigration." *Science* 235: 645–51.

Bould, Sally, Beverly Sanborn, and Laura Reif. 1989. *Eighty-Five Plus: The Oldest Old.* Belmont, CA: Wadsworth.

Bourgeois-Pichat, Jean. 1979. "La transition démographique: Vieillissement de la population." (The demographic transition: Aging of population). In *La science de la population au service de l'homme* (Population science in the service of mankind), 211–39. Liège, Belgium: Institut de la Vie (International Union for the Scientific Study of Population).

Branch, Laurence G., Robert F. Coulam, and Yvonne A. Zimmerman. 1995. "The PACE Evaluation: Initial Findings." *Gerontologist* 35: 349–59.

Branch, Lawrence, and Alan M. Jette. 1982. "A Prospective Study of Long-Term Care Institutionalization among the Aged." *American Journal of Public Health* 72: 1373–79.

Branch, Laurence, Sidney Katz, Kathleen Kniepmann, and Joseph Papsidero. 1984. "A Prospective Study of Functional Status among Community Elders." *American Journal of Public Health* 74: 266–68.

Branch, Laurence G., and K. T. Nemeth. 1985. "When Elders Fail to Visit Physicians." *Medical Care* 23: 1265–75.

Brody, Elaine. 1981. "Women in the Middle." *Gerontologist* 21: 471–80.

———. 1990. *Women in the Middle: Their Parent Care Years.* New York: Springer.

Brody, Stanley J., Walter P. Poulshock, and Carla F. Masciocchi. 1978. "The Family Caring Unit: A Major Consideration in the Long-Term Support System." *Gerontologist* 18:556–61.

Bryant, Sharon, and William Rakowski. 1992. "Predictors of Mortality among Elderly African-Americans." *Research on Aging* 14: 50–67.

Burke, M., T. Hudson, and E. Eubanks. 1990. "Number of Adult Day Care Centers Increasing, but Payment Is Slow." *Hospitals* 11: 34–42.

Burkhauser, Richard, J. S. Butler, and Karen C. Holden. 1991. "How the Death of a Spouse Affects Economic Well-Being after Retirement: A Hazard Model Approach." *Social Science Quarterly* 72: 504–19.

Burr, Jeffrey A. 1990. "Race/Sex Comparisons of Elderly Living Arrangements: Factors Influencing the Institutionalization of the Unmarried." *Research on Aging* 12: 507–30.

Burr, Jeffrey A., and Jan E. Mutchler. 1992. "The Living Arrangements of Unmarried Elderly Hispanic Females." *Demography* 29: 93–112.

Burton, Linda M. 1992. "Black Grandparents Rearing Children of Drug-Addicted Parents: Stressors, Outcomes, and Social Service Needs." *Gerontologist* 32: 744–51.

Burton, Linda M., and Vern L. Bengtson. 1985. "Black Grandmothers: Issues of Timing and Continuity of Roles." In *Grandparenthood,* ed. Vern L. Bengtson and Joan Robertson, 61–77. Beverly Hills, CA: Sage.

Burwell, Brian O., E. Kathleen Adams, and Mark R. Meiners. 1990. "Spend-Down of Assets before Medicaid Eligibility among Elderly Nursing-Home Recipients in Michigan." *Medical Care* 28: 349–62.

Callahan, J. J., Jr., L. Diamond, J. Giele, and R. Morris. 1980. "Responsibility of Families Caring for Their Severely Disabled Elders." *Health Care Financing Review* 1: 29–48.

Cantor, Marjorie H. 1979. "The Informal Support System of New York's Inner City Elderly: Is Ethnicity a Factor?" In *Ethnicity and Aging,* ed. D. E. Gelfand and A. J. Kutzik, 153–74. New York: Springer.

———. 1983. "Strain among Caregivers: A Study of Experience in the United States." *Gerontologist* 23: 597–604.

Cantor, Marjorie H., and Virginia Little. 1985. "Aging and Social Care." In *Handbook of Aging and the Social Sciences,* ed. Robert H. Binstock and Ethel Shanas, 745–81. New York: Van Nostrand Reinhold.

Cantor, Majorie H., Karen Rosenthal, and Louis Wilker. 1979. "Social and Family Relationships of Black Aged Women in New York City." *Journal of Minority Aging* 4: 50–61.

Capitman, John A. 1986. "Community-Based Long-Term Care Models, Target Groups, and Impacts on Service Use." *Gerontologist* 26: 389–97.

Capitman, John A., and Mark Sciegaj. 1995. "A Contextual Approach for Understanding Individual Autonomy in Managed Community Long-Term Care." *Gerontologist* 3: 533–40.

Catchen, Harvey. 1989. "Generational Equity: Issues of Gender and Race." *Women and Health* 14: 21–38.

Center for Disease Control. 1990. "Trends in Lung Cancer Incidence and Mortality—United States, 1980–1987." *Morbidity and Mortality Weekly Report* 39: 875–83.

Cetron, M. 1985. "The Public Opinion of Home Care: A Survey Report Executive Summary." *Caring* 4: 12–15.

Chapa, Jorge. 1991. "Special Focus: Hispanic Demographic and Educational Trends." In *Ninth Annual Status Report on Minorities in Higher Education,* ed. Deborah J. Carter and Reginald Wilson. Washington, DC: American Council of Education.

Chappell, N. L. 1985. "Social Support and the Receipt of Home Care Services." *Gerontologist* 25: 47–54.

———. 1990. "Aging and Social Care." In *Handbook of Aging and Social Sciences,* ed. Robert H. Binstock and Linda K. George, 438–54. San Diego, CA: Academic.

Chavez, Linda. 1989. "Tequila Sunrise: The Slow but Steady Progress of Hispanic Immigrants." *Policy Review,* Spring, 64–67.

———. 1991. *Out of the Barrio: Toward a New Politics of Hispanic Assimilation.* New York: Basic.

Cherlin, Andrew J. 1991. *Divided Families: What Happens to Children When Parents Part.* Cambridge: Harvard University Press.

Chesney, Alan P., Juan A. Chavira, Rogers P. Hall, and Howard E. Gary, Jr. 1982. "Barriers to Medical Care of Mexican-Americans: The Role of Social Class, Acculturation, and Social Isolation." *Medical Care* 20: 883–91.

Child, Irving L. 1943. *Italian or American? The Second Generation in Conflict.* New Haven: Yale University Press.

Chiplin, Alfred J. 1989. "The Older Americans Act: Current Problems and Developments." *Clearinghouse Review,* October, 677–90.

Chiswick, Barry. 1990. "Opening the Golden Door." *Washington Post,* October 7, 1990, D3.

Choi, Namkee G. 1992. "Correlates of Economic Status of Widowed and Divorced Elderly Women." *Journal of Family Issues* 13: 38–54.

Clark, Robert L. 1990. "Income Maintenance Policies in the United States." In *Handbook of Aging and the Social Sciences,* 3rd ed., ed. Robert H. Binstock and Linda K. George, 362–81. New York: Academic.

Clark, Robert L., and A. McDermed. 1988. "Pension Wealth and Job Changes: The Effect of Vesting, Portability, and Lump-Sum Distributions." *Gerontologist* 28: 524–32.

———. 1989. *Pension Regulation and Pension Structure.* Washington, DC: American Enterprise Institute.

Cohen, Marc A., Nanda Kumar, Thomas McGuire, and Stanley S. Wallack. 1992. "Financing Long-Term Care: A Practical Mix of Public and Private." *Journal of Health Politics, Policy, and Law* 17: 403–23.

Cohen, Marc A., Eileen J. Tell, Christine E. Bishop, Stanley S. Wallack, and Laurence G. Branch. 1989. "Patterns of Nursing Home Use in a Prepaid Managed Care System: The Continuing Care Retirement Community." *Gerontologist* 29: 74–80.

Cohen, Marc A., Eileen J. Tell, Jay N. Greenberg, and Stanley S. Wallack. 1987. "The Financial Capacity of the Elderly to Insure for Long-Term Care." *Gerontologist* 27: 494–502.

Cohen, Marc, Eileen J. Tell, and Stanley S. Wallack. 1986. "The Risks and Costs of Nursing Home Care among the Elderly." *Medical Care* 24: 1161–72.

Concord Coalition. 1993. *The Zero Deficit Plan.* Washington, DC: Concord Coalition.

Connidis, Ingrid. 1983. "Living Arrangement Choices of Older Residents: Assessing Quantitative Results with Qualitative Data." *Canadian Journal of Sociology* 8: 359–75.

Consumer Reports. 1991. "An Empty Promise to the Elderly?" June, 421–42.

Corin E. 1987. "The Relationship between Formal and Informal Social Support Networks in Rural and Urban Contexts." In *Aging in Canada: Social Perspectives,* 2d ed., ed. V. W. Marshall, 367–94. Markham, Ontario: Fitzhenry and Whiteside.

Cornoni-Huntley, Joan, Dan G. Blazer, Mary E. Lafferty, Donald F. Everett, Dwight B. Brock, and Mary E. Farmer. 1990. *Established Populations for Epidemiologic Studies of the Elderly: Resource Data Book.* Vol. 2. National Institutes of Health, Publication No. 90–495. National Institute on Aging.

Cowart, Marie E. 1994. "Long-Term Care Policy and American Family Values." Paper presented at the Gerontological Association Annual Meetings, Atlanta, November.

Cowgill, D. 1986. *Aging around the World.* Belmont, CA: Wadsworth.

Cox, Carole. 1993. *The Frail Elderly: Problems, Needs, and Community Responses.* Westport, CT: Auburn House.

Crimmins, Eileen M., Mark D. Hayward, and Yasuhiko Saito. 1994. "Changing Mortality and Morbidity Rates and the Health Status and Life Expectancy of the Older Population." *Demography* 31: 159–75.

———. In press. "Differentials in Active Life Expectancy in the Older Population of the United States." *Journal of Gerontology: Social Sciences.*

Crystal, Stephen. 1982. *America's Old Age Crisis.* New York: Basic.

Crystal, Stephen, and Dennis Shea. 1990a. "Cumulative Advantage, Cumulative Disadvantage, and Inequality among Elderly People." *Gerontologist* 30: 437–43.

———. 1990b. "The Economic Well-Being of the Elderly." *Review of Income and Wealth* 36: 227–47.

Crystal, Stephen, Dennis Shea, and Shreeram Krishnaswami. 1992. "Educational Attainment, Occupational History, and Stratification: Determinants of Later-

Life Economic Outcomes." *Journal of Gerontology: Social Sciences* 47: S213–21.

Danziger, Sheldon. 1984. "Implications of the Relative Economic Status of the Elderly for Transfer Policy." In *Retirement and Economic Behavior,* ed. H. J. Aaron and G. Burtless, 175–193. Washington, DC: Brookings Instititution.

Davis, Karen. 1975. "Equal Treatment and Unequal Benefits: The Medicare Program." *Milbank Memorial Fund Quarterly* 53: 449–88.

———. 1990. *National Survey of Hispanic Elderly People, 1988.* Ann Arbor, MI: Inter-University Consortium for Political and Social Research.

———. 1992. *National Survey of Problems Facing Elderly Americans Living Alone, 1986.* Ann Arbor, MI: Inter-University Consortium for Political and Social Research.

Day, Christine. 1990. *What Older Americans Think: Interest Groups and Aging Policy.* Princeton: Princeton University Press.

Day, Jennifer Cheeseman. 1993. "Population Projections of the United States, by Age, Sex, Race, and Hispanic Origin: 1993–2050." U.S. Bureau of the Census, *Current Population Reports,* P25–1104. Washington, DC: U.S. Government Printing Office.

Diamond, Timothy. 1992. *Making Gray Gold: Narratives of Nursing Home Care.* Chicago: University of Chicago.

Doty, P. 1986. "Family Care of the Elderly: The Role of Public Policy." *Milbank Quarterly* 64. 1: 34–75.

Dressel, Paula L. 1988. "Gender, Race, and Class: Beyond the Feminization of Poverty in Later Life." *Gerontologist* 28: 177–80.

Dunkelberg, Anne. 1992. *Expanding the Medicaid Program in Texas: Funding Issues and Alternatives.* Austin: Lyndon B. Johnson School of Public Affairs, University of Texas at Austin.

Dutton, Diana B. 1986. "Social Class, Health, and Illness." In *Applications of Social Science to Clinical Medicine and Health Policy,* ed. Linda H. Aiken and David Mechanic, 31–62. New Brunswick, NJ: Rutgers University Press.

Easterlin, Richard A. 1980. *Birth and Fortune: The Impact of Numbers upon Personal Welfare.* London: Grant McIntyre.

Easterlin, R. A., C. Macdonald, and D. J. Macunovich. 1990a. "How Have American Baby Boomers Fared? Earnings and Economic Well-Being of Young Adults, 1964–87." *Journal of Population Economics* 3: 277–90.

———. 1990b. "Retirement Prospects of the Baby-Boom Generation: A Different Perspective." *Gerontologist* 30: 776–83.

Edelman, P., and S. Hughes. 1990. "The Impact of Community Care on Provision of Informal Care to Homebound Elderly Persons." *Journal of Gerontology: Social Sciences* 45: S74–84.

Easterlin, Richard A., Diane J. Macunovich, and Eileen M. Crimmins. 1993.

"Economic Status of the Young and Old in Working-Age Population, 1964–1987." In *The Changing Contract across Generations*, ed. Vern L. Bengtson and W. Andrew Achenbaum 67–85. New York: Aldine de Gruyter.

Eggebeen, David J., and Dennis P. Hogan. 1990. "Giving between Generations in American Families." *Human Nature* 1: 211–32.

Elo, Irma T., and Samuel H. Preston. 1994. "Estimating African-American Mortality from Inaccurate Data." *Demography* 31: 427–58.

Eribes, Richard A., and Martha Bradley-Rawls. 1978. "The Underutilization of Nursing Home Facilities by Mexican-American Elderly in the Southwest." *Gerontologist* 18: 363–71.

Erikson, Erik H. 1963. *Childhood and Society.* New York: Norton.

Espino, David V., and David Maldonado. 1990. "Hypertension and Acculturation in Elderly Mexican Americans: Results from 1982–84 Hispanic HANES." *Journal of Gerontology* 45: M209–13.

Espino, David V., Carlos A. Moreno, and Melissa Talamantes. 1993. "Hispanic Elders in Texas: Implications for Health Care." *Texas Medicine* 89: 58–61.

Espino, David V., Richard R. Neufeld, Michael Mulvihill, and Leslie S. Libow. 1988. "Hispanic and Non-Hispanic Elderly on Admission to the Nursing Home: A Pilot Study." *Gerontologist* 28: 821–24.

Espino, David V., Ernesto O. Parra, and Rod Kriehbiel. 1994. "Mortality Differences between Elderly Mexican Americans and Non-Hispanic Whites in San Antonio, Texas." *Journal of the American Geriatric Society* 42: 604–8.

Estrada, Antonio L., Fernando M. Trevino, and Laura A. Ray. 1991. "Health Care Utilization Barriers among Mexican American: Evidence from HHANES 1982–84." *American Journal of Public Health* 80 (supplement): 27–31.

Evans, Jeffrey. 1987. "Migration and Health." *International Migration Review* 31: 5–14.

Even, William E. 1994. "Gender Differences in Pensions." *Journal of Human Resources* 29: 555–88.

Fannie Mae. 1995. *Home Keeper: It Pays to Keep You in Your Home.* 390 Wisconsin Ave., NW, Washington, DC 20016-2899.

Feder, Judith, Diane Rowland, John Holahan, Alina Salganicoff, David Heslam. 1993. *The Medicaid Cost Explosion: Causes and Consequences.* Baltimore: Kaiser Commission on the Future of Medicaid.

Feder, Judith, and William Scanlon. 1982. "The Underused Benefit: Medicare's Coverage of Nursing Home Care." *Health and Society* 60: 604–32.

Feinson, Marjorie Chary. 1985. "Aging and Mental Health: Distinguishing Myth from Reality." *Research on Aging* 7: 155–74.

Findley, Sally E. 1988. "The Directionality and Age Selectivity of the Health-

Migration Relation: Evidence from Sequences of Disability and Mobility in the United States." *International Migration and Review* 22: 4–29.

Fischer, David Hackett. 1978. *Growing Old in America.* New York: Oxford University Press.

Flowers, Marilyn R. 1977. *Women and Social Security: An Institutional Dilemma,* Washington, DC: American Enterprise Institute for Public Policy Research.

Foner, Anne. 1986. *Aging and Old Age.* Englewood Cliffs, NJ: Prentice-Hall.

Forbes, Douglas, and W. Parker Frisbie. 1981. "Spanish Surname and Anglo Infant Mortality: Differentials of a Half-Century." *Demography* 28 (4): 639–61.

Franco, Laerico J., Michael P. Stern, Marc Rosenthal, Steven M. Haffner, Helen P. Hazuda, and Paul J. Comeaux. 1985. "Prevalence, Detection, and Control of Hypertension in a Biethnic Community." *American Journal of Epidemiology* 121: 684–96.

Frerichs, R. R., J. M. Chapman, and E. F. Maes. 1984. "Mortality Due to All Causes and Cardiovascular Diseases among Seven Race-Ethnic Populations in Los Angeles County." *International Journal of Epidemiology* 13: 291–98.

Friedman, Eugene A., and Harold L. Orbach. 1974. "Adjustment to Retirement." In *The Foundations of Psychiatry,* ed. Silvano Arieti vol. 1, *American Handbook of Psychiatry,* 2d ed. 609–45. New York: Basic.

Frisbie, W. Parker. 1991. *Final Report, NICHD Grant No. 22490.* Austin: Population Research Center, University of Texas at Austin.

Frisbie, W. Parker, Frank D. Bean, and Dudley L. Poston. 1985. "Household and Family Demography of Hispanics, Blacks and Anglos." Prepared for the Demographic and Behavioral Sciences Branch Center for Population Research, National Institute of Child Health and Human Development, National Institutes of Health. Population Research Center, University of Texas at Austin.

Fuguitt, Glenn V, David L. Brown, and Calvin L. Beale. 1989. *Rural and Small Town America.* New York: Russell Sage.

Garfinkel, Irwin, and Sara S. McLanahan. 1986. *Single Mothers and Their Children: A New American Dilemma.* The Changing Domestic Priorities Series. Washington, DC: Urban Institute Press.

Gelfand, Donald. 1984. *The Aging Network.* New York: Springer.

George, Linda K. 1988. "Social Participation in Later Life: Black-White Differences." In *The Black Elderly American: Research on Physical and Psychological Health,* ed. James Jackson, 99–106. New York: Springer.

Gibson, Rose. 1994. "The Age-by-Race Gap in Health and Mortality in the Older Population: A Social Research Agenda." *Gerontologist* 34: 454–63.

Giddens, Anthony. 1991. *Moderning and Self-Identity: Self and Society in the Later Modern Age.* Stanford, CA: Stanford University Press.

Gjorup, T., C. Hendrickson, E. Lund, and E. Stromgard. 1987. "Is Growing Old a Disease? A Study of the Attitudes of Elderly People to Physical Symptoms." *Journal of Chronic Diseases* 40: 1095–98.

Glazer, Nathan, and Daniel P. Moynihan. 1970. *Beyond the Melting Pot: The Negroes, Puerto Ricans, Jews, Italians and Irish of New York City.* Cambridge, MA: MIT Press.

Goffman, Erving. 1961. *Asylums: Essays on the Social Situation of Mental Patients and Other Inmates.* Garden City, NJ: Anchor.

Goldscheider, Frances K., and Calvin Goldscheider. 1989. "The New Family Economy: Residential and Economic Relationships among the Generations." In *Ethnicity and the New Family Economy: Living Arrangements and Intergenerational Financial Flows,* ed. Frances K. Goldscheider and Calvin Goldscheider. 1–16. Boulder, CO: Westview.

———. 1991. "The Intergenerational Flow of Income: Family Structure and the Status of Black Americans." *Journal of Marriage and Family* 53: 499–508.

Gordon, Milton. 1964. *Assimilation and American Life.* New York: Oxford University Press.

Grad, Susan. 1992. *Income of the Population 55 or Older.* U.S. Department of Health and Human Services, Social Security Administration, Office of Research and Statistics, Publication No. 13–11871. Washington, DC: Government Printing Office.

Graebner, William. 1980. *A History of Retirement: The Meaning and Function of an American Institution, 1885–1978.* New Haven: Yale University Press.

Grason, Holly, and Bernard Guyer. 1995. "Rethinking the Organization of Children's Programs: Lessons from the Elderly." *Milbank Quarterly* 73: 565–97.

Gratton, Brian. 1987. "Familism among the Black and Mexican-American Elderly: Myth or Reality?" *Journal of Aging Studies* 1: 19–32.

Greeley, Andrew. 1971. *Why Can't They Be like Us? America's White Ethnic Groups.* New York: Dutton.

Greenberg, Jay S., and M. B. Becker. 1988. "Aging Parents as Family Resources." *Gerontologist* 28: 786–96.

Greene, Vernon L., Mary E. Lovely, and Jan I. Ondrich. 1993a. "The Cost-Effectiveness of Community Services in a Frail Elderly Population." *Gerontologist* 33: 177–89.

———. 1993b. "Do Community-Based Long-Term Care Services Reduce Nursing Home Use? A Transition Probability Analysis." *Journal of Human Resources* 28. 2: 288–317.

Greene, Vernon L., and Deborah J. Monahan. 1984. "Comparative Utilization of Community-Based Long-Term Care Services by Hispanic and Anglo Elderly in a Case Management System." *Journal of Gerontology: Social Sciences* 39: S730–35.

Greene, Vernon L., and Jan I. Ondrich. 1990. "Risk Factors for Nursing Home Admissions and Exits: A Discrete-Time Hazard Function Approach." *Journal of Gerontology* 45: S250–58.

Groger, Lisa. 1994. "Decision as Process: A Conceptual Model of Black Elders' Nursing Home Placement." *Journal of Aging Studies* 8: 77–94.

Guendelman, Sylvia, and Joan Schwalbe. 1986. "Medical Care Utilization by Hispanic Children." *Medical Care* 24: 925– 37.

Guralnik, Jack M., Kenneth C. Land, Dan Blazer, Gerda G. Fillenbaum, and Laurence G. Branch. 1993. "Educational Status and Active Life Expectancy among Older Blacks and Whites." *New England Journal of Medicine* 329: 110–17.

Haber, Carole, and Brian Gratton. 1994. *Old Age and the Search for Security.* Bloomington and Indianapolis: University of Indiana Press.

Hambour, J. 1987. "Economic Policy, Intergenerational Equity, and the Social Security Trust Fund Buildup." *Social Security Bulletin* 50: 13–18.

Ham-Chande, Roberto. 1994. "Conceptos para estudio sociodemografico del envejecimiento en America Latina y el Caribe." Manuscript, Universida El Colegio de la Frontero Norte, Baja, CA/Tiajuana, Mexico.

Handlin, Oscar. 1951. *The Uprooted: The Epic Story of the Great Migrations That Made the American People.* Boston: Little, Brown.

Hanley, R. J., and J. M. Wiener. 1991. "Use of Paid Home Care by the Chronically Disabled Elderly." *Research on Aging* 13: 310–32.

Hanley, Raymond J., Joshua M. Wiener, and Katherine M. Harris. 1991. "Will Paid Home Care Erode Informal Support?" *Journal of Health Politics, Policy, and the Law* 16: 507–21.

Hanson, S. M., and W. J. Sauer. 1985. "Children and Their Elderly Parents." In *Social Support Networks and the Care of the Elderly.* ed. W. J. Sauer and R. T. Coward, 41–66. New York: Springer.

Harris, Louis, and Associates, Inc. 1986. "Problems Facing Elderly Americans Living Alone: Field Work, June–July, 1986." In *Final Report to The Commonwealth Fund Commission on Elderly People Living Alone.* Commonwealth Fund.

Hasler, Bonnie, S. 1991. "Report on Characteristics of Clients Receiving Community-Based Long-Term Care." In *Ageline,* 60. Washington, DC: National Association of State Units on Aging,

Hayes-Bautista, David E., Werner O. Schink, and Jorge Chapa. 1988. *The Burden of Support: Young Latinos in an Aging Society.* Stanford, CA: Stanford University Press.

Hayes-Bautista, David E. 1992. "Young Latinos, Older Anglos, and Public Policy: Lessons from California." In *Diversity: New Approaches to Ethnic Minority Aging* ed. E. Percil Stanford and Fernando M. Torres-Gil, 73–80. Amityville, NY: Baywood Publishing.

Health Insurance Association of America. 1995. *Who Buys Long-Term Care Insurance? 1994–95 Profiles and Innovations in a Dynamic Market.* Washington, DC: Health Insurance Association of America.

Heclo, Hugh. 1988. "Generational Politics." In *The Vulnerable,* ed. John L. Palmer, Timothy Smeeding, and Barbara Boyle Torrey, 381–411. Washington, DC: Urban Institute.

Hess, B., and B. Soldo. 1985. "Husband and Wife Networks." In *Social Support Networks and the Care of the Elderly,* ed. W. J. Sauer and R. T. Coward, 67–92. New York: Springer.

Hess, Beth B., and Joan. M. Waring. 1978. "Parent and Child in Later Life: Rethinking the Relationship." In *Child Influences on Marital and Family Interaction,* ed. R. Lerner and G. Spanier. 241–73. New York: Academic.

Holden, Karen, and Timothy M. Smeeding. 1990. "The Poor, the Rich, and the Insecure Elderly Caught in Between." *Milbank Quarterly* 68: 191–219.

Holden, Karen C., and Pamela J. Smock. 1991. "The Economic Costs of Marital Dissolution: Why Do Women Bear a Disproportionate Cost?" *Annual Review of Sociology* 17: 51–78.

Holmes, Douglas, Jeanne Teresi, and Monica Holmes. 1983. "Differences among Black, Hispanic, and White People in Knowledge about Long-Term Care Services." *Health Care Financing Review* 5: 51–67.

Holstein, Martha. 1995. "The Normative Case: Chronological Age and Public Policy." *Generations* 19: 11–14.

Holstein, Martha, and Meredith Minkler. 1991. "The Short Life and Painful Death of the Medical Catastrophic Coverage Act." In *Critical Perspectives on Aging: The Political and Moral Economy of Growing Old,* ed. Meredith Minkler and Carroll L. Estes, 189–206. Amityville, NY: Baywood.

Horwitz, Amy, and Lois W. Shindelman. 1983. "Social and Economic Incentives for Family Caregivers." *Health Care Financing Review* 5: 25–33.

Hough, Richard L., John A. Landsverk, Marvin Karno, Audrey Burnam, Dianne M. Timbers, Javier I. Escobar, and Darrel A. Regier. 1987. "Utilization of Health and Mental Health Services by Los Angeles Mexican Americans and Non-Hispanic Whites." *Archives of General Psychiatry* 44: 702–9.

House J. S., K. R. Landis, and D. Umberson. 1988. "Social Relationship and Health." *Science* 241: 540–45.

House, J. S., J. C. Robbins, and H. L. Metzer. 1982. "The Association of Social Relationships and Activities with Morality: Perspective Evidence from the Tecumseh Community Health Study." *American Journal of Epidemiology* 116: 123–40.

Houseknecht, Sharon K., and Saad Z. Nagi. 1994. "Aging and Clustering of Problems: Implications for the Organization of Services." Paper presented at the American Sociological Association Meetings, Los Angeles, CA, August.

Hudson, Robert B. 1995. "Social Protection and Services." In *Handbook of*

Aging and the Social Sciences, ed. Robert H. Binstock and Linda K. George, 446–64. San Diego, CA: Academic Press.

Hughes, S. 1985. "Apples and Oranges? A Review of Community-Based Long-Term Care." *Health Services Research* 20: 461–87.

Idler, Ellen, and Ronald Angel. 1990. "Age, Pain, and Self-Assessments of Health." In *Advances in Medical Sociology,* ed.Gary L. Albrecht, vol. 1, 127–48. Greenwich, CT: JAI.

Irvine, Audrey, Elayne Kornblatt Phillips, Patricia Cloonan, James C. Torner, Mary E. Fisher, and Gary A. Chase. 1991. "Impact of Medicare Payment Policy on Home Health Resources Utilization." *Health Care Financing Review* 13: 13–18.

Jackson, James S., Toni C. Antonucci, and Rose C. Gibson. 1991. "Cultural, Ethnic, and Racial Influences on Productive Aging: A Life-Course Framework." In *Achieving a Productive Aging Society,* ed. S. A. Bass, F. G. Caro, and B. Chen, 249–68. Westport, CT: Auburn House.

Jasso, Guillermina, and Mark Rosenzweig. 1990. *The New Chosen People.* New York: Russell Sage.

Jepson, Christopher, Larry G. Kessler, Barry Portnoy, and Tyson Gibbs. 1991. "Black-White Differences in Cancer Prevention Knowledge and Behavior." *American Journal of Public Health* 81: 501–4.

Jette, Alan M., Sharon Tennstedt, and Sybil Crawford. 1995. "How Does Formal and Informal Community Care Affect Nursing Home Use?" *Journal of Gerontology* 50B: S4–12.

Johnson, Colleen L., and Barbara M. Barer. 1990. "Families and Networks among Older Inner-City Blacks." *Gerontologist* 30: 726–33.

Juster, Thomas F. 1993. "The Health and Retirement Survey." *ICPSR Bulletin* 14: 1–2.

Kamerman, Sheila, and Alfred Kahn. 1978. *Family Policy: Governments and Families in Fourteen Countries.* New York: Columbia University Press.

Kane, Robert L., Laurel Hixon Illston, and Nancy A. Miller. 1992. "Qualitative Analysis of the Program of All-Inclusive Care for the Elderly (PACE)." *Gerontologist* 32: 771–80.

Kane, Robert L., and Rosalie A. Kane. 1990. "Health Care for Older People: Organizational and Policy Issues." In *Handbook of Aging and the Social Sciences,* 3d ed., ed. Robert H. Binstock and Linda K. George, 415–37. New York: Academic.

Kane, Rosalie A., and Robert L. Kane. 1987. *Long-Term Care: Principles, Programs, and Policies.* New York: Springer.

Kane, Rosalie A., Robert L. Kane, Laurel Hixon Illston, John A. Nyman, and Michael D. Finch. 1991. "Adult Foster Care for the Elderly in Oregon: A Mainstream Alternative to Nursing Homes?" *American Journal of Public Health* 81: 1113–20.

Kasarda, John D. 1993. *The Impact of Skill Mismatches, Spatial Mismatches, and Welfare Incentives on City Joblessness and Poverty.* Cambridge, MA: Lincoln Institute on Land Policy.

Kasl, Stanislav V., and Lisa F. Berkman. 1983. "Health Consequences of the Experiences of Migration." *Annual Review of Public Health* 4: 69–90.

Katz, S., L. G. Branch, M. H. Branson, J. A. Papsidero, J. C. Beck, and D. S. Greer. 1983. "Active Life Expectancy." *New England Journal of Medicine* 309: 1218–24.

Kaye, Lenard, and Patricia M. Kirwin. 1990. "Adult Day Care Services for the Elderly and Their Families: Lessons from the Pennsylvania Experience." *Journal of Gerontological Social Work* 15: 167–83.

Kayel, L., and Patricia Kerwin. 1990. "Adult Day Care Services for the Elderly and Their Families: Lessons from a Pennsylvania Experience." *Journal of Gerontological Social Work* 4: 167–83.

Keefe, Susan E., and Amado M. Padilla. 1987. *Chicano Ethnicity.* Albuquerque: University of New Mexico Press.

Keith, Jennie. 1990. "Age in Social and Cultural Context." In *Handbook of Aging and the Social Sciences,* 2d ed., 231–66. New York: Van Nostrand.

Keith, Jennie, Christine L. Fry, Anthony P. Glascock, Charlotte Idels, Jeanette Dickerson-Putnam, Henry C. Harpending, and Patricia Draper, eds., 1994. *The Aging Experience: Diversity and Commonality across Cultures.* Thousand Oaks, CA: Sage.

Kemper, Peter. 1988. "The Evaluation of the National Long-Term Care Demonstration: Overview of the Findings." *Health Services Research* 23: 161–74.

———. 1990. "Case Management Agency Systems of Administering Long-Term Care: Evidence from the Channeling Demonstration." *Gerontologist* 30: 817–24.

———. 1992. "The Use of Formal and Informal Home Care by the Disabled Elderly." *Health Services Research* 27: 421–51.

Kendig, Hal L., Akiko Hashimoto, and Larry C. Coppard. 1992. *Family Support for the Elderly: The International Experience.* New York: Oxford University Press.

Kendig, David A., and Guo Yan. 1993. "Physician Supply in Rural Areas with Large Minority Communities." *Health Affairs* 12 (supplement): 177–84.

Kenney, Genevieve M. 1993. "Rural and Urban Differences in Medicare Home Health Use." *Health Care Financing Review* 14: 39–57.

Kingson, Eric R., Barbra A. Hirshorn, and John M. Cornman. 1986. *Ties That Bind: The Interdependence of Generations.* Washington, DC.: Seven Locks Press.

Kingson, Eric, and Jill Quadagno. 1995. "Social Security: Marketing Radical Reform." *Generations* Fall: 43–49.

Kinsella, Kevin. 1992. "Population and Health Transitions." U.S. Bureau of the Census, *Current Population Reports,* series P95/92–2. Washington, DC: Government Printing Office.

Kirwin, Patricia. 1991. *Adult Day Care: The Relationship between Formal and Informal Systems of Care.* New York: Garland.

Kittner, Steven J., Lon R. White, Katalin G. Losonczy, Philip A. Wolf, and J. Richard Hebel. 1990. "Black-White Differences in Stroke Incidence in a National Sample." *Journal of the American Medical Association* 264: 1267–70.

Kleinman, Arthur. 1986. *Social Origins of Distress and Disease: Depression, Neurasthenia, and Pain in Modern China.* New Haven, CT: Yale University Press.

Kobrin, Frances E. 1976. "The Fall of Household Size and the Rise of the Primary Individual in the U.S." *Demography* 13: 127–38.

Koff, Theodore H. 1988. *New Approaches to Health Care for an Aging Population.* San Francisco: Jossey-Bass.

Kosloski, Karl, and Rhonda J. V. Montgomery. 1992. "Perceptions of Respite Services as Predictors of Utilization." *Research on Aging* 15: 399–413.

Kotlikoff, Laurence J. 1989. *What Determines Savings?* Cambridge: Massachusetts Institute of Technology.

Krause, Neal. 1990. "Illness Behavior in Later Life." In *Handbook of Aging and the Social Sciences,* 3d ed., ed. Robert H. Binstock and Linda K. George, 227–44. New York: Academic.

Krout, John A., Stephen J. Cutler, and Raymond T. Coward. 1990. "Correlates of Senior Center Participation: A National Analysis." *Gerontologist* 30: 72–79.

Kutza, Elizabeth A. 1995. "Medicaid: The Shifting Place of the Old in a Needs-Based Health Program." *Generations* 19; 54–57.

Land, Kenneth C., Jack M. Guralnik, and Dan Blazer. 1994. "Estimating Increment-Decrement Life Tables with Multiple Covariates from Panel Data: The Case of Active Life Expectancy." *Demography* 31: 297–321.

Lasch, Christopher. 1979. *The Culture of Narcissism: American Life in an Age of Diminishing Expectations.* New York: Warner.

Laslett, Peter. 1972. *Household and Family in Past Time: Comparative Study in the Size and Structure of the Domestic Group over the Last Thirty Years.* Cambridge, England: Cambridge University Press.

———. 1989. *A Fresh Map of Life: The Emergence of the Third Age.* London: Weidenfeld and Nicolson.

Laslett, Peter, and James S. Fishkin, eds. 1992. *Philosophy Politics, and Society: Justice between Age Groups and Generations.* New Haven, CT: Yale University Press.

Lawton, M. Powell, Elaine M. Brody, and Avalie R. Saperstein. 1989. "A Controlled Study of Respite Service for Caregivers of Alzheimer's Patients." *Gerontologist* 29: 8–16.

Lawton, M. Powell, Doris Rajagopal, Elaine Brody, and Morton H. Kleban. 1992. "The Dynamics of Caregiving for a Demented Elder among Black and White Families." *Journals of Gerontology: Social Sciences* 47: S156–64.

Leavitt, T. and James H. Schulz. 1988. *Time to Reform the SSI Asset Test?* American Association of Retired Persons Public Policy Institute. Publication No. 8802. Washington, DC: AARPPI.

Lee, David J., and Kyriakos S. Markides. 1991. "Health Behaviors, Risk Factors, and Health Indicators Associated with Cigarette Use in Mexican Americans: Results from the Hispanic HANES." *American Journal of Public Health* 81: 859–64.

Lee, Gary R., Jeffrey W. Dwyer, and Raymond T. Coward. 1990. "Residential Location and Proximity to Children among Impaired Elderly Parents." *Rural Sociology* 55: 579–89.

Leutz, Walter. 1986. "Long-Term Care for the Elderly: Public Dreams and Private Realities." *Inquiry* 23: 134–40.

Leutz, Walter, Mark Sciegaj, John Capitman, and Mary Ellen Henry. 1995. *Service Planning Guidelines in Community Long-Term Care Programs.* Waltham, MA: National Resource Center: Diversity and Long-Term Care, Heller Graduate School, Brandeis University.

Lewin, Tamar. 1994. "Keeping Elderly at Home and Care Affordable." *New York Times.* February 14, A1, A12.

Lieberson, Stanley, and Mary C. Waters. 1990. *From Many Strands: Ethnic and Racial Groups in Contemporary America.* New York: Russell Sage.

Link, Bruce G. and Joe Phelan. 1995. "Social Conditions as Fundamental Causes of Diseases." *Forty Years of Medical Sociology: The State of the Art and Directions for the Future, Journal of Health and Social Behavior.* (Extra Issue): 80–94.

Litwak, Eugene. 1985. *Helping the Elderly: The Complementary Role of Informal Networks and Formal Systems.* New York: Guilford.

Liu, Korbin, Pamela Doty, and Kenneth Manton. 1990. "Medicaid Spenddown in Nursing Homes." *Gerontologist* 30: 7–15.

Liu, Korbin, and Kenneth Manton. 1991. "Nursing Home Length of Stay and Spenddown in Connecticut, 1977–1986." *Gerontologist* 31: 165–73.

Liu, K., K. G. Manton, and B. M. Liu. 1985. "Home Care Expenses for the Disabled Elderly." *Health Care Financing Review* 7: 51–58.

Lock, Margaret. 1987. "Introduction: Health and Medical Care as Cultural and Social Phenomena." In *Health, Illness, and Medical Care in Japan,* ed. E. Norbeck and M. Lock, 1–23. Honolulu: University of Hawaii Press.

———. 1993. "Ideology, Female Midlife, and the Greying of Japan." *Journal of Japanese Studies* 19: 43–78.

Lockery, Shirley A. 1992. "Caregiving among Racial and Ethnic Minority Elders: Family and Social Supports." In *Diversity: New Approaches to Minority Aging*, ed. E. Percil Stanford and F. M. Torres-Gil, 113–22. Amityville, NY: Baywood.

Logue, Barbara J. 1991. "Women at Risk: Predictors of Financial Stress for Retired Women Workers." *Gerontologist* 31: 657–65.

Longman, Philip. 1985. "Justice between Generations." *Atlantic Monthly* 255: 73–81.

Lopata, Helen Z. 1970. "The Social Environment of American Widows." In *Aging and Contemporary Society*, ed. E. Shanas. Beverly Hills, CA: Sage.

Lopez, David. 1978. "Chicano Language Loyalty in an Urban Setting." *Sociology and Social Research* 62: 267–78.

Lubben, James E., and Rosina M. Becerra. 1987. "Social Support among Black, Mexican, and Chinese Elderly." In *Ethnic Dimensions of Aging*, ed. Donald E. Gelfand and Charles M. Barresi, 130–44. New York: Springer.

Lubitz, James, James Beebe, and Colin Baker. 1995. "Longevity and Medicare Expenditures." *New England Journal of Medicine* 332: 999–1003.

Lubitz, J., and R. Prihoda. 1984. "The Use and Costs of Medicare Services in the Last Two Years of Life." *Health Care Financing Review* 5: 117–31.

Lubitz, James D., and Gerald F. Riley. 1993. "Trends in Medicare Payments in the Last Year of Life." *New England Journal of Medicine* 328: 1092–96.

Manton, Kenneth G. 1993. "Forecasts of Active Life Expectancy: Policy and Fiscal Implications." *Journal of Gerontology* 48: 11–27.

Manton, Kenneth G., and James W. Vaupel. 1995. "Survival after the Age of 80 in the United States, Sweden, France, England, and Japan." *New England Journal of Medicine* 333: 1232–35.

Manton, Kenneth G., Larry S. Corder, and Eric Stallard. 1993. "Estimates of Change in Chronic Disability and Institutional Incidence and Prevalence Rates in the U.S. Elderly Population from the 1982, 1984, and 1989 national Long Term Care Survey." *Journal of Gerontology: Social Sciences* 48: S153–66.

Manton, Kenneth G., Clifford H. Patrick, and Katrina W. Johnson. 1989. "Health Differentials between Blacks and Whites: Recent Trends in Mortality and Morbidity." In *Health Policies and Black Americans*, ed. D. P. Willis, 129–99. New Brunswick, NJ: Transaction.

Manton, Kenneth G., Burton H. Singer, and Richard M. Suzman, eds. 1993. *Forcasting the Health of Elderly Populations*. New York: Springer-Verlag.

Manton, Kenneth G., Eric Stallard, and Korbin Liu. 1993. "Frailty and Forecasts of Active Life Expectancy in the United States." In *Forecasting the Health of Elderly Populations*, eds. Kenneth G. Manton, Burton H. Singer, and Richard M. Suzman, 159–81. New York: Springer-Verlag.

Marcus, A. C., and L. A. Crane. 1985. "Smoking Behavior among U.S. Latinos: An Emerging Challenge for Public Health." *American Journal of Public Health* 75: 169–72.

Markides, Kyriakos S. 1992. *A Longitudinal Study of Mexican American Elderly Health*. Washington, DC: National Institute on Aging.

Markides, Kyriakos S., and Sandra A. Black. 1996. "Race, Ethnicity, and Aging: The Impact of Inequality." In *Handbook of Aging and the Social Sciences* 4th ed., 153–70. New York: Van Nostrand.

Markides, Kyriakos S., J. S. Boldt, and Laura A. Ray. 1986. "Sources of Helping and Intergenerational Solidarity: A Three Generations Study of Mexican Americans." *Journal of Gerontology* 41: 506–11.

Markides, Kyriakos S., Jeannine Coreil, and Laura A. Ray. 1987. "Smoking among Mexican Americans: A Three Generation Study." *American Journal of Public Health* 77: 708–11.

Markides, Kyriakos, and Neal Krause. 1985. "Intergenerational Solidarity and Psychological Well-Being maong Older Mexican Americans: A Three Generational Study." *Journal of Gerontology* 40: 390–92.

Markides, Kyriakos S., Jeffrey S. Levin, and Laura A. Ray. 1985. "Determinants of Physician Utilization among Mexican-Americans: A Three-Generations Study." *Medical Care* 23: 236–46.

Markides, Kyriakos S., Harry W. Martin, and Ernesto Gomez. 1983. *Older Mexican Americans: A Study in an Urban Barrio*. Austin: University of Texas Press.

Markides, Kryiakos S., Laura A. Ray, Christine A. Stroup-Benham, and Fernando Trevino. 1990. "Acculturation and Alcohol Consumption in the Mexican American Population of the Southwestern United States: Findings from HHANES 1982–84." *American Journal of Public Health* 80 (supplement): 42–46.

Markides, Kryiakos S., Laura Rudkin, Ronald J. Angel, and David V. Espino. In press. "Health Status of Hispanic Elderly in the United States." In *Racial and Ethnic Differences in Late Life Health in the United States,* ed. Linda G. Martin, Beth J. Soldo, and Karen Foote. Washington, DC: National Academy Press.

Marks, Gary, Melinda Garcia, and Julia Solis. 1990. "Health Risk Behaviors of Hispanics in the United States: Findings from HHANES, 1982–1984." *American Journal of Public Health* 80 (supplement): 20–26.

Marmor, Theodore R., J. L. Mashaw, and P. L. Harvey. 1990. *America's Misunderstood Welfare State*. New York: Basic.

Marmor, Theodore R., Timothy M. Smeeding, and Vernon L. Greene. 1994. *Economic Security and Intergenerational Justice: A Look at North America*. Washington, DC: Urban Institute.

Marshall, Victor W., Fay Lomax Cook, and Joanne Gard Marshall. 1993. "Conflict over Intergenerational Equity: Rhetoric and Reality in a Comparative Context." In *Changing Contract across Generations,* ed. Vern L. Bengtson and W. Andrew Achenbaum, 119–40. New York: Aldine de Gruyter.

Marshall, Victor W., Carolyn J. Rosenthal, and Joanne Daciuk. 1987. "Older Parents' Expectations for Filial Support." *Social Justice Research* 1: 405–24.

Martin, Linda G., and Samuel H. Preston, ed. 1994. *Demography of Aging.* Washington, DC: National Academic Press.

Martin, Teresa Castro, and Larry L. Bumpass. 1989. "Recent Trends in Marital Disruption." *Demography* 26: 37–51.

Massey, Douglas S. 1993. "Latino Poverty Research: An Agenda for the 1990s." *Items* 47. 1: 7–11.

McAuley, W. J., and R. Bleiszner. 1985. "Selection of Long-Term Care Arrangements by Older Community Residents." *Gerontologist* 25: 188–93.

McCarthy, Kevin, and R. B. Valdez. 1985. *Current and Future Effects of Mexican Immigration in California.* Publication R-3365-CR. Santa Monica, CA: Rand Corporation.

McCoy, John L., and Ronald W. conley. 1990. "Surveying Board and Care Homes: Issues and Data Collection Problems." *Gerontologist* 30: 147–53.

McLaughlin, Diane K., and Leif Jensen. 1991. "Poverty among the Elderly: The Plight of Nonmetropolitan Elders." *Journal of Gerontology: Social Sciences* 48: S44–54.

McSteen, Martha. 1995. "Medicare Reform." Statement to the Senate Democratic Policy Committee on behalf of the National Committee to Preserve Social Security and Medicare, October 5.

Mechanic, David. 1980. "The Experience and Reporting of Common Physical Complaints." *Journal of Health and Social Behavior* 21: 146–55.

Mechanic, David, and Ronald J. Angel. 1987. "Some Factors Associated with the Report and Evaluation of Back Pain." *Journal of Health and Social Behavior* 23: 131–39.

Meiners, M. R., and A. K. Tave. 1984. "Consumer Interest in Long-Term Care Insurance: A Survey of Elderly in Six States." Rockville, MD: National Center for Health Services Research.

Menagh, Melanie. 1993. "Heroes of Health Care." *Omni* 15: 34–41.

Mendelson, Daniel N., and William B. Schwartz. 1993. "The Effects of Aging and Population Growth on Health Care Costs." *Health Affairs* 12 (Spring): 119–125.

Mendes de Leon, Carlos F. 1988. "Acculturation and Alcohol Consumption among Mexican Americans: A Three Generation Study." *American Journal of Public Health* 78: 1178–81.

Menefee, J., B. Edwards, and S. Schieber. 1981. "Analysis of Nonparticipation in the SSI Program." *Social Security Bulletin* 44: 3–21.

Meyer, Madonna Harrington. 1990. "Family Status and Poverty among Older

Women: The Gendered Distribution of Retirement Income in the United States." *Social Problems* 37: 551–63.

Miller, Baila, Richard T. Campbell, Lucille Davis, Sylvania Furner, Aida Giachello, Thomas Porhaska, Julie E. Kaufman, Min Li, and Carmen Pereze. 1996. "Minority Use of Community Long-Term Care Services: A Comparative Analysis." *Journal of Gerontology: Social Sciences* 51B: S70–81.

Mindel, Charles H. 1979. "Multigenerational Family Households: Recent Trends and Implications for the Future." *Gerontologist* 19: 456–63.

Minkler, Meredith. 1992. "Generational Interdependence." In *Diversity: New Approaches to Ethnic Minority Aging,* ed. E. Percil Stanford and Fernando M. Torres-Gil, 65–71. Amityville, NY: Baywood.

Minkler, Meredith, Kathleen M. Roe, and Marilyn Price. 1992. "The Physical and Emotional Health of Grandmothers Raising Grandchildren in the Crack Cocaine Epidemic." *Gerontologist* 32: 752–61.

Mitchell, Braxton D., Michael P. Stern, Steven M. Haffner, Helen P. Hazuda, and Judith K. Patterson. 1990. "Risk Factors for Cardiovascular Mortality in Mexican Americans and Non-Hispanic Whites." *American Journal of Epidemiology* 131: 423–33.

Mitchell Jim, and Jasper C. Register. 1984. "An Exploration of Family Interaction with the Elderly by Race, Socioeconomic Status, and Residence." *Gerontologist,* 24: 48–54.

Moon, Marilyn. 1977. *The Measurement of Economic Welfare: Its Application to the Aged Poor.* New York: Academic.

———. 1993. *Medicare Now and in the Future.* Washington, DC: Urban Institute.

———. 1995. "Medicare: An Appropriate Age-Related Program?" *Generations* 19: 50–53.

Mor, Vincent, Orna Intrator, and Linda Laliberte. 1993. "Factors Affecting Conversion Rates to Medicaid among New Admissions to Nursing Homes." *Health Services Research* 28: 2–25.

Morgan, James N. 1983. "The Redistribution of Income by Families and Institutions and Emergency Help Patterns." In *Five Thousand American Families—Patterns of Economic Progress* ed. Gregory J. Duncan and James. N. Morgan, 1–59. Ann Arbor: Institute for Social Research, University of Michigan.

Morgan, Leslie A. 1989. "Economic Well-Being Following Marital Termination: A Comparison of Widowed and Divorced Women." *Journal of Family Issues* 10: 86–101.

Morrison, Barbara Jones. 1983. "Sociocultural Dimensions: Nursing Homes and the Minority Aged." In *Gerontological Social Work Practice in Long-Term Care,* ed. George S. Getzel and M. Joanna Mellor, 127–45. New York: Haworth.

Moscovice, I., G. Davidson, and D. McCaffrey. 1988. "Substitution of Formal and Informal Care for Community-Based Elderly." *Medical Care* 26: 971–81.

Murphy, E., R. Smith, J. Lindesay, and J. Slattery. 1988. "Increased Mortality Rates in Later-Life Depression." *British Journal of Psychiatry* 152: 347–53.

Mutchler, Jan E., and Parker Frisbie. 1987. "Household Structure among the Elderly: Racial/Ethnic Differentials." *National Journal of Sociology* 1: 3–23.

Mutran, Elizabeth. 1985. "Intergenerational Family Support among Blacks and Whites: Response to Culture or to Socioeconomic Differences?" *Journals of Gerontology* 40: 382–89.

Myers, George C. 1990. "Demography of Aging." In *Handbook of Aging and the Social Sciences,* ed. Robert H. Binstock and Linda K. George, 3d ed., 19–44. San Diego: Academic.

Myers, Robert J. 1982. "Incremental Change in Social Security Needed to Result in Equal and Fair Treatment of Men and Women." In *A Challenge to Social Security,* ed. Robert Burkhauser and Karen Holden, 235–45. New York: Academic.

Myers, Samuel L. 1995. "Racial Differences in Home Ownership and Mortgage Financing among Pre-Retirement Aged Households." Paper presented at the Health and Retiremetn Survey Minority Perspectives Workshop, University of Michigan, Ann Arbor, May 26.

Myles, J. 1984. *Old Age in the Welfare State: The Political Economy of Public Pensions.* Boston: Little, Brown.

Nagi, Saad Z. 1979. "The Concept and Measurement of Disability." In *Disability Policies and Government Programs,* ed. Emil D. Berkowitz, 1–15. New York: Praeger.

———. 1991. "Disability Concepts Revisited: Implications for Preventions." In *Disability in America: Toward a National Agenda for Prevention,* ed. A. M. Pope and A. R. Tarlov, 309–27. Washington, DC: National Academy.

National Academy on Aging. 1995. "Facts on . . . the Older Americans Act." *Gerontology News* November: 5–6.

National Association of State Units on Aging. 1992. *How Healthy Is Your Community Care System? An Eldercare Assessment Guide.* Washington, DC: National Eldercare Institute on Long Term Care.

National Center for Health Statistics. 1983. "Americans Needing Help to Function at Home." Department of Health and Human Services. In *Advance Data from Vital and Health Statistics.* Publication 83–1250. Hyattsville, MD: DHHS.

National Council of la Raza (NCLR). 1992. *Hispanics and Health Insurance.* Washington, DC: Labor Council for Latin American Advancement.

National Council on the Aging. 1988. *Long-Term Care Choices: A Manual for Organizing a Successful Consumer Education Campaign.* Vol. 13. Washington, DC: National Council on the Aging.

Neidert, Lisa, and Farley Reynolds. 1985. "Assimilation in the United States: An Analysis of Ethnic and Generation Differences in Status and Achievement." *American Sociological Review* 50: 840–50.

Nelson, Gary M. 1983. "A Comparison of Title XX Services to the Urban and Rural Elderly." *Journal of Gerontological Social Work* 6: 3–23.

Neugarten, Bernice L. 1974. "Age Groups in American Society and the Rise of the Young-Old." *Annals of the American Academy of Political and Social Science* 415 (September): 187–98.

Newhouse, Joseph P. 1993. "An Iconoclastic View of Health Cost Containment." *Health Affairs* 12 (Supplement): 152–71.

Newman, Sandra J. 1995. "Housing Policy and Home-Based Care." *Milbank Quarterly* 73: 407–42.

Nocks, Barry C., R. Max Learner, Donald Blackman, and Thomas E. Brown. 1986. "The Effects of a Community-Based Long-Term Care Project on Nursing Home Utilization." *Gerontologist* 26: 150–57.

Nutting, Paul A., William L. Freeman, David R. Risser, Steven D. Helgerson, Roberto Paisano, John Hisnanick, Shelli K. Beaver, Irene Peters, John P. Carney, and Marjorie A. Speers. 1993. "Cancer Incidence among American Indians and Alaska Natives, 1980 through 1987." *American Journal of Public Health* 83: 1589–98.

O'Brien Thomas R., W. Dana Flanders, Pierre Decoufle, Coleen A. Boyle, Frank DeStefano, and Steven Teutsch. 1989. "Are Racial Differences in the Prevalence of Diabetes in Adults Explained by Differences in Obesity?" *Journal of the American Medical Association* 262: 1485–88.

Oppenheimer, Valerie K. 1974. "The Life Cycle Squeeze: The Interaction of Men's Occupational and Family Life Cycles." *Demography* 11: 227–45.

Oriol, William. 1994. *Social Policy and Mexican American Aging.* Washington, DC: National Council on Aging.

Orloff, Ann Shola. 1988. "The Political Origins of America's Belated Welfare State." In *The Politics of Social Policy in the United States,* ed. Margaret Weir, Ann Shola Orloff, and Theda Skocpol, 38–80. Princeton: Princeton University Press.

Pampel, Fred C. 1981. *Social Change and the Aged: Recent Trends in the United States.* Lexington, MA: Lexington.

Pappas, Gregory, Peter J. Gergen, and Margaret Carroll. 1990. "Hypertension Prevalence and the Status of Awareness, Treatment, and Control in the Hispanic Health and Nutrition Examination Survey (HHANES), 1982–84." *American Journal of Public Health* 80: 1431–36.

Pappas, Gregory, Susan Queen, Wilbur Hadden, and Gail Fisher. 1993. "The Increasing Disparity in Mortality between Socioeconomic Groups in the United States, 1960 and 1986." *New England Journal of Medicine* 329: 103–9.

Passel, Jeffrey, and Barry Edmonston, 1992. "Immigration and Race in the United States: The 20th and 21st Centuries." Washington, DC: Urban Institute (PRIP-UI-20).

Peterson, Peter G. 1995. "Reform Proposal of Commissioner Peter G. Peterson: Reforming Entitlements and Tax Expenditures." In *Bipartisan Commission on Entitlement and Tax Reform: Final Report to the President,* 47–79. Washington, DC: Superintendent of Documents.

Pierson, Paul, and Miriam Smith. 1994. "Shifting Fortunes of the Elderly: The Comparative Politics of Retrenchment." In *Economic Security and Intergenerational Justice: A Look at North America,* ed. Theodore R. Marmor, Timothy M. Smeeding, and Vernon L. Greene, 21–59. Washington, DC: Urban Institute.

Plankans, Andrejs. 1989. "Stepping Down in Former Times: A Comparative Assessment of Retirement in Traditional Europe." In *Age Structure in Comparative Perspective,* ed. David I. Kertzer and K. Warner Schaie, 175–95. Hillsdale, NJ: Lawrence Erlbaum.

Polednak, Anthony P. 1989. *Racial and Ethnic Differences in Disease.* New York: Oxford University Press.

———. 1990. "Mortality from Diabetes Mellitus, Ischemic Heart Disease, and Cerebrovascular Disease among Blacks in a Higher Income Area." *Public Health Reports* 105: 393–99.

———. 1993. "Lung Cancer Rates in the Hispanic Population of Connecticut, 1980–88." *Public Health Reports* 108: 471–76.

Popenoe, David. 1994. "The Family Condition of America: Cultural Change and Public Policy." In *Values and Public Policy,* ed. Henry J. Aaron, Thomas E. Mann, and Timothy Taylor, 81–112. Washington, DC: Brookings Institution.

Portes, Alejandro, and R. Bach. 1985. *Latin Journey.* Berkeley: University of California Press.

Portes, Alejandro, and R. Rumbaut. 1990. *Immigrant America: A Portrait.* Berkeley: University of California Press.

Preston, Samuel H. 1984. "Children and the Elderly: Divergent Paths for America's Dependents." *Demography* 21: 435–57.

Preston, Samuel H., and Paul Taubman. 1995. "Socioeconomic Differences in Adult Mortality and Health Status." In *Demography of Aging,* ed. Linda G. Martin and Samuel H. Preston, 279–318. Washington, DC: National Academic.

Quadagno, Jill. 1982. *Aging in Early Industrial Society: Work, Family, and Social Policy in Nineteenth-Century England.* New York: Academic.

———. 1990. "Generational Equity and the Politics of the Welfare State." *International Journal of Health Services Research* 20: 632–49.

Quadagno, Jill, W. Andrew Achenbaum, and Vern L. Bengtson. 1993. "Setting the Agenda for Research on Cohorts and Generations: Theoritical, Political, and Policy Implications. In *The Changing Contract across Generations,* ed. Vern L. Bengtson and W. Andrew Achenbaum, 259–72. New York: Aldine de Gruyter.

Quinn, Joseph F., and Richard V. Burkhauser. 1990. "Work and Retirement." In *Handbook of Aging and the Social Sciences,* 3d ed., ed. Robert H. Binstock and Linda K. George, 307–27. New York: Academic.

Quinn, Joseph F., Richard V. Burkhauser, and Daniel A. Myers. 1990. *Passing the Torch: The Influence of Economic Incentives on Work and Retirement.* Kalamazoo: MI: W. E. Upjohn Institute for Employment Research.

Rakowski, William, and Tom Hickey. 1992. "Mortality and the Attribution of Health Problems to Aging among Older Adults." *American Journal of Public Health* 82: 1139–41.

Redfoot, Donald L. 1987. "On the Separatin' Place": Social Class and Relocation among Older Women." *Social Forces* 66: 486–501.

Reid, Barbara V. 1992. " 'It's like You're Down on a Bed of Affliction': Aging and Diabetes among Black Americans." *Social Science and Medicine* 34: 1317–23.

Reno, Virginia P. 1993. "The Role of Pensions in Retirement Income: Trends and Questions." *Social Security Bulletin* 56: 29–43.

Research Triangle Institute. 1989. *SUDAAN: Professional Software for Survey Data Analysis.* P.O. Box 12194, Research Triangle Park, NC.

Rice, D., and J. Feldman. 1983. "Living Longer in the United States: Demographic Changes and Health Needs of the Elderly." *Milbank Memorial Fund Quarterly* 61: 363–96.

Rich, Spencer. 1991. "90,000 Could Need Long-Term Care." *Washington Post,* March 8, 1991, A13.

Riley, Matilda White, and Anne Foner. 1968. *Aging and Society.* vol. 1, *An Inventory of Research Findings.* New York: Russell Sage.

Rivlin, Alice M., and Joshua M. Wiener. 1988a. *Caring for the Disabled Elderly: Who Will Pay?* Washington, DC: Brookings Institution.

———. 1988b. "Home Equity Conversions." *Consumers' Research* 71: 24–27.

Robine, J. M., D. Bucquet, and K. Ritchie. 1991. "L'espérance de vie sans incapacité, un indicateur de l'évolution des conditions de santé au cours du temps: vingt ans de calcul." *Cahiers Québécois de Démographie* 20: 205–36.

Rogers, A., R. Rogers, and A. Belanger. 1990. "Longer Life but Worse Health? Measurement and Dynamics." *Gerontologist* 30: 640–49.

Rogers, Richard G. 1991a. "Demographic Characteristics of Cigarette Smokers in the United States." *Social Biology* 38: 1–12.

———. 1991b. "Health-Related Lifestyles among Mexican-Americans, Puerto

Ricans, and Cubans in the United States." In *Mortality of Hispanic Populations: Mexicans, Puerto Ricans, and Cubans in the United States and in the Home Countries,* ed. Ira Rosenwaike, 145–60. New York: Greenwood.

Rogers, Richard G., and John Crank. 1988. "Ethnic Differences in Smoking Patterns: Findings from NHIS." *Public Health Reports* 103: 387–93.

Rogler, Lloyd H., Douglas T. Gurak, and Rosemary S. Cooney. 1987. "The Migration Experience and Mental Health: Formulations Relevant to Hispanics and Other Immigrants." Simon Bolivar Research Monograph No. 1. In *Health and Behavior: Research Agenda for Hispanics,* ed. M. Gaviria and J. D. Arana, 72–84. Chicago: University of Chicago Press.

Rogot, Eugene, Paul D. Sorlie, Norman J. Johnson. 1992. "Life Expectancy by Employment Status, Income, and Education: The National Longitudinal Mortality Study." *Public Health Reports* 107: 457–62.

Roos, Noralou P., and Evelyn Shapiro. 1981. "The Manitoba Longitudinal Study of Aging: Preliminary Findings on Health Care Utilization by the Elderly." *Medical Care* 19: 644–57.

Rosenwaike, I. 1987. "Mortality Differentials among Persons Born in Cuba, Mexico, and Puerto Rico Residing in the United States, 1979–81." *American Journal of Public Health* 77: 603–6.

Rowland, Diane, Judith Feder, Barbara Lyons, and Alina Salganicoff. 1992. "Medicaid at the Crossroads." Baltimore: Kaiser Commission on the Future of Medicaid.

Rowland, Diane, and Barbara Lyons. 1987. *Medicare's Poor: Filling the Gaps in Medical Coverage for Low-Income Elderly Americans.* Baltimore: Commonwealth Fund.

Ruggles, Steven. 1987. *Prolonged Connections: The Rise of the Extended Family in Nineteenth-Century England and America.* Madison: University of Wisconsin Press.

Russell, Louis B. 1989. *Medicare's New Hospital Payment System: Is It Working?* Washington, DC: Brookings Institute.

Saluter, Arlene F. 1994. "Marital Status and Living Arrangements: March 1993." U.S. Bureau of the Census, *Current Population Reports,* series P20–478. Washington, DC: Government Printing Office.

Samet, Jonathan M., David B. Coultas, Cheryl A. Howard, Betty J. Skipper, and Craig L. Hanis. 1988. "Diabetes, Gallbladder Disease, Obesity, and Hypertension among Hispanics in New Mexico." *American Journal of Epidemiology* 128: 1302–11.

Samet, J. M., S. D. Schraag, C. A. Howard, C. R. Key, and D. R. Pathak. 1982. "Respiratory Disease in a New Mexico Population Sample of Hispanic and Non-Hispanic Whites." *American Review of Respiratory Diseases* 125: 152–57.

Savitz, David A. 1986. "Changes in Spanish Surname Cancer Rates Relative to Other Whites, Denver Area, 1969–71 to 1979–81." *American Journal of Public Health* 76: 1210–15.

Schlesinger, Arthur, Jr. 1992. *The Disuniting of America.* New York: Norton.

Schneider, Ira S., and Ezra Huber. 1989. *Financial Planning for Long-Term Care.* New York: Human Sciences.

Schulz, James H. 1995. *The Economics of Aging.* 6th ed. Westport, CT: Auburn House.

Schwenk, F. N. 1992. "Income and Expenditures of Older Widowed, Divorced, and Never-Married Women Who Live Alone." *Family Economics Review* 5: 2–8.

Scruggs, David W. 1995. *The Future of Continuing Care Retirement Communities.* Washington, DC: American Association of Homes and Services for the Aging.

Shanas, Ethel. 1979. "The Family as a Support System in Old Age." *Gerontologist* 19: 169–74

Shanas, Ethel, Peter Townsend, Dorothy Wedderburn, Henning Friis, Poul Milhoj, and Jan Stehouwer. 1968. *Old People in Three Industrial Societies.* New York: Atherton.

Short, Pamela Farley, Peter Kemper, Llewellyn J. Cornelius, and Daniel C. Walden. 1992. "Public and Private Responsibility for Financing Nursing-Home Care: The Effect of Medicaid Asset Spend-Down." *Milbank Quarterly* 70: 277–98.

Siegel, Paul Z., Larry C. Deeb, Loretta E. Wolfe, Dwain Wilcox, and James S. Marks. 1993. "Stroke, Mortality, and Its Socioeconomic, Racial, and Behavioral Correlates in Florida." *Public Health Reports* 108: 454–58.

Smeeding, Timothy M. 1990. "Economic Status of the Elderly." In *Handbook of Aging and the Social Sciences,* 3d ed., ed. Robert H. Binstock and Linda K. George, 362–81. New York: Academic.

Social Security Administration. 1994. *Supplemental Security Income* (No. 05–11000). Washington, DC: Department of Health and Human Services.

Soldo, Beth J. 1985. "In-Home Services for the Dependent Elderly: Determinants of Current Use and Implications for Future Demand." *Research on Aging* 7: 281–304.

Soldo, Beth J., Reynolds Farley, Kenneth G. Manton, and Anne Pebley. "The Demography of Aging: A Framework for Evaluating Survey Data Requirements." Report prepared by an ad hoc committee of the Population Association of America, at the request of T. Franklin Williams. Washington, DC: Population Association of America.

Soldo, Beth J., Douglas A. Wolf, and Emily M. Agree. 1990. "Family, Households, and Care Arrangements of Frail Older Women: A Structural Analysis." *Journal of Gerontology* 45: S238-49.

Somers, Anne R., and Nancy L. Spears. 1992. *The Continuing Care Retirement Community: A Significant Option for Long-Term Care*. New York: Springer.

Sorel, Janet E., David R. Ragland, and S. Leonard Syme. 1991. "Blood Pressure in Mexican Americans, Whites, and Blacks." *American Journal of Epidemiology* 134: 370–78.

Sorensen, Aage B. 1989. "Old Age, Retirement, and Inheritance." In *Age Structure in a Comparative Perspective,* ed. David I. Kertzer and K. Warner Schaie, 197–213. Hillsdale, NJ: Lawrence Erlbaum.

Sorlie, Paul D. 1993. "Mortality by Hispanic Status in the United States." *Journal of the American Medical Association* 270: 2464–68.

Sorlie, Paul, Eugene Rogot, Roger Anderson, Norman Johnson, and Eric Backlund. 1992. "Black-White Differences by Family Income." *Lancet* 340: 346–50.

Sowell, Thomas. 1981. *Ethnic America: A History.* New York: Basic.

Speare, Alden, Roger Avery, and Leora Lawton. 1991. "Disability, Residential Mobility, and Changes in Living Arrangements." *Journal of Gerontology* 46: S133–42.

Spence, Denise A., and Joshua M. Wiener. 1990a. "Estimating the Extent of Medicaid Spend-Down in Nursing Homes." *Journal of Health Politics, Policy and Law* 15: 607–26.

———. 1990b. "Nursing Home Length of Stay Patterns: Results from the 1985 National Nursing Home Survey." *Gerontologist,* 30: 16–20.

Stack, Carol B. 1974. *All Our Kin: Strategies for Survival in a Black Community.* New York: Harper and Row.

Stone, Robyn. 1986. "Aging in the Eighties, Age 65 and Over—Use of Community Services." Advance Data from Vital and Health Statistics, No. 124. Washington, DC: National Center for Health Statistics.

Stone, Robyn, Gail Lee Cafferata, and Judith Sangl. 1987. "Caregivers of the Frail Elderly: A National Profile." *Gerontologist,* 27: 616–26.

Strauss, Melania, and Gretchen Dee. 1995. "No Serious Dialogue." *Future Focus: Third Millennium Newsletter,* July, 1–2.

Stroup-Benham, Christine A., Fernando M. Trevino, and Dorothy B. Trevino. 1990. "Alcohol Consumption Patterns among Mexican American Mothers and among Children from Single- and Dual-Headed Households: Findings from HHANES 1982–84." *American Journal of Public Health* 80 (supplement): 36–41.

Suttles, Gerald D. 1968. *The Social Order of the Slum: Ethnicity and Territory in the Inner City* Chicago: University of Chicago Press.

Suzman, Richard M., David P. Willis, and Kenneth G. Manton. 1992. *The Oldest Old.* New York: Oxford University Press.

Taeuber, Cynthia. 1990. "Diversity: The Dramatic Reality." In *Diversity in*

Aging, ed. Scott A. Bass, Elizabeth A. Kutza, and Fernando M. Torres-Gil, 1–25. Glenview, IL: Scott, Foresman.

Taylor, Robert J. 1985. "The Extended Family As a Source of Support to Elderly Blacks." *Gerontologist* 25: 488–95.

———. 1988. "Aging and Supportive Relationships among Black Americans." In *The Black American Elderly: Research on Physical and Psychosocial Health,* ed. James Jackson, 259–81. New York: Springer.

Taylor Robert J. and Linda M. Chatters. 1986. "Church-Based Informal Support among Aged Blacks." *Gerontologist,* 26: 637–42.

———. 1988. "Correlates of Education, Income, and Poverty among Aged Blacks." *Gerontologist* 28: 435–41.

Taylor, Robert J., Linda M. Chatters, and Vickie M. Mays. 1988. "Parents, Children, Siblings, In-laws, and Non-Kin As Sources of Emergency Assistance to Black Americans." *Family Relations,* 298–304.

Tennstedt, Sharon L., Sybil L. Crawford, and John B. McKinlay. 1993. *Milbank Quarterly* 71: 601–24.

Third Millennium. N.D. *Become an Advocate for the Future.* Newsletter. P.O. Box 20866, New York.

Thomas, Kausar, and Andrew Wister. 1984. "Living Arrangements of Older Women: The Ethnic Dimension." *Journal of Marriage and the Family* 46: 301–11.

Thomas, William I., and Florian Znaniecki. 1927. *The Polish Peasant in Europe and America.* Vol. 2. New York: Knopf.

Thompson, David. W. 1991. *Selfish Generations? The Aging of New Zealand's Welfare State.* Manchester: Manchester University Press.

———. 1993. "A Lifetime of Privilege? Aging and Generations at Century's End." In *Changing Contract across Generations*, ed. Vern L. Bengtson and W. Andrew Achenbaum, 215–37. New York: Aldine de Gruyter.

Tissue, Thomas, and John L. McCoy. 1981. "Income and Living Arrangements among Poor Aged Singles." *Social Security Bulletin* 44: 3-13.

Torres-Gil, Fernando M. 1993. "Interest Group Politics: Generational Changes in the Politics of Aging." In *The Changing Contract across Generations,* ed. Vern L. Bengtson and W. Andrew Achenbaum, 239–57. New York: Aldine de Gruyter.

Torres-Gil, Fernando, and Eve Fielder. 1986–87. "Long-Term Care Policy and the Hispanic Population." *Journal of Hispanic Studies* 2: 49–66.

Trapido, Edward J., Clyde B. McCoy, Nancy Strickman Stein, Stacy Engel, H. Virginia McCoy, and Stan Olejniczak. 1990. "The Epidemiology of Cancer among Hispanic Women." *Cancer* 66: 2435–41.

Treas, Judith. 1995. *Older Americans in the 1990s and Beyond.* Washington, DC: Population Reference Bureau.

Treas, Judith, and Michele Spence. 1989. "Intergenerational Economic Obligations in the Welfare State." In *Aging Parents and Adult Children,* ed. Jay A. Mancini, 181–95. Lexington, MA: Lexington Books/D.C. Heath.

Trevino, Fernando M., Eugene Moyer, R. Burciaga Valdez, and Christine Stroup-Benham. 1991. "Health Insurance Coverage and Utilization of Health Services by Mexican American, Mainland Puerto Ricans, and Cuban Americans." *Journal of the American Medical Assocation* 265: 233–37.

Tuma, Nancy B., and Gary Sandefur D. 1988. "Trends in the Labor Force Activity of The Elderly in the United States, 1940–1980." In *Issues in Contemporary Retirement,* ed. R. Ricardo-Campbell and E. P. Lazear, 38–74. Stanford, CA: Hoover Institution.

Twentieth Century Fund. 1995. *Medicare Reform: A Twentieth Century Fund Guide to the Issues.* New York: Twentieth Century Fund.

U.S. Bureau of the Census. 1991. Preliminary Results from the 1990 Census on Race and Ethnicity. Washington, DC: Governmetn Printing Office.

———. 1992a. "Population and Health Transitions." Current Population Reports, series P95/92–2. Washington, DC: Government Printing Office.

———. 1992b. "An Aging World II." In *International Population Reports,* P59/92-3, appendix A. Washington, DC: U.S. Bureau of the Census.

———. 1992c. "Who's Helping Out? Support Networks among American Families: 1988." *Current Population Reports,* series P-70, no. 28. Washington, DC: Government Printing Office.

U.S. General Accounting Office. 1992. *Access to Health Care—Significant Gaps Exist.* GAO/PEMD-92-6. Washington, DC: U.S. Government Printing Office.

U.S. Senate. 1995. *Medicaid Estate Recoveries, Section 1971(b)(1)(B) of the Social Security Act.* Bill read by Mr. Feingold in the 104th Congress, January 4, 1995.

Valdez, R. Burciaga, Hal Morgenstern, E. Richard Brown, Roberta Wyn, W. Chao, and William Cumberland. 1993. "Insuring Latinos against the Cost of Illness." *Journal of the American Medical Association* 269: 889–95.

Valdivieso, Rafael, and Cary Dains. 1988. "U.S. Hispanics: Challenging Issues for the 1990s." *Population Trends and Public Policy,* December, 1–16.

Van Nostrand, Joan F. 1993. "Common Beliefs about the Rural Elderly: What Do National Data Tell Us?" In *Vital and Health Statistics,* National Center for Health Statistics. series 92–412, Washington, DC: Government Printing Office.

Van Nostrand, Joan F., Sylvia E. Furner, and Richard Suzman, eds. 1993. *Chartbook on Health Data on Older Americans: United States, 1992.* Vital and Health Statistics, series 3, no. 27. Washington, DC: National Center for Health Statistics.

Verbrugge, Lois J. 1987. "From Sneezes to Adieux: Stages of Health for American Men and Women." In *Health and Aging: Sociological Issues and Policy Directions,* ed. R. Ward and S. Tobin, 17–57. New York: Springer.

———. 1989. "The Twain Meet: Empirical Explanations of Sex Differences in Health and Mortality." *Journal of Health and Social Behavior* 30: 282–304.

———. 1994. "Disability in Late Life." In *Aging and the Quality of Life,* ed. R. Abeles, H. Gift, and M. Ory, 79–98. New York: Springer.

Verbrugge, Lois M., and Alan M. Jette. 1994. "The Disablement Process." *Social Science and Medicine* 38: 1–14.

Vertrees, James C., Kenneth G. Manton, and Gerald S. Adler. 1989. "Cost Effectiveness of Home and Community-Based Care." *Health Care Financing Review,* 10: 65–78.

Vinovskis, Maris. 1989. "Stepping Down in Former Times: The View from Colonial and 19th-Century America." In *Age Structurein in Comparative Perspective,* ed. David I. Kertzer and K. Warner Schaie, 215–25. Hillsdale, NJ: Lawrence Erlbaum.

Waid, Mary Onnis. 1996. "Brief Summaries of Title XVIII and Title XIX of the Social Security Act as of 6/24/95 (with 1994 data)." Html 3.0//EN,/gifs/hcfabnr2.gif. Office of the Actuary, Health Care Financing Administration, N3-01-23, 7500 Security Blvd. Baltimore, MD 21244-1851.

Waldo, Daniel R. 1994. "Estimating the Cost of a Medicare Outpatient Prescription Drug Benefit." *Health Care Financing Review* 15: 103–12.

Waldo, Daniel R., Sally T. Sonnefeld, David R. McKusick, and Ross H. Arnett III. 1989. "Health Expenditures by Age Group, 1977 and 1987." *Health Care Financing Review* 111–20.

Wallace, Steven P., and Chin-Yin Lew-Ting. 1992. "Getting by at Home: Community-Based Long-Term Care of Latino Elders." *Western Journal of Medicine* 157: 337–44.

Wallace, Steven P., Lene Levy-Storms, and Linda R. Ferguson. 1995. "Access to Paid In-Home Assistance among Disabled Elderly People: Do Latinos Differ from Non-Latino Whites?" *American Journal of Public Health* 85: 970–75.

Walls, Carla T., and Steven H. Zarit. 1991. "Informal Support from Black Churches and the Well-Being of Elderly Blacks." *Gerontologist* 31: 490–95.

Warner, David C., and Kevin Reed. 1993. *Health Care across the Border: The Experiences of U.S. Citizens in Mexico.* Austin, TX: Lyndon B. Johnson School of Public Affairs.

Waters, Mary C. 1990. *Ethnic Options: Choosing Identities in America.* Berkeley: University of California Press.

Weeks, John R., and Jose B. Cuellar. 1981. "The Role of Family Members in the Helping Networks of Older People." *Gerontologist* 21: 388–94.

———. 1983. "Isolation of Older Persons: The Influence of Immigration and Length of Residence." *Research on Aging* 5: 369–88.

Weissert, William G., Cynthia M. Cready, and James E. Pawelak. 1988. "The Past and Future of Home- and Community-Based Long-Term Care." *Milbank Quarterly* 66. 2: 309–88.

Weissert, William G., Jennifer M. Elston, Elise J. Bolda, Cynthia M. Creedy, William N. Zelman, Phil D. Sloane, William D. Kalsbeek, Elizabeth Mutran, Thomas H. Rice, and Gary C. Koch. 1989. "Models of Adult Day Care: Findings from a National Survey." *Gerontologist* 29: 640–50.

Weissert, William G., and Susan C. Hedrick. 1994. "Lessons Learned from Research on Effects of Community-Based Long-Term Care." *Journal of the American Geriatrics Society* 42: 348–53.

Wells, Kenneth B., Jacqueline M. Golding, Richard L. Hough, M. Audrey Burnam, and Marvin Karno. 1989. "Acculturation and the Probability of Use of Health Services by Mexican Americans." *Health Services Research* 24: 237–57.

Westat, Inc. 1989. *A Survey of Elderly Hispanics: Final Report to the Commonwealth Fund Commission on Elderly People Living Alone*. Rockville, MD.

White-Means, Shelley I., and Michael C. Thornton. 1990. "Ethnic Differences in the Production of Informal Home Health Care." *Gerontologist* 30: 758–68.

Wiener, Joshua M., and Raymond J. Hanley. 1992a. "Caring for the Disabled Elderly: There's No Place like Home." In *Improving Health Policy and Management: Nine Critical Research Issues for the 1990's*, ed. Stephen M. Shortell and Uwe E. Reinhardt, 75–110. Ann Arbor, MI: Health Administration Press.

———. 1992b. "Long-Term Care and Social Insurance: Issues and Prospects." In *Social Insurance Issues for the Nineties*, ed. Paul N. Van DeWater, 101–19. Dubuque, IA: Kendall/Hunt.

Wiener, Joshua M., Raymond J. Hanley, and Laurel Hixon Illston. 1992. "Financing Long-Term Care: How Much Public? How Much Private?" *Journal of Health Politics, Policy, and Law* 17: 425–35.

Wiener, Joshua M., and Katherine M. Harris. 1990. "Myths and Realities: Why Most of What Everybody Knows about Long-Term Care Is Wrong." *Brookings Review*, Fall, 29–34.

Wiener, Joshua M., and L. H. Illston 1993. "Options for LTC Financing Reform: Public and Private Insurance Strategies." *Journal of Long-Term Care Administration* 21: 46–57.

Wiener, Joshua M., Laurel Hixon Illston, and Raymond J. Hanley. 1994. *Sharing the Burden: Strategies for Public and Private Long-Term Care Insurance*. Washington, DC: The Brookings Institution.

Williams, Norma. 1990. *The Mexican American Family: Tradition and Change*. Dix Hills, NY: General Hall.

Wilson, C., and W. Weissert. 1989. "Private Long-Term Care Insurance: After Coverage Restrictions, Is There Anything Left?" *Inquiry* 26: 493–507.

Wisensale, Steven K., and Michael D. Allison. 1988. "An Analysis of 1987 State Family Leave Legislation: Implications for Caregivers of the Elderly." *Gerontologist* 28: 779–85.

Woehrer, Carol E. 1978. "Cultural Pluralism in American Families: The Influence of Ethnicity on Social Aspects of Aging." *Family Coordinator* October: 329–39.

Wolf, Douglas A., and Beth J. Soldo. 1988. "Household Composition Choices of Older Unmarried Women." *Demography* 25: 387–403.

Wolinsky, Fredric D., Benigno E. Aguirre, Lih-Jiuan Fann, Verna M. Keith, Connie L. Arnold, John C. Niederhauer, and Kathy Dietrich. 1989. "Ethnic Differences in the Demand for Physician and Hospital Utilization among Older Adults in Major American Cities: Conspicuous Evidence of Considerable Inequalities." *Milbank Quarterly* 67: 412–49.

Wolinsky, Frederic D., Steven D. Culler, Christopher M. Callahan, et al. 1994. "Hospital Resource Consumption among Older Adults: A Prospective Analysis of Episodes, Length of Stay, and Charges over a Seven-Year Period." *Journal of Gerontology* 49: S240–52.

World Bank. 1994. *Averting the Old Age Crisis: Policies to Protect the Old and Promote Growth*. New York: Oxford University Press.

Worobey, Jacqueline L., and Ronald J. Angel. 1990a. "Functional Capacity and Living Arrangements of Unmarried Elderly Persons." *Journal of Gerontology: Social Sciences* 45: 95–101.

———. 1990b. "Poverty and Health: Older Minority Women and the Rise of the Female-Headed Household." *Journal of Health and Social Behavior* 31: 370–83.

Yankelovich, Daniel. 1994. "How Changes in the Economy are Reshaping American Values." In *Values and Public Policy,* ed. Henry J. Aaron, Thomas E. Mann, and Timothy Taylor, 16–53. Washington, DC: Brookings Institution.

Ycas, M., and S. Grad. 1987. "Income of Retirment-Aged Persons in the United States," *Social Security Bulletin* 50: 5–14.

Yordi, Cathleen, and Jacqueline Waldman. 1985. "Consolidated Model of Long-Term Care: Service Utilization and Cost Impacts." *Gerontologist,* 25. 4: 389–97.

Zawadski, Rick T., and Catherine Eng. 1988. "Case Management in Capitated Long-Term Care." *Health Care Financing Review* (annual supplement): 75–81.

Zick, Cathleen D., and Ken R. Smith. 1991. "Patterns of Economic Change Surrounding the Death of a Spouse." *Journal of Gerontology: Social Sciences* 46: S310–20.

INDEX

AARP. *See* American Association of Retired Persons
Active life expectancy, 35–38
Activities of daily living (ADLs)
  adult day care and, 147
  assistance with, 118–19, 122, 136
  continuing care retirement communities and, 118–19
  disablement process model and, 34
  informal networks and, 93–94
  long-term care insurance and, 122
  problems with, by age, ethnicity, and gender, 39–40
Administration on Aging (AOA), 142–43
Adult day care facilities, 147
Adult foster care, 147–48
Affirmative action programs, *xx*
AGE. *See* Americans for Generational Equity
Age-based conflict
  ethnic conflict and, 3–4, 163–67
  inequities in social welfare system and, 6–7
  potential for, 4, 159–63
Aging population. *See* Older population
AIME. *See* Average indexed monthly earnings
Alba, Richard, *xix*
American Association of Retired Persons (AARP)
  heterogeneity of the elderly and, 165
  lobbying by, 159–60
  "Medigap" policies and, 72
American political culture, *xvi–xx, xxv–xxvi*
Americans for Generational Equity (AGE), 6, 161, 166
AOA. *See* Administration on Aging
Asians, 96. *See also* Ethnicity
Asset accumulation. *See also* Financial resources; Inheritance
  concept of the "third age" and, 169–70
  ethnic differences in, 49, 50
  intergenerational transfer of assets and, 15–16, 170–72
  marriage patterns and, 15, 16
  by non-Hispanic white *vs.* minority Americans, 10–11
  reverse annuity mortgages and, 149–50
  socioeconomic status and, 50–52
Assisted living plans, 118–19

Austin, Texas, project, 185
Average indexed monthly earnings (AIME), 56

"Baby bust" cohort, 163
Bilingual education, *xviii*
Blacks. *See also* Ethnicity; Race
 access to health insurance and, 73–76
 health insurance coverage among, 66–67, 68, 77–81
 health of, compared with Mexican Americans, 38–44
 life expectancy and, 44
 preretirement resources of, 78–79
 retirement income and, 47–49
 role of family and, 8–9, 91–92
 social support networks among, 96–97, 98
 use of nursing home care and, 126–30
"Board and care" arrangements, 147–48
Brandeis University, 119

Case management, 145, 151
Catastrophic illness, 71, 159–60, 168
CCRCs. *See* Continuing care retirement communities
Chinese Americans. *See* Asians
Chronic conditions
 by age, ethnicity, and gender, 40, 42
 ethnicity and, 26–28, 40, 42
 increased prevalence of, 37, 64
 long-term care insurance and, 122
 preventive care and, 84
 quality of life and, 37
Churches. *See* Community organizations
Citizenship, and health insurance, 76. *See also* Immigrants
Collateral families, 91
Community-based programs. *See also* On Lok program, in San Francisco's Chinatown
 adult day care facilities, 147
 "board and care" arrangements and, 147–48
 case management and, 145
 characteristics of, 137
 compared with nursing home care, 136–38
 as complement to institutionalization, 138–39
 cost-effectiveness of, *xxiii–xxiv,* 140–41, 153–57
 cultural appropriateness and, 22, 137–38, 153
 family involvement and, *xxiv,* 21–22, 135, 138–39, 146
 and federal programs, 142–43
 financial arrangements and, 149–50
 in hierarchy of support networks, 95
 housing programs and services, 148–49
 institutionalization and, 131
 On Lok program and, 150–53
 nutrition services and, 145–46
 potential for, *xxiii–xxiv*
 potential of induced demand and, 139–41
 preferences of the elderly and, *xxiv,* 132, 154
 quality of life and, 138
 respite care and, 146
 transportation services and, 143–45
 use of, by race and ethnicity, 143, 144
Community organizations, 137–38, 156
Congregate Housing Act, 148–49
Continuing care retirement communities (CCRCs), 118–19
 life-care-at-home option, 119–21
 life-care communities and, 149
Cost containment
 in health care financing, and minorities, 81–87
 impacts of proposed Social Security reforms and, 173–76
 On Lok program and, 151–53
 for Medicare and Medicaid, 69, 71–72, 81–87, 175–76
 need for community-based programs and, *xxiii*
Costs
 effectiveness of community-based programs and, *xxiii–xxiv,* 140–41, 153–57
 incurred by older population, *xxi–xxiii*
 of long-term care, *xiii,* 18–19, 20–21, 121–25
 nursing home care and, 123, 124, 131–32
 public expenditures for health care and, *xxii–xxiii,* 37, 71

Cultural factors. *See also* Ethnicity; Social change; Socioeconomic status; *entries for specific ethnic groups*
appropriateness of community support and, 22, 137–38, 153
conflation of socioeconomic status and, 98–99
cultural change, and options for elder care, 19–22
differences in family size and, 19–20, 90
differences in social support and, 91–92, 95–97
in disability, 30–34
long-term care arrangements and, 120–21, 126–27
multigenerational households and, 90–92, 101–2
role of family and, *xiv,* 8–9, 90–92, 110–12

Defined benefit plans, 53–54
Defined contribution plans, 53, 54–55
Delco, Wilhelmina, 185
Depression in old age, 33, 93–94, 109
Developing nations, 4, 115. *See also* Global aging of populations
DI. *See* Disability Insurance
Disability. *See also* Functional capacity; Health; Illness
active life expectancy and, 35–38
"intrinsic" *vs.* "actual," 33–34
risk of, and age, 135
Social Security programs and, 55
sociocultural factors in, 30–34
Disability Insurance (DI), 55
"Disablement process" model, 30–34
Diversity, *xvi–xviii, xxvi*
Divorce, and economic disadvantage, 11, 14–16
Domestic economy, slowing of growth in, *xxi–xxiii,* 163
Domiciliary care homes, 147–48
Durenberger, David, 161

Easterlin, Richard, 163, 167
Economic success. *See also* Asset accumulation; Financial resources; Poverty; Socioeconomic status
barriers to, *xix–xx, xvix–xvxx,* 11, 13–14, 44, 111–12, 168
individual differences in, *xix–xx*
intergenerational asset accumulation and, 11, 16, 170–72
size of birth cohort and, 163
Elderly, the. *See* Older population
Emotional support, 93–94. *See also* Social support
Employment status
health insurance coverage and, 66–68, 81, 83–85
retirement income and, 52–55, 66
Entitlement programs, cuts in, 172–73. *See also* Cost containment; Medicaid; Medicare; Social Security
Erikson, Eric, 178
Ethnic conflict, and age-based politics, 3–4, 163–67
Ethnicity. *See also* Blacks; Diversity; Hispanics; Mexican Americans; Minority group status; Non-Hispanic whites
access to health care and, 167–68
active life expectancy and, 36
advantages associated with, 8, 27, 44–45
age differences among ethnic groups and, 3–4, 165
chronic conditions and, 26–28, 40, 42
concept of, *xvi–xx*
cultural change and, 19–20
disablement process and, 32–33
future of family role in elder care and, 110–12
within group heterogeneity and, 99, 183
health differences and, 24–28, 38–44
life expectancy differences and, 23–24
living arrangements and, 101–2
mobility impairment and, 40, 41
preretirement economic resources and, 50–52
problems with activities of daily living and, 39–40
as risk factor, 8
self-assessments of health and, 40, 42–44
social support differences and, 91–92, 95–97, 98–100
sources of retirement income and, 47–49
use of community-based programs and, 143, 144
European ethnic identity, concept of, *xix*

Family, role of
  as alternative to institutionalization, 114–17, 129
  centrality of, 181
  community-based programs and, *xxiv,* 21–22, 135, 138–39, 145, 146, 156–57
  cultural factors and, *xiv,* 8–9, 90–92, 110–12
  in the future, 110–12, 113–14
  hierarchy of support and, 94–95
  immigrants and, 106, 108, 109
  Japanese policy on aging and, *xiv*
  options for involvement of, 111, 112, 181
  respite care and, 146
  social change and, 88–89, 113–14
  socioeconomic factors and, *xiv–xv*
  as source of informal support, 90, 93–94
Family size, 17, 19–20, 62, 90
Family structure, changes in, 179–80. *See also* Female-headed households; Single mothers
Federal Civil Service Retirement System, 53
Federal Council on Aging, 143
Federal government. *See also* Medicaid; Medicare; Older Americans Act; Public policy; Social Security; Social welfare system
  community-based programs and, 142–43, 148–49
  financial support of the elderly and, *xiv,* 18, 89–90, 114–15
Federal housing services, 148–49
Female-headed households
  economic disadvantage and, 50–51
  headed by grandmothers, 12–14
  health insurance coverage and, 66–67
  informal networks and, 97–98
  preretirement resources and, 78–79
  retirement health insurance and, 80
  single mothers and, 14–16
Fertility rate, decrease in, 17
Fictive kin, 98
Financial resources. *See also* Asset accumulation; Economic success; Retirement income
  age-bias in distribution of, 6–7
  heterogeneity of, among the elderly, 8
  of minority elderly, 10–11, 51–52
  preretirement, by gender and ethnicity, 50–52, 78–79
  reverse annuity mortgages and, 149–50
  of single individuals, 9–10
  of working-age adults, 90
Financial support of the elderly. *See also* Medicaid; Medicare; Social Security; Social support; Social welfare system; Supplemental Security Income
  families of immigrants and, 106, 108–9
  federal government and, *xiv,* 18, 89–90
Focus groups. *See* Policy forums
Formal retirement contracts, 92–93
Formal support. *See* Financial support of the elderly; Institutionalization; Nursing home care; Social support
Functional capacity
  community-based programs and, 152, 154
  cultural factors in disability and, 30–34
  health monitoring and, 152
  institutionalization and, 129, 130, 132–33
  living arrangements and, 102, 129
  meaning of, 28–34
  nature of environmental challenge and, 37–38
  social support and, 27–28, 37–38, 152, 154
  socioeconomic status and, 27–28

Gender. *See also* Female-headed households; Women
  active life expectancy and, 36
  chronic conditions and, 40, 42
  composition of informal networks and, 97
  early retirement and, 47
  economic disadvantage and, 11, 12–14, 50–51
  interaction with minority status, 8, 50–51
  life expectancy and, 24
  mobility impairment and, 40, 41
  preretirement economic resources and, 50–52, 78–79
  problems with activities of daily living and, 39–40

retirement health insurance and, 80
self-assessments of health and, 40, 42–44
Generational equity
political power of the elderly and, 160–61
public discourse and, 178–79
Generativity, theory of, 178
Global aging of populations, 4, 5, 166. *See also* Developing nations
Grandmother, as head of household, 12–14, 97

Halfway houses, 147–48
Health. *See also* Chronic conditions; Disability; Functional capacity; Illness
active life expectancy and, 35–38
of black *vs.* Mexican American elderly, 38–46
of Hispanics *vs.* non-Hispanic whites, 128
meaning of, 28–34
self-assessments of, by age, ethnicity, and gender, 40, 42–44
socioeconomic status and, 44–45
Health and Retirement Survey (HRS), 50
Health care. *See also* Health insurance coverage; Home health care services; Long-term care; Medicaid; Medicare; Nursing home care
case management model and, 145
cultural factors in seeking, 32–33, 85–86
future financing of, 81–87
inequalities in access to, 85–86, 167–68
quality of, and health insurance, 68
rural/urban distinctions and, 104–5
Health care reform proposals, *xxv,* 28, 133, 167–68
Health insurance coverage. *See also* Long-term care insurance; Medicaid; Medicare
access to, 167–68
for the elderly, by immigrant status, 76
for the elderly, by race and ethnicity, 75–76, 79–81
employer-paid health insurance and, 66–68, 73–74, 79, 83–84
group differences in private insurance and, 64–65, 73–74
importance of, 63–64
preretirement, and minority status, 77–81
by race, ethnicity, and gender of household head, 66–67, 68
for working-age *vs.* elderly populations, 65–66
Health maintenance organizations (HMOs), 82, 118, 119
Heterogeneity of older population, *xv, xxi,* 7–9
differences in needs and, *xxv,* 28, 133, 163–66, 181–82, 183
within group differences and, 85–86, 99, 100, 105–9, 183
health-care reform proposals and, *xxv,* 28, 133, 167–68
public forums and, 182–84
Hispanics. *See also* Ethnicity; Mexican Americans
age of immigration and, 105–9
asset accumulation and, 50–52
within group differences and, 85–86, 99, 100, 105–9, 183
health insurance coverage among, 73–76, 77–81, 84–85
health risk and, 44–45
Medicaid and, 74, 131
Medicare and, 74–75, 131
preretirement resources of, 78–79
retirement income and, 47–49
role of family and, 8–9, 113–14
use of community-based programs and, 143, 144
use of nursing home care and, 126–30
HMOs. *See* Health maintenance organizations
Home-based care. *See* Community-based programs; Family, role of
Home equity conversions. *See* Reverse annuity mortgages
Home health care services
as alternative to institutionalization, 136–37
family involvement and, *xxiv*
preferences of the elderly and, *xxiv,* 132, 136, 154
Housing Act of 1959, Section 202, 148
HRS. *See* Health and Retirement Survey

Illness. *See also* Chronic conditions; Disability; Functional capacity; Health

Illness *(Continued)*
biological *vs.* social factors in, 29–30
catastrophic, 71, 159–60, 168
vs. disease, 29
Immigrants. *See also* Mexican Americans
Americans of European *vs.* non-European ancestry and, *xviii–xix*
cultural change and, 19–20
health insurance coverage and, 76
impact of age and, 105–9
"Personal Responsibility Act" and, 62
retirement income of, 61–62
social support and, 105–9
Income and assets test, 60–62
Individual differences, and economic success, *xix–xx,* 183–84
Induced demand
community-based programs and, 139–41
long-term care insurance and, 121
Informal social support. *See* Community-based programs; Family, role of; Social support
Information
on long-term care options, 182, 184–85
policy forums and, 182–84
Inheritance. *See also* Asset accumulation; Pact between generations; Reverse annuity mortgages
changing marriage patterns and, 15, 16
costs of long-term care and, 21
formal retirement contracts and, 92–93
intergenerational reciprocity and, 170–72
Institutionalization. *See also* Continuing care retirement communities; Long-term care; Nursing home care
as alternative in long-term care, 114–17, 129, 130–33
community-based programs as complement to, 138–39
community-based programs compared with, 136–38
decision-making process for, 128
functional capacity and, 129, 130, 132–33
in hierarchy of support networks, 95, 130–33
lack of informal network and, 113–14, 129–30
preferences of the elderly and, *xxiv,* 132, 134, 154
Instrumental activities of daily living (IADLs), 34
Intergenerational relations. *See also* Age-based conflict; Pact between generations
cultural change and, 19
economic interdependence and, 170–72
ethnic heterogeneity of the elderly and, 3–4, 163–66
generational equity and, 162–63, 165
political power of the elderly and, 159–61
potential for conflict in, 4, 159–63

Japan
policy on aging in, *xiii–xiv*
population aging in, 4
Jette, Alan, 30–34
Johnson, Lyndon B., 142

Kingson, Eric, 174

Labor-force participation
decline in, among older men, 47
of women, 16–19
Lasch, Christopher, 186
Laslett, Peter, 169
Life care communities, 149
Life-course perspective
age of immigration and, 105–9
concept of the "third age" and, 169–70
impacts of increased in life expectancy, 4–6
impacts of social changes and, 9–12
individual emphasis of terminology in, 186
intergenerational interdependence and, 83, 84, 86
persistence of inequalities and, 77
potential for intergenerational conflict and, 164
public discourse and, 178–79
"Life-cycle," as term, 186–87
Life expectancy, increase in, 1–2, 44
active life expectancy and, 35–38
at birth *vs.* age sixty-five, 24
changes in life course and, 4–6
ethnic differences in, 23–26

importance of retirement income and, 169–70
Lineal families, 91
Living arrangements. *See also* Community-based programs; Home health care services; Institutionalization; Long-term care; Nursing home care
availability of informal support and, 100–102
"board and care" arrangements, 147–48
continuing care communities and, 118–21
cultural appropriateness and, 120–21
federal housing services, 148–49
nursing home care and, 117–18
Living wills, 184
Lobbying groups, 159–60
Long-term care. *See also* Community-based programs; Family, role of; Institutionalization; Nursing home care
case management model and, 145
continuing care retirement communities and, 118–19
contributions by children to, 18–19, 173
costs of, *xiii,* 18–19, 20–21, 121–25
expansion of alternatives for, 116–17
group differences in use of nursing home care and, 126–30
information on options for, 182, 184–85
institutional options and, 117, 156–57
life-care-at-home option, 119–21
On Lok program and, 150–53
Medicaid and, *xiii,* 72–73, 123, 124–25
Medicare and, 69, 70–71
risk of two-tiered system in, 83, 157
role of community-based programs in, 136–39
Long-term care insurance, 20–21, 79, 121–24. *See also* Health insurance coverage
Low-Income Home Emergency Program, 148

Managed care. *See* Continuing care retirement communities; Health maintenance organizations; Social health maintenance organizations
Marriage patterns, 12–16
economic resources in retirement and, 11, 51–52
informal support networks and, 101–2
public discourse and, 179–80
MCCA. *See* Medicare Catastrophic Coverage Act
Means-testing, 59, 60, 140, 174–75
Medicaid, 72–73
adult day care and, 147
"board and care" arrangements and, 148
case management and, 145
eligibility for, 76, 125
growth in expenditures under, *xxii–xxiii*
Hispanics and, 74
immigrant status and, 76
impacts of cost-saving measures and, 81–83, 175–76
long-term care and, *xiii,* 72–73, 124–25, 130–33
recipients of, *xxii*
Medicare
in Canada *vs.* U.S., 166
cost of, 71–72
equitability and, 166–67
growth in expenditures under, *xxii*
Hispanics and, 74–75
impacts of cuts in, 81–83, 172, 175–76
long-term care and, 69, 70–71
participation in, 67, 69
private health insurance as supplement to, 68
services covered by, 69–70
Medicare Catastrophic Coverage Act (MCCA), 71, 159–60, 168
Medicare Hospital Insurance Trust Fund, 175
"Medigap" coverage, 72, 83. *See also* Medicaid
Mexican Americans
access to health care and, 104–5
economic disadvantage and, 50
fictive kin and, 98
health insurance coverage among, 66–67, 68, 74, 76, 77–81
health of, compared with other groups, 38–46
life-course stage at migration and, 106–9
Medicaid and, 74, 76, 131
Medicare and, 69, 131
retirement income and, 61–62
use of community-based programs and, 144
use of nursing home care and, 126–27

Middle class
asset accumulation and, 50
cuts in entitlement programs and, 172, 174–75
labor-force participation of women and, 16–17
Minority group status
access to health insurance and, 66–68, 73–76
age-based social conflict and, 3–4, 163–67
asset accumulation and, 15–16
changes in health care financing and, 81–87
concept of "minority group" and, *xx*
consequences of proposed Social Security reforms and, 173–76
employer-paid benefits and, 49, 52, 66–68, 73–74, 79, 83–84
female-headed households and, 12–14
interaction with gender, 8, 50–51
labor-force participation of women and, 17
long-term care insurance and, 79
needs of minorities and, 60–62, 135
preretirement health insurance coverage and, 77–81
reliance on Social Security income and, 10
retirement income and, 47–49, 61–62
use of nursing home care and, 130–31
Mobility impairment, by age, ethnicity, and gender, 40, 41
Moral foundation of pact between generations, 177–80
Moral hazard, and long-term care insurance, 121
Mortality rates, 26–28
Multidisciplinary assessment, and community-based programs, 151
Multigenerational households
cultural factors and, 90–92, 101–2
headed by women in poverty and, 12–14, 97–98
social support and, 101–2

NARFE. *See* National Association of Retired Federal Employees
National Association of Retired Federal Employees (NARFE), 159
National Committee to Preserve Social Security and Medicare (NCPSSM), 159
National Council of La Raza (NCLR), 73
National Council of Senior Citizens (NCSC), 159
National Council on Aging (NCOA), 159
National intergenerational awareness campaign, 184
National Mass Transportation Assistance Act of 1974, 144–45
NCLR. *See* National Council of La Raza
NCOA. *See* National Council on Aging
NCPSSM. *See* National Committee to Preserve Social Security and Medicare
NCSC. *See* National Council of Senior Citizens
Non-Hispanic whites
health insurance coverage among, 66–67, 68
health of, compared with other ethnic groups, 38–44
life expectancies among, 24
as percentage of total population, 3–4
reliance on Social Security income, 10
use of nursing home care and, 126–30
Nursing home care
as alternative for long-term care, 116–17
community-based programs compared with, 136–38, 153–55
cost of long-term care and, 123, 124, 131–32, 153–55
cultural environment of, 128
duration of stay and, 117, 123–24
group differences in use of, 126–30
in hierarchy of support networks, 95, 130–33, 134
Medicaid and, 82, 130–33
predictors of admission and, 117, 154, 155–56
preferences of the elderly and, *xxiv,* 126–27, 129, 132, 134, 154
Nutrition services, 145–46

OAA. *See* Older Americans Act
OAA program. *See* Old Age Assistance program
OAI. *See* Old Age Insurance
Old Age Assistance program (OAA; Title I), 59

Old Age Insurance (OAI; Title II), 55. *See also* Social Security
Older Americans Act (OAA)
  Administration on Aging and, 142–43
  case management and, 145
  nutrition services and, 145–46
  transportation services and, 144–45
Older population
  attitudes about responsibility for, 89–90, 116
  as challenge for social institutions, 4–7
  conflict within, 165–66
  costs incurred by, *xxi–xxiii*
  demographic transition and, 1–4
  as global issue, *xx–xxi*
  inequalities in retirement income in, 47–49
  long-term care preferences of the elderly and, *xxiv*, 126–27, 129, 132, 134, 154
  problems with activities of daily living among, by age, ethnicity, and gender, 39–40
  projections of, by country, 4, 5
  projections of, by race and ethnicity, 2–4
  as ratio of total U.S. population, *xx–xxi*, 2–3
  self-assessments of health among, by age, ethnicity, and gender, 40, 42–44
"Old-old," the, *xx–xxi*, 1
On Lok program, in San Francisco's Chinatown, 22, 150–53

PACE. *See* Program of All-Inclusive Care for the Elderly
Pact between generations. *See also* Inheritance
  cultural change in, 20
  materialistic orientation and, 150, 170–72
  moral foundations of, 177–80
  socialization of costs of long-term medical care and, 67–68, 173
  threats to, 158–59, 165
Pensions, private
  effects of lack of, 49–50
  ethnic differences and, 49, 52
  introduction of, 52–53
  types of, 53–55
"Personal Responsibility Act," 62
Planning and service area (PSA), 142
Policy forums, 182–84
Political power
  of the elderly, 159–61, 164
  generational equity and, 160–61
  of the middle class, and reform proposals, 180
Population Association of America, 161
Poverty. *See also* Financial resources; Retirement income; Socioeconomic status
  among the elderly, *xxii*, 46
  among young families, *xxii–xxiii*, 46
  informal networks and, 97–98
  intergenerational asset accumulation and, 15–16, 170–72
  medical coverage and, *xxii–xxiii*, 82–83, 167–68
  options for elder care and, 21–22, 111–12
  risk factors for, 49
PPS. *See* Prospective payment system
Preston, Samuel, 161
Preventive care
  chronic conditions and, 84
  cost control and, 152
Private-public partnerships, 184, 185
Program of All-Inclusive Care for the Elderly (PACE), 152–53
Prospective payment system (PPS), 71
PSA. *See* Planning and service area
Public advocacy agenda, 185–86
Public discourse
  on cuts in entitlement programs, 172–73
  from life-course perspective, 178–79
  policy forums and, 182–84
Public policy
  community-based long-term care options and, 141–57
  moral foundations and, 177–80
  recommendations for intergenerational policy, 180–87

Quadagno, Jill, 174
Quality of life, 138, 153–54

Race. *See also* Blacks; Ethnicity; Minority group status
  access to health care and, 167–68
  in American political culture, *xvi–xvii*
  asset accumulation and, 15–16

Race *(Continued)*
economic disadvantage and, 50
equity of Social Security reforms and, 176
health risk and, 25–28
life expectancy and, 24
role of family and, 8–9
sources of retirement income and, 47–49
use of community-based programs and, 143, 144
RAMs. *See* Reverse annuity mortgages
Respite care, 146
Retirement
age of, 20, 56–57
attitudes toward, 46–47
concept of, 5–6
dual purpose of, 53
early, and gender, 47, 56
Retirement income. *See also* Asset accumulation; Financial resources; Pensions, private; Social Security; Supplemental Security Income
changing social context and, 9–12
employment status and, 52–55
reverse annuity mortgages and, 149–50
before Social Security, 46
sources of, by race and ethnicity, 47–49
Reverse annuity mortgages (RAMs), 21, 149–50
Ritchie, K., 36
Robine, J. M., 36
Rural/urban differences, 103–5, 127, 144, 145

Sale/leaseback arrangements, 149
San Francisco, California, 150–53
Schlesinger, Arthur, Jr., *xvii,* 180
Shared housing, 149
Sheltered care, 147–48
SHMOs. *See* Social health maintenance organizations
SI. *See* Survivors Insurance
Single mothers, 14–16, 113
Social change. *See also* Immigrants
availability of family for care and, 113, 135–36
context of aging and, 9–12
family structure and, 12–16, 88–89, 135
options in elder care and, 19–22, 132, 135–36
rate of, and public discourse, 179–80
women in the work force and, 16–19, 135
Social class. *See* Middle class; Poverty
Social conflict. *See* Age-based conflict
Social health maintenance organizations (SHMOs), 119–20
Social Security. *See also* Medicaid; Medicare; Retirement income
Disability Insurance program and, 55
elimination of, 176
equitability and, 166–67
features of, 55–58
funding for, *xxi–xxii,* 57–58, 161
generational inequity in returns on, 6–7, 162–63
immigrants and, 108, 109
indexing to inflation, 47, 55–56
means-testing and, 59, 60, 174–75
needs of minorities and, 60–62
needs of women and, 60–62
participation by Hispanics and, 75
proposed reforms to, 58, 173–76
public opinion on responsibility for elder care and, 18–19, 89
qualification for benefits, 56
replacement rate of, 56
as sole source of retirement income, 10–11
solvency of, 175
Survivors Insurance and, 55
taxation of, 172
Social Security Act, 18
amendments to, 47, 55–56
Old Age Assistance (OAA) program (Title I), 59
Old Age Insurance (OAI) component (Title II), 55
Title XX, and rural states, 103
Social support. *See also* Community-based programs; Family, role of
class differences in, 95–97
composition of informal networks and, 97–100
context of, 92–94
continuing care retirement communities and, 118–19
cultural differences in, 33, 91–92, 95–97
functional capacity and, 27–28, 37–38, 129

future of the family in, 109–12
hierarchical systems of, 94–95
immigrants and, 105–9
induced demand for community-based services and, 139–41
informal *vs.* formal, 92
lack of, and formal support, 113–14, 129–30
living arrangements and, 100–102
On Lok program and, 150–53
marital status and, 101–2
need for formal support and, 113–17, 129–30
rural/urban differences in, 103–5
transportation services and, 143–45
Social welfare system. *See also* Medicaid; Medicare; Social Security
competition for programs in, *xxi–xxiii*
dilemmas of, 61
elimination of rural/urban distinctions and, 103–4
equitability of, 6–7, 166–67
population aging as challenge for, 4–7
potential for intergenerational conflict and, 162–63
public expectations for elder care and, 18–19
as reflection of pact between generations, 173
Socioeconomic status. *See also* Poverty
asset accumulation and, 50–52
barriers to success and, *xix–xx, xvix–xvxx,* 11, 13–14, 111–12, 168
conflation of culture patterns with, 98–99
consequences of cost-saving policy reforms and, 82–83, 173– 76
consequences of female labor-force participation and, 17–18
culture as adaptation to, 92
family ability to contribute to elder care and, 16
health risk and, 24–28, 44–45
impact of functional impairments and, 27–28
long-term care insurance and, 121–22, 123
mortality rate and, 26, 27
role of family and, *xiv–xv,* 92
style of informal support and, 93–94
SSI. *See* Supplemental Security Income
State agencies, 142–43
State of residence, and Medicaid, 76
"Stepping down" process, 92–93
Supplemental Security Income (SSI), 59–60
eligibility for, 60–61
eligibility for other federal programs and, 149
ethnic differences in reliance on, 10
immigrants and, 108, 109
minority elderly and, 47, 49
nonparticipation in, 60–62
nutrition services and, 146
Support networks. *See* Community-based programs; Family, role of; Social support
Surface Transportation Assistance Act of 1978, 145
Survivors Insurance (SI), 55
Sweden, 36

Taylor, Robert J., 97
Texas, 104–5, 127
"Third age," concept of, 169–70
Third Millennium, 6, 185–86
Thompson, David, 162–63, 178
Title I. *See* Old Age Assistance program
Title II. *See* Old Age Insurance
Title XX. *See under* Social Security Act
Torres-Gil, Fernando, 164–65
Transportation services, 143–45
Two-tiered system, risk of, 83, 157

University of Michigan Survey Research Center, Health and
Retirement Survey, 66, 86–87
Urban Mass Transit Act of 1964, 144

Verbrugge, Lois, 30–34
"Vision Village" project, 185

Weatherization Assistance Program, 148
Whites. *See* Non-Hispanic whites
Widowhood, 49, 101–2
Women
active life expectancy and, 36
asset accumulation and, 14–15, 16
consequences of proposed Social Security reforms and, 173–76

Women *(Continued)*
- early retirement and, 56
- grandmother as head of household and, 12–14, 97–98
- immigrant, income sources for, 108–9
- labor-force participation of, 16–19
- long-term care needs of, 183
- marital status of, 14–15, 16, 101
- needs of, and Social Security, 60–62
- preretirement resources of, 78–79
- retirement income and, 47–49, 50–51
- single mothers and, 14–16, 113
- social support and, 101–2
- use of nursing home care and, 130
- widowhood and, 49, 101–2

Working-age population. *See also* Age-based conflict; Family, role of; Intergenerational relations; Pact between generations
- generational equity and, 6–7, 160–61, 178–79
- health insurance coverage among, 77–81
- preretirement financial resources, by gender and ethnicity, 50–52, 78–79